DATE DUE

JUN 0 9 1993			
SEP 0 8 1993			
ILL 4-3-96			

DEMCO 38-297

The Prevention of Genocide

The Prevention of
GENOCIDE

LEO KUPER

Yale University Press
NEW HAVEN AND LONDON

Published with assistance from the
Mary Cady Tew Memorial Fund.

Designed by James J. Johnson
and set in Aster Roman type by
Graphic Composition Inc., Athens Georgia.
Printed in the United States of America by
The Alpine Press, Inc., Stoughton, Massachusetts.

Library of Congress Cataloging in Publication Data

Kuper, Leo,
   The prevention of genocide.

   Bibliography: p.
   Includes index.
   1. Genocide. I. Title.
JX5418.K864 1985   341.7'7   85–40465
ISBN 0–300–03418–0 (alk. paper)

*The paper in this book meets the guidelines for
permanence and durability of the Committee on
Production Guidelines for Book Longevity of the
Council on Library Resources.*

10 9 8 7 6 5 4 3 2 1

Contents

Preface

In the course of many years' work on race and ethnic relations, I kept coming across charges of genocide and complaints of the indifference of the outside world. I did not credit these reports, or perhaps I felt they were too painful to investigate. But when I finally turned to a study of the problem, I was overwhelmed to find that genocides were a continuing phenomenon of our times and that there was virtually no protection against the crime, notwithstanding the Genocide Convention of 1948 and the resolve of the United Nations to liberate mankind from its "odious scourge."

The findings in this study were reported in my book *Genocide* and in a paper for the Minority Rights Group on International Action against Genocide. I have drawn on these publications and on earlier work on the polarization of race and ethnic relations, incorporating some excerpts in the present text.

I imposed two limitations on the scope of the present study. I draw a distinction between types of genocide, with a broad division between genocides arising on the basis of internal divisions within a society, that is, the "domestic" genocides, and genocides arising in the course of international warfare. For reasons mentioned in the epilogue, the genocides of international warfare are not a central focus in this study. Instead, I am concerned here almost exclusively with the domestic genocides, though there is some broadening of subject matter in the inclusion of reference to political mass murder. This is in part because it is often difficult to distinguish between genocide and the political mass murders of racial, ethnic, and religious groups, but in part also because contemporary political mass murder takes at least as heavy a toll of human lives as genocide.

The second limitation is in terms of the recommendations advanced for prevention of genocide. I discuss the different types of domestic genocide and theories of genocide, as well as the performance of the United Nations and its failure to provide protection against genocide and other gross violations of human rights. But I do not derive from these discussions ideal prescriptions for the prevention of genocide, such as the abolition of warfare and the redistribution of funds from armaments to peaceful development of impoverished nations, or the elimination of discrimination, or the establishment of truly democratic societies, and other transformations of states and their international relations at deep structural levels. Instead, I take the perspective of what might be accomplished in the more immediate future by an activating secretariat or similar body, working, with the cooperation of nongovernmental organizations, within the United Nations but also outside the United Nations from an independent base. With the possible exception of the suggestions in regard to self-determination, the proposals are for a short-term and immediately practicable program of action.

It is generally accepted that the United Nations has failed to secure the effective implementation by its member states of their obligations in the field of human rights, particularly as they relate to genocide and political mass murder. Much of the discussion that follows is devoted to an analysis of the factors that account for the appreciable failure in implementation. But I am not pursuing this analysis simply in its own right. It is subsidiary to the main purpose of the book, which is to devise strategies for the prevention of genocide. If there is to be effective preventive action under present conditions, some contribution from the United Nations is indispensable. It is in the strongest position to bring international pressure to bear on offending states, and it represents potentially the most effective channel for action to eradicate genocide. Moreover, the record is not totally negative. There have been positive contributions, as well as recent encouraging developments, from preoccupation with standard setting to concern for implementation.

My objective, then, is to derive from the analysis suggestions for effective strategies within the United Nations that can be used as part of a general, and more broadly based, campaign against genocide. I hope that sustained pressure on this issue, and successful action in some cases, will help to sensitize international public opinion and reawaken sentiment against the crime, as has happened with the governmental practice of "disappearances"—the torture and murder of victims and the secret disposal of their bodies.

I should like to thank the University of California, Los Angeles, for the facilities made available to me as a retired professor and the Ford Foundation for support of this research. I also wish to thank my wife, Hilda, my nephew, Adam Kuper, Ben Whitaker of the Minority Rights Group, and Dr. Bertrand Ramcharan of the United Nations Center for Human Rights for their comments on the manuscript; Paul Hoffman for the stimulus derived from his work on behalf of Amnesty International; Colonel Patrick Montgomery and Peter Davies of the Anti-Slavery Society; Gerald Knight of the Bahá'í International Community; Leah Levin for her suggestions and creative ideas; Gary Remer for his contribution as my research assistant; Lillian Chodar for her excellent secretarial work; Terry Joseph for her expert revision of the bibliography; and Marian Neal Ash and Alexander Metro, of Yale University Press, for their highly appreciated editorial support.

For the rest, I can only hope that this volume will make some contribution to the prevention of genocide.

PART ONE

THE RIGHT TO LIFE

1

The Individual's Right to Life

There must surely be unanimity among the members of the United Nations on the primacy of the right to life. The emphasis on human rights would be quite meaningless without the survival of living subjects to be the carriers of these rights. And the circumstances of the founding of the United Nations, as well as its Charter, declarations, and covenants, seem to establish without doubt that in the midst of the sharpest conflict of ideologies, of values, and of national interest there is unanimity among the member states on the primacy of the right to life.

The United Nations Charter (1945) makes no explicit reference to this right, but in the opening chapter on purposes and principles the promotion of human rights and of fundamental freedoms is emphasized. In the Universal Declaration of Human Rights (1948), there is an early affirmation of the right to life. The first paragraph of the preamble falls back on the doctrine of natural rights in its assertion that "recognition of the inherent dignity and of the equal and inalienable rights of all members of the human family is the foundation of freedom, justice and peace in the world." In similar vein, the first article declares that "all human beings are born free and equal in dignity and rights." The second article is also very general in scope, assuring universal entitlement to all the rights and freedoms set forth in the declaration, without distinction of any kind. Then follows a list of specific rights, civil and political, economic, social, and cultural. The first of these, article 3, is the right of everyone to life, liberty, and security of the person.

The Declaration on the Elimination of All Forms of Racial Discrimination (1963) sets out a series of provisions against discrimination and declares in article 1 that everyone has the right to security of person and protection by the state against violence or bodily harm.

United Nations resolutions, conventions, declarations, and covenants often recall Mao's "Little Red Book," with its repetition of basic ideas and the slow infiltration of new ideas. In the U.N. documents, this role is performed by the preambles, which read like a doctrinal liturgy. I suppose it is a way of creating new international customary law. So we have, in the preamble to the International Covenant on Civil and Political Rights (1966), reiteration of the natural law doctrine of the inherent dignity, and of the equal and inalienable rights, of all members of the human family and recognition "that these rights derive from the inherent dignity of the human person." Part I then deals with the right of all peoples to self-determination, including the right to dispose of their natural wealth and resources.

Part II provides for nondiscrimination and lays down procedures to give effect to the rights recognized in the covenant. Part III details specific civil and political rights, beginning in article 6 with the assertion that "every human being has the inherent right to life. This right shall be protected by law. No one shall be arbitrarily deprived of his life." In times of public emergency threatening the life of the nation, states that are parties to the covenant may take measures derogating from their obligations in respect of civil and political rights to the extent strictly required by the emergency. However, certain provisions are protected from this power of derogation, and the first of these is the inherent right to life. Indeed, there is an implication in article 6, paragraph 6, of the covenant that the abolition of capital punishment is desirable. For further measure, we might refer to the International Convention on the Elimination of All Forms of Racial Discrimination (1969), which, in article 5, guarantees the right of everyone to security of person and protection against violence or bodily harm.

Moving outside the United Nations, we might seek evidence of unanimity in the undertakings of member states of regional organizations. Thus, in the European Convention for the Protection of Human Rights and Fundamental Freedoms (1953), the first specific right mentioned is the right to life, and the permitted exceptions are narrowly specified and carefully defined. Moreover, no derogation from this right is permitted in times of war or other public emergency threatening the life of the nation, except for deaths resulting from lawful acts of war. In the American Declaration of the Rights and Duties of Man (1948), article 1 asserts the right to life. Curiously, in the American Convention on Human Rights (1969), the chapter on civil and political rights opens with the right of every person to recognition as a person before the law. Then follows the right to life, which "shall be protected by law and, in general, from the moment of conception." No suspension of the right to juridical recognition and to life, among other rights, is permitted in time of war, public danger, or other emergencies. There is also an implication, or rather a clear indication, that the abolition of the death penalty is desirable.

Given such concerns for the security and protection of individual life, it seems to follow that there should be an even greater commitment to the protection of human groups, of individual life writ large. And indeed the circumstances of the founding of the United Nations and its declarations, resolutions, and conventions all seem to indicate the strength of this commitment.

The horror at the vast destruction of human life in the Second World War, extending far beyond the mass slaughter of conventional warfare, was expressed, from the victors' point of view, in the Four-Power Agreement of 8 August 1945 between the governments of England, France, the Soviet Union, and the United States. This agreement established the Charter for the International Military Tribunal that tried the major war criminals at Nuremberg. Article 6 specified three types of crime falling under the jurisdiction of the tribunal, namely, crimes against peace, including the waging of a war of aggression; war crimes, such as murder of civilian populations, killing of hostages, wanton destruction of cities, towns, or villages; and crimes against humanity, which were specified as "murder, extermination, enslavement, deportation and other inhumane acts committed against any civilian population, before or during the war, or persecutions on political, racial or religious grounds in execution of or in connection with any crime within the jurisdiction of the Tribunal, whether or not in violation of the domestic law of the country where perpetrated."

The founding Charter of the United Nations (1945) declares the determination of the peoples of the United Nations "to save succeeding generations from the scourge of war, which twice in our lifetime has brought untold sorrow to mankind." The opening clause of the first article binds them "to maintain international peace and security, and to that end: to take effective collective measures for the prevention and removal of threats to the peace, and for the suppression of acts of aggression or other breaches of the peace, and to bring about by peaceful means, and in conformity with the principles of justice and international law, adjustment or settlement of international disputes or situations which might lead to a breach of the peace."

During its very first session, the General Assembly passed a resolution for the prevention and punishment of *genocide*. This was a newly coined term to describe the destruction of human groups. The resolution noted the parallel between genocide and homicide in its explanatory introduction that "genocide is a denial of the right of existence of entire human groups, as homicide is a denial of the right to live of individual human beings." It declared that such denial of the right of existence of human groups shocked the conscience of mankind, resulted in great losses to humanity in cultural and other contributions, and was contrary to moral law and to the spirit and aims of the United Nations. Many instances of such crimes had occurred when racial, religious, political, and other groups had been destroyed entirely or in part; and the resolution declared that the punishment of genocide was a matter of international concern.

The depth of concern, to use a favorite word in the United Nations' vocabulary of horror, is shown by the fact that the resolution was passed unanimously and that the Convention on the Prevention and Punishment of the Crime of Genocide was adopted by the General Assembly two years later. It was a remarkable achievement to have agreed on the terms and phrasing of this convention so expeditiously, particularly when one reflects that the United Nations was a new organization, still establishing its procedures; that the draft convention was exposed to the deliberations of member states, with their different national and ideological interests; that its provisions were also subjected to the critical examination of a legal committee, whose members reflected greatly varied philosophies of law but a common preoccupation with the minutiae of precise formulation; and that even for the purpose of outlawing aggressive war and framing a Code of Offenses against the Peace and Security of Mankind, the United Nations repeatedly failed to arrive at an acceptable definition of aggression until 1974.

The preamble to the convention expressed itself strongly in its description of genocide as an "*odious scourge*." Article II defines genocide in terms of specified acts committed "with intent to destroy, in whole or in part, a national, ethnical, racial or religious group, as such," and the convention declares genocide to be a crime under international law that the contracting parties undertake to prevent and to punish.

There are other declarations and conventions that protect the right to existence of human groups, as for example the protection extended to racial and ethnic groups against acts of violence or bodily harm, under the provision of articles 4 and 5 of the Convention on the Elimination of All Forms of Racial Discrimination (1969). And there is the further reassurance in the United Nations' record for humanitarian relief to the victims of famine, flood, and war and to the survivors of genocide.

Given the strength of the commitment of the United Nations to the protection of the right to life of individuals and of groups, why has performance in response to genocidal conflicts been so negative, a history for the most part of inaction and evasion?

2

The Genocide Convention
The Group's Right to Life

The negative performance of the United Nations in the prevention and punishment of the crime of genocide is to be explained in part by the provisions of the Genocide Convention itself, and in part by conflicts of values among member states, extending to the very concept of human rights. But above all the failure to implement the convention reflects the primacy that member states accord to their political interests over the protection of the most basic human rights.[1]

Because the Genocide Convention deals with the group aspect of the right to life, protection of the right to life would extend automatically to genocide. But genocide is also a denial of the cultural and other contributions of human groups. There was thus a need for a Genocide Convention, irrespective of the particular historical circumstances of German crimes in the Second World War, which led to the adoption by the General Assembly of the United Nations, on 9 December 1946, of a resolution recommending international cooperation for the speedy prevention and punishment of the crime of genocide.

Major war crimes were tried under the authority of the Charter for an International Military Tribunal, established at Nuremberg, pursuant to the Four-Power Agreement of 8 August 1945 between England, France, the Soviet Union, and the United States. The Charter,

1. An extended discussion of the convention will be found in United Nations, *Study of the Question of the Prevention and Punishment of the Crime of Genocide*, E/CN.4/ Sub. 2/416, 4 July 1978; Robinson, 1960; and Kuper, 1981: chap. 2.

as we have seen, specified three types of crime falling within the jurisdiction of the tribunal: crimes against peace, war crimes, and crimes against humanity. The crimes against humanity included genocide (in the reference to the extermination of any civilian population), though the term was not used. However, the Nuremberg Charter linked the crimes against humanity to aggressive war or conventional war crimes. In this historical context, then, the Genocide Convention made the further contribution of freeing the concept from its association with war and rendering it applicable to the crimes of governments against their own nationals, whether committed in time of war or in time of peace.

The term *genocide* was coined by the jurist Raphael Lemkin, who effectively campaigned for the convention. It was derived from the Greek word *genos* (race, tribe) and the Latin *cide* (killing), and thus denoted the destruction of a nation or an ethnic group. In his book *Axis Rule in Occupied Europe*, Lemkin explained the concept as follows:

Generally speaking, genocide does not necessarily mean the immediate destruction of a nation, except when accomplished by mass killings of all members of a nation. It is intended rather to signify a coordinated plan of different actions aiming at the destruction of essential foundations of the life of national groups, with the aim of annihilating the groups themselves. The objectives of such a plan would be the disintegration of the political and social institutions, of culture, language, national feelings, religion, and the economic existence of national groups, and the destruction of the personal security, liberty, health, dignity, and even the lives of the individuals belonging to such groups. Genocide is directed against the national group as an entity, and the actions involved are directed against individuals, not in their individual capacity, but as members of the national group.[2]

As for the more detailed objectives of the genocidal plan, Lemkin based these on his analysis of the German techniques of genocide, which he listed comprehensively under the following headings: political, social, cultural, economic, biological, physical, religious, and moral.

It is clear from Lemkin's use of the words *a coordinated plan* of different actions *aiming* at the destruction of essential foundations of the life of national groups, with the *aim* of annihilating the groups themselves, that an essential element of the crime is the *intent* to

2. 1944:79.

destroy. This question of intent, and its definition, became a highly controversial issue in the framing of the convention.

So, too, the principle of the universal repression of the crime, emphasized by Lemkin, was vigorously contested. Lemkin had advocated that, in addition to provisions in national laws for punishment of genocide, the principle of universal repression should be accepted because of the special implications of genocide for international relations. "According to this principle," he wrote, "the culprit should be liable to trial not only in the country in which he committed the crime, but also, in the event of his escape therefrom, in any other country in which he might have taken refuge."

Lemkin was one of the experts consulted by the secretariat of the Human Rights Division on the first draft of the convention, and the influence of his ideas is very marked. The secretariat's draft was then thrown "into the high seas" of debate. Here it was exposed to extreme political buffeting, as was to be expected, given the different historical experiences and sensitivities to human suffering, the different world perspectives and political ideologies, the different state interests, and the different vulnerabilities calling for protective formulations and exclusions. The final convention bears all the marks of its difficult passage.

The convention was designed to prevent, as well as to punish, the crime, but the debates were not guided by any general theory of genocide. The Russian delegation argued that genocide was essentially bound up with fascist and Nazi ideologies and other, similar racial theories spreading national and racial hatred and aiming at the domination of the so-called superior races and the extermination of the so-called inferior races.[3] This argument drew attention to one element in many genocides, that of racial and ethnic prejudice. But although there was indeed an explicit relationship between Nazi ideology and genocide, this is not true for fascism, nor can the many genocides throughout history be explained in the context of Nazism-fascism and racist or ethnic exterminatory ideologies. I therefore interpret the Soviet argument as protective, and not as serious advocacy of a theory. The debates took place during the Stalinist era, and the many crimes of mass murder under that regime could hardly be attributed to Nazism-fascism.

A proposed amendment by the French delegate emphasized an-

3. ECOSOC, session 7, 26 Aug. 1948, pp. 721–22.

other element in the crime of genocide. He wished the definition to include the conception that genocide was a crime committed, encouraged, or tolerated by the heads of a state.

The theoreticians of nazism and fascism, who had taught the doctrine of the superiority of certain races, could not have committed their crimes if they had not had the support of their rulers; similarly, pogroms had occurred frequently only in countries where no severe legal measures were taken against the perpetrators. Thus the experience of history showed the way; it was inconceivable that human groups should be exterminated while the Government remained indifferent; it was inadmissible that the central authority should be powerless to put a stop to mass assassination when homicide was the first of punishable crimes. When the crime of genocide was committed, it was committed either directly by the Governments themselves or at their behest; alternatively, they remained indifferent and failed to use the power which every Government should have in order to ensure public order. Thus, whether as perpetrator or as accomplice, the Government's responsibility was in all cases implicated.[4]

It is certainly true that, in the great majority of cases, genocide is committed by, or with the complicity of, governments, and the argument for the amendment is valuable in drawing attention to the intimate relationship between state power and genocide. However, in some cases, though this is rare, genocide is committed without the involvement of the state. In any event, a general theory of genocide would need to specify the conditions under which state power takes on genocidal manifestations.

In the absence of any general theory of genocide, it is difficult, if not impossible, to devise measures for the prevention of the crime. The convention, in fact, makes only two perfunctory references to prevention. It is essentially directed to punishment of the crime, with the possibly deterrent effect of the threat of punishment as the main contribution to prevention.

The definition of genocide in the convention reflects the emphasis on punishment of the crime, along the lines of national (municipal) law. It reads as follows:

In the present Convention, genocide means any of the following acts committed with intent to destroy, in whole or in part, a national, ethnical, racial or religious group, as such:
   (a) Killing members of the group;
   (b) Causing serious bodily or mental harm to members of the group;

4. A/C.6/78, p. 146.

    (c) Deliberately inflicting on the group conditions of life calculated to
        bring about its physical destruction in whole or in part;
    (d) Imposing measures intended to prevent births within the group;
    (e) Forcibly transferring children of the group to another group.

The crime is thus defined, not in general terms, but by reference
to specific acts. These read rather strangely, being derived neither
logically nor theoretically, but by compromise and controversy. However, the first three categories of acts relate to physical extermination, the prevention of births to biological extermination (in
Lemkin's discussion), while the transfer of children is a relic of the
original formulation by the secretariat of acts constituting cultural
genocide.

The precise listing of genocidal acts would certainly assist a
court to arrive at a just assessment of guilt. Unfortunately, there are
ambiguities in the core of the definition relating to the phrase *in
whole or in part* and to the nature of the specific intent necessary to
constitute the crime.

The phrase *in whole or in part* appears in the secretariat's first
draft. It was omitted in the second draft by the Ad Hoc Committee
and then reinstated by the Legal Committee. The ambiguity lies in
determining what number or what proportion would constitute a
part for purposes of the definition. This would not be a serious difficulty if there were an international penal court, or effective national
courts, to deal with the crime of genocide. Presumably the convention is intended to deal with acts against large numbers, relative to
the size of the persecuted group, and it would rest with the courts to
adjudicate on this issue.

The inclusion of *intent*, and the manner in which it is defined,
raise more serious problems. In the first place, there are difficulties
in proof, and the denial of intent is readily available as a defense.
Thus, the defense minister of the government of Paraguay, in answer-
ing charges of genocide against the Aché Indians, replied that there
was no intention to destroy them. "Although there are victims and
victimizer, there is not the third element necessary to establish the
crime of genocide—that is 'intent.' Therefore, as there is no 'intent,'
one cannot speak of 'genocide.'"

There are also problems in determining the conditions under
which intention can be imputed. I will assume that intent is established if the foreseeable consequences of an act are, or seem likely to
be, the destruction of a group. But this may be controversial. The

problem is discussed, from varied perspectives, by Roger Clark with reference to the Indonesian massacres of the people of East Timor,[5] and by H. A. Bedau with reference to the role of the United States in the Vietnam War.[6] Here again, it would be for a court to decide the issue in the circumstances of the particular case.

Proof of intent is complicated further by the requirement of a specific intent, as the result of the introduction of the words *as such*. It is not sufficient that there should be an intent to destroy the group; there must be an intent to destroy the group *as such*. The phrase was adopted as a compromise amendment to the draft of the Ad Hoc Committee, which had introduced in addition to intent the requirement of a specific motive, namely, that the intended destruction should be "on grounds of national or racial origin, religious belief, or political opinion of its members." But what does the phrase mean? It is clearly ambiguous, and indeed the ambiguity was such for the members of the Sixth Committee that there was a serious proposal to appoint a working group to study the problem raised by the adoption of the amendment, the nature of the problem being that the vote had given rise to three interpretations.

The issue is not "purely academic." Thus, the permanent representative of Brazil to the United Nations replied as follows to charges of genocide against Indians in the Amazon River region of Brazil:

The crimes committed against the Brazilian indigenous population cannot be characterized as genocide, since the criminal parties involved never eliminated the Indians as an ethnic or cultural group. Hence there was lacking the special malice or motivation necessary to characterize the occurrence of genocide. The crimes in question were committed for exclusively economic reasons, the perpetrators having acted solely to take possession of the lands of their victims.

Or again, in my book *Genocide*, I had described the atomic bombing of the Japanese cites of Hiroshima and Nagasaki by the United States and the pattern bombing of the Allies of Hamburg and Dresden, as genocide. This interpretation was rejected by General Telford Taylor on the ground that these bombings were not genocidal within the meaning of the convention, which limits genocide to acts committed with intent to destroy a national, ethnical, racial or religious group, as such. "Berlin, London and Tokyo were not bombed because their inhabitants were German, English or Japanese, but be-

5. 1981:321–28.
6. 1978:5–46.

cause they were *enemy* strongholds. Accordingly, the killing ceased when the war ended and there was no longer any enemy."[7]

I cannot accept the view that the atomic bombing, in time of war, of such civilian enemy populations as those of Hiroshima, Nagasaki, Hamburg, and Dresden does not constitute genocide within the terms of the convention. But in any event, it seems to me that General Telford Taylor is equating the phrase "as such" with the original formulation "on grounds of national or racial origin" or assigning it the meaning "because of national or racial origin." I prefer to interpret the phrase to mean "using the national or racial origin, or religious belief, as the criterion for selecting the individuals killed."[8]

Since the Genocide Convention is primarily concerned with the judicial punishment of the crime, authoritative interpretations might be expected to emerge from court decisions. But proposals for effective institutions and procedures to punish the crime were greatly watered down, and there are no authoritative decisions to which reference might be made.

The original draft of the convention called on states parties to the convention to provide in their laws for effective punishment of the crime, and it conferred universal jurisdiction, the parties undertaking to punish offenders "within any territory under their jurisdiction, irrespective of the nationality of the offender or of the place where the offense" was committed. It also included two alternative draft statutes: one for an international criminal court with general competence, and the other for a special international court to deal with acts of genocide.

Bearing in mind that it is mostly governments which commit the crime of genocide, and that the member states participate through their governments in the councils of the United Nations, the emphasis in the convention on punishment of the crime would be threatening. Hence, it is not surprising that protective action should have been taken against the more effective provisions for enforcement of the convention.

The obligation of the parties to legislate against genocide and to provide penalties for punishment is included in the final draft, and a small number of states have passed the necessary measures, including states that are not parties to the convention.[9] Others considered

7. *New York Times Book Review*, 28 Mar. 1982, pp. 9, 18, 19.
8. Interpretation suggested by Peter Archer.
9. See E/CN.4/Sub.2/416, pp. 141–54.

that their laws already provided for punishment of the crime. But the whole process of legislation and of prosecution is under the control of the governments themselves, and domestic jurisdiction in cases of genocide has the bizarre consequence that, in the large majority of cases, governments would be expected to prosecute their own members—presidents, cabinet ministers, general secretaries, juntas, and so on. In other words, governments would have nothing to fear unless they were overthrown by revolution or by outside intervention.

The real threat to governments would have come from the acceptance of universal jurisdiction and the establishment of an international penal court. Universal jurisdiction, however, was eliminated from the convention; protection against genocide would seem to rank below protection against piracy or the counterfeiting of money. The provision for trial by a competent international tribunal was also eliminated, only to be reinstated later in the greatly weakened form of "such international penal tribunal as may have jurisdiction with respect to those Contracting Parties which shall have accepted its jurisdiction." And even this reference to a hypothetical penal court with optional jurisdiction was bought at great cost by the exclusion of political groups from the "protection" of the convention.

The original United Nations resolution, which affirmed that genocide was a crime under international law, referred to the many instances of that crime "when racial, religious, political and other groups" were destroyed entirely or in part. This was a natural response to the annihilation of racial, ethnic, religious, and political groups in Germany under the Nazis. And both the first and second drafts of the convention extended "protection" to political groups. But the inclusion of political groups came under vigorous attack.[10]

Many of the arguments for deletion of the reference to political groups do not seem very cogent, as for example the argument that political groups were too unstable, and lacking in identifiability, for protection under the convention or that, by reason of voluntary membership, they belonged to a different order from racial, religious, or national groups, whose distinctive features were permanent. Neither the Nazis nor the Soviets under Stalin had difficulty in identifying and murdering their political opponents, and under certain conditions for example, in the labor camps of the Pol Pot regime in

10. See Kuper, 1981:24–30.

Democratic Kampuchea or in Indonesian villages at the time of the large-scale massacres of communists), political affiliation can be as permanent and as immutable as racial origin.

The real issue was the freedom of governments to dispose of political opposition without interference from the outside world. The comment of the Swedish representative that the proposed provision in the draft convention "applied only to the most horrible form of the crime against a group, that of its physical destruction," and "that it seemed that all States could guarantee that limited measure of protection to political groups"[11] seems curiously naive. The French representative was much more realistic. He warned that "whereas in the past crimes of genocide had been committed on racial or religious grounds, it was clear that in the future they would be committed mainly on political grounds."[12] And indeed, his warning was prophetic. At the present time, political groups are a special target for assassination in many member states of the United Nations, with a massive toll of victims. At a recent conference of Amnesty International (Holland), Extra-Legal Executions as a Means of Political Persecution, extensive documentation was presented on political mass murder by governments in many parts of the world, often taking the most horrendous forms—of disappearances, or of torture and the terroristic display of mutilated bodies, or the contemptuous discarding of the dead in mass graves.[13]

However, anxiety lest the inclusion of political groups should seriously affect ratification of the convention finally prevailed, and reference to political groups was eliminated. This made it possible to reinstate reference to trial by an international penal tribunal, but only in the conditional and optional form mentioned above.

No international penal court has as yet been established, and of the enforcement procedures originally envisaged in the draft conventions, there remains only trial by a competent tribunal of the state in the territory of which the crime was committed. Aside from prosecutions of war criminals, there have been only two such trials. In Equatorial Guinea, the tyrant Macías had been slaughtering his subjects and pillaging his country for a number of years. He was finally overthrown, found guilty of a number of crimes, including genocide, and executed. In a report on the trial, however, the legal officer of the

11. A/C.6/75, p. 114.
12. U.N. ECOSOC (cited in n. 3), p. 723.
13. See *Political Killings by Governments*, 1983.

International Commission of Jurists concluded that he had been wrongly convicted of genocide.[14] In Kampuchea, when the Khmer Rouge regime was overthrown by the Vietnamese invasion, the successor government instituted criminal proceedings against the former prime minister, Pol Pot, and the deputy prime minister on charges of genocide, and the accused were found guilty of the crime, in absentia, by a people's revolutionary tribunal. But Pol Pot is still at large, protected by his army and by the continued recognition of his regime in the United Nations as the accredited representative of the Cambodian people. In April 1973 the government of Bangladesh announced its intention to proceed with the trial of 195 Pakistani nationals "for serious crimes, which include genocide, war crimes, crimes against humanity, breaches of Article 3 of the Geneva Conventions, murder, rape and arson." But this projected prosecution was later abandoned under extreme pressure.[15]

There can be no doubt as to the many defects in the framing of the Genocide Convention. It is primarily concerned with punishment, and yet there is serious ambiguity in the definition of the crime, a somewhat illogical specification of the acts by which it is committed, and, above all, inadequate provision for enforcement. Whether one applies the test of the number of genocides that have run their seemingly uninhibited course since the adoption of the convention, or the test of the prosecutions for genocide during the same period, it is impossible to escape the conclusion that the convention has been quite ineffective.

Some of the assessments of the convention have been exceedingly negative. I quote two such assessments from the "Views on the Effectiveness of the 1948 Convention as a Whole," presented in the United Nations report on genocide.[16]

The whole Convention is based on the assumption of virtuous Governments and criminal individuals, a reversal of the truth. . . . In any event even if this assumption were correct, the criminal law of every civilized State provides sufficiently against individual acts of the kind which are enumerated in the Convention. . . . Thus the Convention is unnecessary where it can be applied and inapplicable where it may be necessary. It is an insult to intelligence and dangerous, because it may be argued *a contrario* by brazen upholders of an

14. *The Trial of Macias in Equatorial Guinea*, 1979.
15. See Paust and Blaustein, 1978:1–38. MacDermot, 1973:476–83, discusses some of the legal issues involved in the proposed prosecution.
16. U.N., *Study of Genocide*, pp. 118–19.

unlimited *raison d'Etat* that acts enumerated in the Convention, but not committed with intent of destroying groups of people "as such" are legal. The Convention . . . is, as has been formulated politely by Professor Brierly, symptomatic of a "tendency to seek a sort of compensation for all that is so terribly discouraging in the international outlook of today by dissipating energies to achieve results which prove on examination to mark no real advance."

In the absence of means to make it effective, the Convention on the Prevention and Punishment of the Crime of Genocide joins all the pacts and international declarations, which, for lack of enforcement provisions, remain pure show and all contain the mental reservation; "unless contrary to the higher interests of the State, of which the State is sole judge."

These comments are, however, much too negative. According to an advisory opinion of the International Court of Justice, genocide was already a crime in international law.[17] The original General Assembly resolution merely *affirmed* that genocide was a crime under international law. It seems then that the convention did not innovate in this respect. But it did give definition to the crime, it made some provisions for punishment, and there is symbolic significance, at the very least, in the denunciation of genocide, and in the steps taken by some member states to legislate against the crime. The convention has been ratified, or acceded to, by 92 states,[18] and it has established genocide, in international awareness and acceptance, as a crime under international law and a matter of international concern. And though a major defect of the convention, given the general involvement of governments in genocide, is the failure to establish an international penal court, the issue is not closed, and the establishment of the court remains on the agenda of the United Nations. Moreover, there are punitive sanctions, other than punishment of the crime by criminal court procedures, that could be invoked within the United Nations by member states.

However, punishment addresses the crime after the event, with its accompanying great loss of life, whereas the priority concern should be to prevent genocide or, failing that, then at least to arrest its catastrophic course. On this more basic problem of prevention, two articles of the convention are relevant. Under article VIII, any of

17. Advisory opinion in the *Reservations to the Genocide Convention Case*, ICJ Reports, 1951:23. I am indebted to Paul Sieghart for drawing my attention to this advisory opinion and its significance. See, however, the critical comments on this advisory opinion by Lane, 1979:263–64.

18. As of June 1983. See A/CN.4/368/Add. 1, p. 3.

the parties to the convention may call upon the competent organs of the United Nations to take such action under the Charter of the United Nations as they consider appropriate for the prevention and suppression of acts of genocide; and under article IX, they may submit to the International Court of Justice disputes relating to the interpretation, application, or fulfillment of the convention.

The convention thus relies on U.N. procedures and institutions for the prevention and suppression of genocide. At the time of its founding, the United Nations was certainly the most appropriate body for this purpose. Its member states, too, were strongly committed to elimination of the crime. But, with a few exceptions, "the competent organs" have failed to respond to well-grounded complaints of genocide; indeed, their responses have usually been protective of offending states. And equally discouraging, the parties to the convention have not availed themselves of the services of the International Court of Justice, under article IX, in circumstances in which it would have been appropriate for them to do so, if suppression of the crime had remained a high priority.[19]

Clearly, the United Nations cannot now be relied upon to initiate and carry out preventive action against genocide. Yet it remains potentially the most effective agent for this purpose, and one might hope to stimulate a more active concern. But it would be a counsel of despair to await this moral renewal. At the same time, it is difficult to see how one can dispense with some active role for the United Nations in a coordinated campaign against genocide. The alternative would be to establish an international grass-roots organization, with even more massive and influential support than the antinuclear movement, in situations in which most people do not feel personally threatened.

However, there is in fact no basis for dismissing the United Nations as irrelevant to preventive action. I have closely observed its performance and the development in recent years of a number of possibilities of preventive action. Some cases may be totally resistant; in others, the genocide or genocidal threat may be more realistically

19. One advisory opinion was sought from the International Court of Justice at the instance of the General Assembly. The action arose out of a dispute in regard to the validity of reservations by some of the ratifying states that they did not consider themselves bound by article IX of the convention, and that they regarded the agreement of all parties to the dispute as essential for the submission of any particular case to the court for decision (E/CN.4/Sub.2/416, pp. 83, 94–99).

approached on the basis of its constituent elements rather than directly confronted in its totality. From the point of view of preventive action, the early detailed indicators of the possibility of genocide become significant—as, for example, mounting repression against a racial, ethnic, or religious group, campaigns of vilification, summary executions, small-scale massacres, and the flight of refugees to neighboring territories. They raise a variety of issues relevant to violations of human rights, as well as problems of humanitarian relief, through which some international pressure, in different contexts, can be mounted against offending states. But if use is to be made of the United Nations in any overall campaign, a first step must be an analysis of the obstacles that have stood in the way of effective action in the past.

The following chapters carry out this analysis at the level of values and of state interests, in the context of the structure and the procedures of the United Nations. In part II, the emphasis is primarily on values relating to human rights in general and to genocide in particular. In part III, the central concern is with implementation.

Part II deals with the constraints on U.N. action for implementation of obligations in the field of human rights, as a result of the conflicts of values and of interests of member states. It opens, in chapter 3, with a general discussion of conflicts of values flowing from different perspectives on human rights and on the scale of values. This is followed by a case study of self-determination in Bangladesh (chap. 4) and by some general observations on the right to self-determination (chap. 5). Self-determination is particularly relevant to the present study. It is one of the most strongly affirmed values within the United Nations, and it played a significant role in the whole process of decolonization. But it has been so redefined in the postcolonial world as to be resistant to the claims of minority groups; and its denial has been, and continues to be, a major source of genocidal conflict. The Bangladesh case study documents this process of redefinition and its implications. It also shows the primacy accorded to values supportive of state power: domestic sovereignty, territorial integrity, and non-intervention; and it throws considerable light on the variability of the commitment to ideologies and values, as well as the role of naked state interests in frustrating action against genocide.

In part III, on implementation, a major theme is the interplay of state interests and values in the deliberations and responses of the

United Nations on human rights issues. The opening chapter (6) outlines major perspectives within the United Nations on the implementation of human rights and discusses some of the general problems arising, but with special reference to genocide. Chapter 7 is a case study of the implementation of the Anti-Slavery Conventions. This was selected in the expectation that the United Nations would be at its most effective in the suppression of slavery, since slavery is the very negation of the Universal Declaration of Human Rights; and it must surely be anathema to Third World countries, which had so often been the victims of the slave trade, and to the East European socialist countries, seeking to eliminate the exploitation of man by man, and to Western capitalist societies, all dedicated to its eradication and some still atoning the guilt of the slave trade. And yet there was great resistance to the provision of even the most minimal procedures for implementation of the Anti-Slavery Conventions. The conclusions in this chapter are relevant to implementation of human rights commitments in general. Also, the form of institutional innovation adopted could be of some relevance for the prevention of genocide.

The final chapters deal with United Nations performance in cases of political mass murder (chap. 8) and genocide (chap. 9). Many case studies were presented in my book on genocide, and I refer briefly to this material. I have, however, added a number of new case studies, and these are discussed in some detail. Political mass murder was included because it is often difficult to draw a clear line between genocide and political mass murder, and its inclusion should help to obviate controversy. There is no authoritative body to declare that a particular series of mass murders constitutes genocide, and readers may consider that some of the cases I cited as genocide are more appropriately categorized as mass murder. Indeed, the two categories shade into each other. Moreover, it was originally contemplated that the "protection" of the Genocide Convention would be extended to political mass murder, which takes at least as heavy a toll of life as genocide.

The book concludes, in part IV, with the discussion of a program of action for the punishment and prevention of the crime of genocide. In this discussion I assume that, realistically, only a small contribution can be expected from the United Nations, at any rate in the immediate future. Even this modest contribution will require activation from the outside. Hence there is a need for some form of

organization, or of collaboration between non-governmental organizations, to stimulate action within the United Nations, but, equally
important, to provide also an independent base for the launching of
a general campaign against genocide.

PART TWO

DYNAMICS OF IDEOLOGICAL CONFLICT

3

Conflicts of Norms and Values

During 1947, when the U.N. Commission on Human Rights was working on the preparation of the Universal Declaration of Human Rights, the United Nations Educational, Scientific and Cultural Organization (UNESCO) carried out a supportive inquiry into the theoretical bases of the rights of man. The result was a great diversity of perspectives, contributed by a large array of thinkers, including some of the leading intellectuals of the day. There were the varied emphases on different categories of human rights; discussions of the rights of man living under liberal, socialist, and communist regimes and in primitive societies; reference to the basic ethical concept of Chinese social political relations as the duty to one's neighbor; and a brief introduction to the five social freedoms, and the five individual possessions or virtues, of Hindu tradition. It would hardly seem possible, with such differences in perspectives, to reach agreement on a Universal Declaration of Human Rights.

In an introduction to the UNESCO report (*Human Rights: Comments and Interpretations*), Jacques Maritain took up the issue. "How," he asks, "can we imagine an agreement of minds between men who are gathered together precisely in order to accomplish a common intellectual task, men who come from the four corners of the globe, and who not only belong to different cultures and civilizations, but are of antagonistic spiritual associations and schools of thought?" (p. 10). And he found the answer in part in a distinction he drew between speculative ideology on the one hand, and practical ideology and ba-

sic principles of action on the other. He argued that the present state
of division among minds, in faith, philosophy, and theory did not permit of agreement on a common speculative ideology. But, given a
pragmatic rather than a theoretical approach, there was nothing to
prevent the achievement of a new and wider declaration of human
rights at the level of practical ideology. However, he warned against
complacency in the mere enumeration of a list of human rights. Over
and above the enumeration of human rights, there was the problem
of implementation, for which the first necessity was agreement on
the scale of values:

To produce a true Charter determining a common way of action, the agreement must also cover the scale of values, the key in which in their practical
exercise in social life, the acknowledged rights of man must be harmo-
nized. . . . The function of language has been so much perverted, the truest
words have been pressed into the service of so many lies, that even the no-
blest and most solemn declarations could not suffice to restore to the peoples
faith in human rights. Thus it is the implementation of these declarations
which is sought from those who subscribe to them; it is the means of securing
effective respect for human rights from States and Governments that it is
desired to guarantee. On this point, I should not venture to express more
than the most guarded optimism. (pp. 16–17)

How disturbingly contemporary these words now sound!

The contributors to the UNESCO inquiry were largely Western
oriented, as was to be expected, the United Nations being very much
under the domination of the West in its early years. Now, more than
thirty years later, the situation is profoundly changed. The United
Nations still excludes large numbers of minority groups. But for the
rest, almost the entire globe is represented with its vast range of cultures and structures; and the diversity of perspectives has been rendered infinitely more complex.

The member states have their own unique historical experience;
member states provide the existential basis for a great variety of
ideologies. Their economic development ranges from largely subsistence agriculture, with great poverty, to the technologically sophisticated industrialization of the most affluent societies. They incorporate varied political forms—semifeudal states, one-party
states, military dictatorships, totalitarian governments, and
Western-type democracies, with greater or lesser predominance of
bureaucracies and mass political parties. There are radical differ-

ences too in their systems of law, in content, elaboration, adjudication, and reliance on authoritative sources—custom, case law, legislation, codification. They differ not only in the nature of the values they pursue, and in their scales of values (to which Maritain referred), but also in the strength of their commitment to these values—rigid or flexible, expedient, cynical, principled, pragmatic. And added to these complexities are the complications of the pursuit of state interests, however crackpot the definition of these interests may be.

It all seems a potential Babel, particularly given the principle of the sovereign equality of member states, though qualified by the right of veto in the Security Council. But clearly the diversity is so structured as to permit the United Nations to function in a vast array of working groups, and to pass, by majority vote and even by an apparent consensus, a plethora of declarations, resolutions, conventions, many of great potential significance for the future of international relations, and for a new world order.

However varied the historical antecedents, the cultures, political forms, and economic development of the member states, there are nevertheless sufficient elements of common interest and experience to provide the basis for a structure of alliances in the United Nation. It has become conventional to view this structure in terms of the industrialized West, the Socialist bloc of East European countries, and the Third World, subdivided for certain purposes into a further category of least developing countries. Decisions are appreciably determined at the present time by an alliance between the socialist bloc and the Third World. From a different aspect, the structure may be viewed in terms of an East-West, and a North-South, division and confrontation. Or one may prefer the Maoist perspective advanced by the Chinese delegate in the General Assembly on 29 September 1977. This is a division into the three worlds of, first, the two superpowers (capitalist-imperialist and social-imperialist, struggling for world hegemony); second, the Western European countries; and, finally, the Third World of developing countries, with which China identifies. There are anomalies in these classifications.[1] Australia, New Zealand, and Japan would be included in the industrialized West, and China in the Third World, though she is a nuclear power, with a prospective capacity to contend for world domination. There

1. See the discussion of this problem of classification in Espiell, 1979:41–65.

is ambiguity too in the concept of the Third World and difficulty in defining it so as to embrace all the countries that claim allegiance.

To these classifications must be added the alliances or groupings falling outside the structure of the United Nations but providing a basis for concerted action within it: the regional intergovernmental associations in Africa, America, Asia, and Europe, NATO, the Warsaw Pact, and similar alliances, which overlap or partly overlap other divisions.

In addition, the United Nations supplies its own internal organization by way of formal structures (the Security Council, General Assembly, Economic and Social Council, commissions, working groups) and by rules and procedures (including, of course, those governing the Commission on Human Rights and the Sub-Commission on Prevention of Discrimination and Protection of Minorities). These rules and procedures, and human rights and other norms, are by no means neutral. They become weapons in political warfare but also instruments for conciliation. Members have established their own traditions for pursuing their political objectives. The framing of an agenda, the allocation of time for discussion, the selection of preambular clauses, and the wording of substantive provisions become arenas of political strife. Opposition may be overruled by majority resolution, or conciliation sought by abstention, or by compromise and consensus, or by noble-sounding, but meaningless, routine formulas.

It is within these structures, formal and informal, and by means of these procedures as defined and as elaborated, that the United Nations acts for the promotion and the protection of human rights. And it is within these structures that conflicts of values and related norms inhibit protective action against gross violations of human rights. From the conflicts of values in the proceedings of the United Nations, I select two of special significance, for the protection of human rights in general and for international protection against genocide.

INDIVIDUAL, STATE, AND SOCIETY

I include, under this heading, conflicts of values concerning (1) the sources of law on human rights; (2) individualism and collectivism, particularly as manifested in different approaches to the relationship between economic, social, and cultural rights on the one hand and civil and political rights on the other; and (3) the scale of values.

In selecting these topics, I leave aside the question of the strength of commitment to the norms. One has only to compare the prohibition of the use of torture in the Universal Declaration of Human Rights and in the Covenant on Civil and Political Rights with the prevalence of this practice by the governments of many member states, to appreciate the wide divergence of routine practice from solemn declaration. Added to this is the complication I have already mentioned, that human rights issues have become, increasingly, political weapons in the international armory. The resulting application of variable, and even double, standards further undermines confidence in the integrity of the commitment.

Norms on human rights are appreciably linked to ideology, and I will discuss the conflict of norms and values in the context of three ideologies—Western capitalist, East European socialist, and Third World development oriented. There is, of course, great variation in each of these categories. One cannot, for example, speak of one socialist conception of human rights or assume that there has been no departure from classic Marxist origins. And there is much overlapping among ideologies. But in presenting these ideologies in a somewhat skeletal and oversimplified form, I am seeking to emphasize broad issues of conflict in their ideological context.

SOURCES OF LAW ON HUMAN RIGHTS

Here, a major antithesis lies between the Western capitalist and the East European socialist societies. The West has a long tradition of human rights derived from natural law, in terms of which the individual as a human being possesses, or has a moral entitlement to, certain fundamental rights. These rights are inherent in the very nature of man, existing, as it were, prior to, and lying outside, any social contract; they are universal, not tied to citizenship in a particular society, and they are inalienable, protecting the individual in perpetuity against governmental interference. They are enshrined in the English Bill of Rights of 1689 and, a hundred years later, in the United States Constitution and the French Declaration of the Rights of Man and Citizen.

In the nineteenth and twentieth centuries, however, the natural law approach to human rights was undermined by legal positivism, that is to say, the conception of human rights as being defined by, and as deriving authority from, custom, legislative enactment, and judicial decision. But the rise of fascism stimulated a revival of natural law concepts. The Nazis had systematically prepared the ground for the destruction of human rights, and ultimately for genocide, by statutory enactment, judicial process, and bureaucratic regulation, thus substituting tyrannical and murderous Rule *by* Law for the Rule *of* Law. Against this assault on human rights with the weapons of legal positivism, natural law doctrines provided some theoretical defense, offering an authoritative source for human rights above, and superior to, positive law;[2] and they are embodied in the United Nations Universal Declaration of Human Rights. The opening preamble declares that "recognition of the inherent dignity and of the equal and inalienable rights of all members of the human family is the foundation of freedom, justice and peace in the world." The first article proclaims that "all human beings are born free and equal in dignity and rights. They are endowed with reason and conscience and should act towards one another in a spirit of brotherhood." And the rights themselves are couched in terms of the rights of individuals.

The socialist critics of natural rights doctrine reject the conception of absolute and eternal rights inherent in the nature of man. They see this as an abstract and ahistorical approach. Human rights are shaped within a specific historical context by the nature of the economic system, the stage of material (and intellectual) development, and the position and relations of economic classes. The meaning of human rights doctrine in any society may be derived from its consequences. In the context of the developing capitalist societies of the seventeenth and eighteenth centuries, it becomes clear, so the argument runs, that the natural rights doctrine provides an ideological statement of the conditions necessary for the accumulation of wealth. It is an ideology of the rising bourgeoisie. Man is viewed in detachment from society, as an egoistic individual pursuing his selfish interests with a minimum of interference. And the rights themselves are essentially formal, abstracted from a content that in fact legitimizes inequality. What is the significance of the right to property for those without any possible means of acquiring property?

Moreover, it is an illusion to view the rights as antecedent to the state. On the contrary, their source *is* the state. One must look beyond the form in which the rights are stated to their actual content, which is determined primarily by the nature of class relations, in effect by the power of the economically ruling class acting through the state.

2. See the discussion by Pétéri, 1966:116–17.

From the perspective I have described as East European socialist, there is no entitlement to human rights existing prior to, and
independent of, the state. The state does not *recognize* rights—it
grants them, linking effective enjoyment to responsible performance.
Moreover, the interests of the socialist state are identified with the
interests of society and rise above human rights.

The conception of the state as the source of human rights, and
the assumption of a harmony of interests between the state and its
subjects, are in sharp contrast with the West's conception of the need
to protect the individual against the tyrannical exercise of state
power. Indeed, in socialist doctrine, the need for such protection falls
away with the abolition of social classes. From a Western perspective,
the subordination to the primacy of the socialist state results in
marked limitations on human rights. The contrast in perspectives
readily appears from the following quotations, taken from the work
of a group of Hungarian socialist scholars.

(1) With reference to the right of combination, the right of assembly, freedom of communication of opinion, and freedom of conscience and worship attaching to the activities of religious communities or churches as organizations, that is, collective freedoms:

Beyond the said collective character these freedoms are characterized by (the
fact) that the citizen exercising them will step out of the sphere of state-
organized social activities and will in a certain sense perform independent
social activities. Owing to its organized character this type of activity has
great political significance. . . . For this reason the conditions for the exercise
of such freedoms are regulated by statutory definitions going into details,
and simultaneously the government organs exercise a systematic tight control over them.[3]

(2) With reference to freedom of religion:

The socialist state applies no coercive measures against the citizens professing religious ideas, it allows the free exercise of religion, yet with the orga-
nizational and educational facilities and institutions of the State propagates
the scientific, materialist ideology and fights with the weapons of science
against religious doctrines, but never against men professing religious
ideas.[4]

(3) With reference to deficiencies in the Universal Declaration of
Human Rights:

3. Schmidt, 1966:245.
4. Ibid., 259.

The generalized formulation of certain provisions of the Declaration, e.g. on the freedom of opinion (Article 19), freedom of assembly and association (Article 20) without the addition of any guiding principles, provides means for the propagation of Fascist doctrines; or by referring to the Declaration—it enables to put forward claims to the formation of organizations with anti-democratic purposes, although the Declaration as a whole ought to serve the reinforcement and safeguard of democracy.[5]

The reinforcement of the power of the state in socialist doctrine has proved attractive to many governments of member states in the United Nations. And I doubt that the doctrine of the long-term withering away of the state has much credibility when the primacy of the state is guaranteed by the centralized concentration of political power, backed by control over the means of production. As a Soviet dissident comments: "The building of communism in the Soviet Union and other Communist countries has made a valuable new contribution to that oldest of sciences, the science of conquering a human society."[6] From a Western European perspective, it is in the theory and practice of East European socialist societies that law attains its fullest expression as an instrument for the enhancement and perpetuation of the power of ruling strata.

INDIVIDUALIST AND COLLECTIVIST IDEOLOGIES

The conflict of norms on the sources of law is related to a much wider conflict of ideological perspectives: that between individualist perspectives in the Western capitalist societies and collectivist in the East European. But this ideological opposition can readily be exaggerated. It is no longer possible to view human rights primarily as a protection against the tyranny of the state. There has been massive intervention by the governments of capitalist states in welfare, social security, and economic planning, as well as a recognition of the necessity for this intervention to secure the common good; and the recognition goes back to the early years of the founding of the United Nations.

In 1941, in a message to the United States Congress, President Roosevelt enunciated the four freedoms (freedom of speech, freedom of religion, freedom from fear, and freedom from want) as the basis of a new world order, and in 1944 he asked Congress to explore the means for implementing an economic bill of rights to secure freedom

5. Bokor, 1966:291.
6. Chalidze, 1975:40.

from want. Though the rights were couched largely in individual terms, implementation called for collective action. The Atlantic Charter of August 1941 referred to the right of self-determination of peoples and to the need for international cooperation to secure economic advancement and social security; and the Yalta Conference of February 1945 emphasized cooperation between peace-loving nations to ensure freedom from fear and freedom from want for all.

In the United Nations the preamble to the founding Charter declared the determination of the signatories to promote social progress and better standards of life in larger freedom and to maintain international peace and security by united action. Following this, the Universal Declaration of Human Rights incorporated economic, social, and cultural rights to be realized through national effort and international cooperation. Though the human rights guaranteed by the declaration are couched in individual terms, many of these rights have a collective aspect.[7] To be sure, there was the influence of the socialist governments in the framing of these documents, but the collective aspects in the declaration were compatible with trends in the capitalist societies.

In socialist societies the collective commitment rests firmly on the primacy of the socialist state and its control of the means of production. The emphasis on the duty to work and on the duty to protect socialist property is curiously reminiscent, at the collective level, of the early Protestant ethic of the nobility of labor and the sanctity of private property. Human rights policy, in theory, is directed to the establishment of the economic and social conditions necessary to render the effective exercise of human rights a reality in everyday life. Thus the right to work is guaranteed by the socialist organization of the economy, by growth in the productive forces, and by elimination of unemployment. Or again, as in article 50 of the Soviet Constitution of 1977, exercise of the political freedoms of speech, the press, and assembly is ensured by the availability of public buildings, streets, and squares to working people and their organizations, by broad dissemination of information, and by the opportunity to use the press, television, and radio.[8]

Creation of the conditions necessary to render human rights effective may be seen as justifying the outright denial, or the severe limitation, of human rights, as in the Soviet commitment to the liq-

7. See the discussion by the former director of the U.N. Division of Human Rights on the individual or collective bias of human rights (van Boven, 1970:386).
8. See Henkin, 1975:68.

uidation of the oppressor classes, in contrast to the privileged position of the workers and the dictatorship of the proletariat. Since the state of human rights in a society is viewed as closely related to its social-economic order, there is an evolutionary, indeed relativistic, approach to human rights. Thus to take a further example from the Soviet Union, the 1977 constitution declares that, the aims of the dictatorship of the proletariat having been fulfilled, the Soviet state has become a state for the whole people.[9] But notwithstanding the collective emphasis, individual human rights are affirmed in the socialist constitutions, though in a somewhat different form than found in the Western constitutions—tending to be descriptive of the state of human rights in the society rather than prescriptive.

Still, even allowing for the exaggerations, the different emphasis on individualism and collectivism constitutes a sharp division in perspectives, and I think there is substance to the comment by the former chairman of the British section of Amnesty International that although the two separate United Nations covenants, on economic, social, and cultural rights and on civil and political rights, are meant to complement each other, they "actually codify what amounts to a major ideological rift."[10]

This ideological rift, of course, preceded the establishment of the United Nations and it immediately found expression in its debates and in the Universal Declaration of Human Rights (1948). The declaration was passed unanimously, in part no doubt because it was conceived as a statement of principles setting a common standard of achievement, a document with moral, not legal, authority. Nevertheless, eight nations abstained from voting: Saudi Arabia, South Africa, the Soviet Union and its socialist European allies. The nature of the socialist objections to the declaration is best conveyed by the statements of their representatives during the debate in the General Assembly.[11]

(a) On implementation:

(i) It was, of course, possible to draft a declaration containing great humanitarian principles, but those principles should bear some relation to the every-day facts of contemporary life in capitalist countries. Each man's right

9. Ibid., 59.
10. Oestreicher, 1979:9
11. General Assembly, 9 and 10 Dec. 1948, pp. (a) 869, 870, 882; (b) 870, 904, 914, 915: (c) 913, 914, 928, 929.

to a luxurious mode of living could be proclaimed; it would, however, remain a fiction for millions of men as long as their living conditions were such that it was impossible for them to enjoy it. In capitalist countries there was and always would be a flagrant contradiction between what was said in the declaration of human rights and reality.

(ii) The declaration proclaimed the right to work; but in real life something quite different happened. [Taking] the United States as an example, that country had nearly two million unemployed.

(iii) The work of the hand made the tool, and the tool permitted the development of the brain and the senses; by means of work man organized himself in society so as to meet his needs and achieve his intellectual and moral development. In its present form, the declaration took no account of the practical aspect of the problem; it simply expressed lofty ideals, making no provision for their implementation in the difficult daily life of the workers.

(b) On the social and economic foundations of human rights:

(i) Before the rights to work, to rest and to education could be put into effect, it was necessary to alter drastically the economic system of private enterprise, the motive power of which was the desire for profit. Unemployment was an essential element of that system.

(ii) In present times, any declaration which failed to establish a close link between political rights and social and economic guarantees, and which did not assure a democratic basis for those rights, was pointless. The victory of the popular forces in several countries of Europe, however, had opened a wide road for the practical application of fundamental human rights by guaranteeing the political, economic and social liberties of the people.

(iii) The economic factor had become decisive in the whole social development of the present time. Consequently, the social status of the individual was not based on juridical instruments but was the result of the social and economic conditions in which that individual lived. That meant that the civil and political status of the individual had become in a very great measure dependent upon his social status.

(iv) The principal objective of the new declaration of human rights should not have been to simply enumerate those rights in terms which were already widely known, but the social and material conditions necessary for their enjoyment.

(c) On the individual, the state, and society:

(i) It (the Declaration) should also provide a more general protection to man, not only as an individual but as a member of social groups, since a number of important human rights resulted from the interdependence existing between man and the community to which he belonged.

The text before the Assembly was based on individualistic concepts which considered man as an isolated individual having rights only as an individual, independently of the social conditions in which he was living and of all the forces which acted upon his social status.

(ii) It had been stated that the USSR wished to subordinate the individual to the State, making of the individual some sort of cog in the powerful, indeed the all-powerful State on the line of Hobbes' Leviathan. Those were hollow arguments which merely went to prove that those who used them did so with insufficient understanding and inadequate analysis of the real meaning of what they had allowed themselves to say about the Union of Soviet Socialist Republics. They had evidently forgotten that the contradiction between the State and the individual was a phenomenon which had occurred, in history, when society had been divided into rival classes. Wherever society was so divided, the ruling class controlled the machinery of government. In such societies the State had become the tool of the ruling classes whose aims and interests were contrary to those of all the other classes. There the State did indeed seek to rule over the individual whose interests were in conflict with its own.

Circumstances were wholly different in a society where there were no rival classes. That was indeed natural, for in such a society, there could not be any contradiction between the government and the individual since the government was in fact the collective individual. That contradiction was eliminated when a society reached the stage when it was no longer divided into classes conflicting with each other, the class of the exploiter and the class of the exploited.

Therefore the problem of the State and the individual, in its historical sense, did not exist. History had already solved that problem in his country. The State and the individual were in harmony with each other; their interests coincided. That relationship was expressed in the formula of which all progressive persons were justly proud: "the Union of Soviet Socialist Republics is the socialist State of workers and peasants." That formula indicated that in their State, the problem of contradiction between the State and the individual did not exist in the form in which it had prevailed at all stages of society's historical development when it was divided into classes: feudal, bourgeois, capitalist and the contemporary socialist-capitalist States. They wished to see other States move closer to that noble ideal which had already been attained in one-sixth of the world.

The conflict of ideologies found further expression in divergent views on the number of covenants necessary to give effect to the Universal Declaration of Human Rights. The socialist arguments in favor of a single covenant emerge readily enough from the emphasis on the socioeconomic conditions necessary for the realization of human rights, and the case for a single covenant originally prevailed. On 4 December 1950 the General Assembly affirmed, in its resolution 421 E(v), that "the enjoyment of civic and political freedoms and of economic, social and cultural rights are interconnected and interdependent" and that "when deprived of economic, social and cultural rights, man does not represent the human person whom the Universal Declaration regards as the ideal of the free man."

However, at the following session of the General Assembly, the opponents of a single covenant succeeded in reversing the decision. The United States representative, Eleanor Roosevelt, summarized the arguments against a single covenant.[12] Economic and social rights were to be achieved progressively: civil and political rights could be made effective rather quickly. The enactment of legislation was generally sufficient to put into effect the civil and political rights, whereas the attainment of economic and social rights called for a broader program of action. There were differences too in the precision with which the rights were formulated and in the machinery for receiving complaints. One might add to these arguments the further argument that the civil and political rights, framed in terms of individual rights, were correlative to negative duties of the state, while the economic and social rights were addressed to states and were correlative to their positive duties.

The arguments are legal and rational, largely procedural rather than substantive, and the issue of one or two covenants seems somewhat formal. But it was a focus for the confrontation of two major ideologies, competing for disciples among the nations of the world. And this same confrontation reappears, though in different form, in the relations between the developing and developed countries.

DEVELOPING AND DEVELOPED COUNTRIES

The terms are not very precise. The developed countries include Great Britain, which has experienced severe economic decline and is now in the midst of a deep recession, with high unemployment mounting to more than 3 million, deliberately used by the government in the fight against inflation. The developing countries cover a wide range. They include, at one extreme, Brazil, a potential economic giant, countries with spectacular growth of wealth, and oil-exporting states with high per capita income. At the other extreme are countries so impoverished and so deficient in resources that they seem to have little potential for development.

Still, the terms can be given a rough connotation in much the same way as North-South (for developed and developing), or East-West, or Third World. The developed countries are those with highly

12. General Assembly, 4 Feb. 1952, 504–05.

industrialized economies, as measured by a variety of indices. They should include the East European Industrialized societies, save that these societies reject identification with the West or inclusion in a division which, in their view, is rooted in the history of colonization.[13]

As for the developing countries, a great number have only recently attained independence, and they share many elements of colonial experience. They are still stabilizing their regimes and feel threatened by neocolonial economic and political domination. Depending greatly on the industrialized countries for sophisticated technology, they experience, for the most part, unequal trade relations in their dealings with these countries. By virtue of their numbers and on the basis of their solidarity, they seek a bargaining counterpoise to the power of the industrialized nations and a transfer of resources from these nations.

The division between the developed and the developing is a division between the rich and the poor. The "least developed countries" have a population of 258 million (1977 estimate) with an average per capita income (for 1977) of $150. For Third World countries as a whole, the World Bank estimated the number of the destitute as 800 million. Extreme deprivation and overwhelming poverty in many of these countries take their toll in a low expectation of life and high death rates from preventable diseases. The United Nations International Children's Emergency Fund (UNICEF) estimated that in 1978 more than 12 million children under the age of five died of hunger. Between 20 and 25 million children below the age of five die every year in developing countries, and one-third of these deaths are from diarrhea contracted from polluted water. Estimates of those who experience hunger and malnutrition number hundreds of millions, with millions either dying from starvation or suffering physical impairment.[14]

Comparable estimates are given by a former United States secretary of state and president of the World Bank: at least one-third to one-half of the world's people suffer from hunger or nutritional deprivation; infant mortality rates are four times as high in the developing countries as in the developed; illiteracy is widespread; there is endemic and growing unemployment; vast numbers of "marginal"

13. See Report of the Independent Commission on International Development Issues (Brandt et al., 1980:31).
14. Ibid., 78, 50, 16, 55, 90. I have taken the figures given in the *North-South* report.

men exist, "wretched strugglers for survival on the fringes of farm and city"; and there is a widening gap between the per capita incomes of the rich nations and the poor nations.[15] A UNESCO volume written by a Third World spokesman emphasizes the sharp contrasts between the developing and the developed nations, observing, for example, that one-third of mankind, representing the most deprived developing countries, receives only 3 percent of world income; or commenting that, "whereas the majority of mankind live in a state of endemic famine, the population of the United States, representing only six percent of the world population, consumes 55 percent of all the natural resources of the earth."[16]

Against this background of poverty and misery in so many areas of the developing countries, it is inevitable that the highest priority should be given to economic development and economic rights. Clearly, the nature and quality of the economic rights attainable are dependent on the level of economic development in a society. This is recognized in the Covenant on Economic, Social and Cultural Rights, which provides for the progressive realization of these rights to the maximum of the available resources. No such reservation is made in the Covenant on Civil and Political Rights. From this circumstance, the American Association for the International Commission of Jurists draws the "clearly evident" conclusion that "the most fundamental civil and political rights, like freedom from torture, arbitrary arrest or cruel and inhuman treatment, can be established immediately if the official resolve and intent to do so are present."[17] But is this the conclusion drawn by member states of the developing countries? Do they see the two sets of rights as compatible and mutually supportive? Or do they view them as competitive, the primacy of economic needs rendering necessary the suspension or derogation of civil and political rights?

It is, in fact, the second point of view that prevails in the counsels of many member states of the developing countries. There are already expressions of this conception written into the Covenant on Economic, Social and Cultural Rights. Article 2, paragraph 3, provides that "developing countries, with due regard to human rights and their national economy, may determine to what extent they would guarantee the economic rights recognized in the present Cov-

15. McNamara, 1973:53–54.
16. Bedjaoui, 1979:26–27.
17. *Toward an Integrated Human Rights Policy*, 1979:7.

enant to non-nationals." Is this provision regarding the derogation of rights a legitimation for the forcing out of, say, Indians from the countries of East Africa? And what is the effect of other permitted derogations, for example, in the very loosely framed articles 4 and 8 (1a)?[18] The permitted derogations of civil and political rights are much more rigorously defined.

Within the human rights sections of the United Nations there is much criticism of the conception that the demands of development are in competition with, or antagonistic to, civil and political rights. Thus, the special assistant to the director of the Division of Human Rights, writing in a purely personal capacity, comments as follows:

The Third World cannot wish away the issue of violations of human rights. It fought for the dignity of its peoples and for their right to self-determination and it strives today for the realization of their right to development. But how does it face up to violations in many parts of the world of the rights of these same peoples? In this paper we shall suggest that while the Third World has made important contributions to the promotion and protection of human rights, and to a better understanding of the human needs of their peoples, there has been a failure of leadership and a certain amount of self-deception in dealing with violations of human rights. We proceed from three basic premises: (i) While recognizing that under-development results in widespread denials of basic human rights and admitting the imperative need for development, we deny that violations of civil and political rights in many countries of the Third World are primarily attributable to under-development. (ii) Governments should be judged by the most exacting standards, especially where human rights are concerned. They fail their peoples when they shrug off the incidence of violations of human rights by saying that these violations are due to under-development or that basic human rights have to be sacrificed for the sake of development. It is a test of the quality of leadership that it should be able to govern fairly and justly even in difficult circumstances. Offering such excuses is a confession of failure. (iii) Third World leaders who shut their eyes to violations of hu-

---

18. These articles are as follows:

4. The States Parties to the present Covenant recognize that in the enjoyment of those rights provided by the State in conformity with the present Covenant, the State may subject such rights only to such limitations as are determined by law only insofar as this may be compatible with the nature of these rights and solely for the purpose of promoting the general welfare in a democratic society.

8.(1a) ... No restrictions may be placed on this right (to form and join trade unions) other than those prescribed by law and which are necessary in a democratic society in the interests of national security or public order or for the protection of the rights and freedoms of others.

man rights occurring within their ranks or offer false excuses for them, betray the moral foundations of the Third World.[19]

On the occasion of the thirtieth anniversary of the Universal Declaration of Human Rights, the director of the Division of Human Rights contributed an article, also in a purely personal capacity, entitled "United Nations Policies and Strategies: Global Perspectives." Here he discusses, at a very general level, some of the constraints of underdevelopment, political instability, and foreign intervention as they affect basic rights and freedoms.

It is certainly in the minds of those who are familiar and concerned with living conditions in many developing countries that poverty, illiteracy, ignorance, hunger, disease, political instability, foreign intervention have such an effect that these countries find themselves virtually in a permanent state of political or economic emergency.

These contextual circumstances are by themselves a threat to human rights or, more directly, they may constitute, as such, gross violations of human rights. They can provide an explanation why human rights are seriously at stake, but they can certainly not be adduced as a justification for the infringements of certain very basic rights and freedoms, such as the right to life, the right to be free from torture or from cruel, inhuman or degrading treatment or punishment, the right not to be held in slavery or in slavery-like conditions and the right to be free from arbitrary arrest or detention. Too often the violations of these very basic rights and freedoms are the result of abuse of power by selfish rulers, of grotesque arrogance of those who claim to be masters, of ill-conceived notions and practices of superiority, of racist ideologies. It is tempting and deceiving on the part of such abusers of power to invoke structural causes and external factors in order to camouflage violations of human rights which they are consistently committing, thus adding immensely to the suffering which is already prevalent as a result of the contextual circumstances.[20]

There is similar criticism by Keba M'Baye (a president of the Supreme Court of Senegal and a distinguished contributor to the work of the U.N. Commission on Human Rights), who reviews, in an article published in 1969, the condition of human rights in the states of black Africa.[21] He describes the initial enthusiasm for the Universal Declaration of Human Rights, and the change upon confrontation with the exigencies of security and of social and economic development to an insistence on giving the rights and liberties defined by the

19. Ramcharan in Cassese, ed., 1979:249.
20. Van Boven in Ramcharan, ed., 1979:86–87.
21. M'Baye, 1969:382–94.

declaration a content compatible with the urgent achievement of a minimum standard of social well-being. He comments on the movement in favor of the legal dictatorship of the executive power and the minimizing of liberty in the name of the general interest. Notwithstanding African condemnation of slavery and the struggle against forced labor, slavery continues in certain forms, forced labor has been rehabilitated under the guise "du boubou de l'interêt general," and freedom of association has been violently and systematically attacked; trade unions are often a simple emanation of the political party in power.

In order to ensure subsistence to the populations they govern and to banish famine, disease, and ignorance, the public authorities conceive of themselves as being in a state of war by reason of which they have the right to impose such restrictions on public rights and liberties as flow from a state of siege, emergency, or exceptional circumstances. In this conception, the black world will return to a normal regime once it has attained economic and social development. "Still, one has the right to ask, whether the current practice of attacks on rights and freedoms, made in the name of the security of the state and of economic and social development, does not run the risk of installing itself irrevocably in the common law, as a result of the habituation of the public authorities and of local opinion to arbitrary rule."[22]

There is thus a convergence between these particular theories of development and theories of socialist reconstruction. Both emphasize the primacy of the collectivity and of economic rights. Both readily sustain the power of strong centralized governments and serve as ideologies for new ruling strata. And both cast individual civil and political rights in a diminished role. From these perspectives, what significance can be attached to the banishment of a Soviet dissident or his confinement in a psychiatric hospital, or arbitrary arrest, or destruction of political opposition as compared with high death rates from malnutrition and preventable disease, or the threat of recurrent famine, or massive unemployment.

We return then to the crucial problem raised by Maritain, the effects of the different salience of human rights among the member states of the United Nations. Let us assume—and this is, of course, an invalid assumption—that ratification of a human rights conven-

22. Ibid., 392.

tion, and incorporation of its provisions in national legislation, implies a serious commitment. Let us assume further that the obligations undertaken have approximately the same meaning in the context of different legal and political systems. And let us ignore, for the moment, the overriding concern with national interests in the international deliberations on human rights. There still remains the problem of the kind of agreement possible, on an ordering and scale of values, among advocates of such diverse ideologies, as well as the need to look at the reality behind the skillful deployment of words and formulas to convey a seeming consensus.

In the chapters that follow on self-determination, the major issues relate to the scale of values and to the role of state interests. There is inevitably a conflict of values because claims for self-determination call for some modification in the structure of state sovereignty, while in the extreme case of demands for secession, there is a challenge to the territorial integrity of the state. And the conflict of values may readily take a highly destructive, indeed genocidal, form because the groups that are exposed to the threat of genocide, namely racial, ethnic, and religious groups, are precisely the groups that would be the claimants in demands for self-determination. In these circumstances, is primacy to be accorded protection against gross violations of human rights, including genocide, or to respect for state sovereignty, territorial integrity, and nonintervention in the internal affairs of sovereign states? And what is the role of state interests in defining or redefining well-accepted principles of international relations and in establishing a hierarchy of values?

4

The Right to Self-Determination
The Secession of Bangladesh

Struggles for greater autonomy by ethnic (and racial) groups in plural societies have been a major source of highly destructive conflict. The ultimate form of autonomy is the establishment of an independent state. Bangladesh is the only case in the postcolonial world in which a people achieved independence by secession. The debates in the United Nations on the Bangladesh conflict illuminate many of the issues that arise in the assertion of the right to self-determination in postcolonial societies.

The conflict had its origin in the establishment of Pakistan as an independent state on the partition of India, a partition accompanied by many genocidal massacres, Hindu-Muslim and Muslim-Hindu, and especially destructive of human life in the Punjab.[1] The partition brought two separate areas of India, and different peoples, into a single state, the basis of unity being brotherhood in Islam and fear of Hindu domination, "the resin of a common hatred."[2] But the initial political and spiritual exhilaration of a new nationalism was beset from the earliest days by the divisive forces of ethnic pluralism.

The main division was between West Pakistan, which was con-

1. This introductory description of the conflict is taken from my book *Genocide* (1981:78–80). I have made one change in my own account to bring out the fact that the Bengali campaign of noncooperation, which preceded the massacres by the Pakistani forces, was accompanied by violence. The extent of this violence was one of the controversial issues.
2. Mascarenhas, 1971:11.

solidated into the four provinces of Baluchistan, the North West Frontier, Punjab, and the Sind, and East Pakistan, which included the eastern half of Bengal, a portion of Assam, and the tribal areas of the Chittagong Hill Tracts.[3] The differences between these two sections were quite extreme. In culture, language, economy, and geography, they were two distinct countries with little communication between them. They were separated by more than 1,000 miles. In East Pakistan, about 95% or more spoke Bengali, compared with fewer than 2% speaking Urdu, the official language of the West.[4] In addition to their different cultural heritages, the peoples themselves are physically distinctive. In climate, West Pakistan is dry, wheat-growing desert country, whereas in the monsoon climate of East Pakistan, with its rice, jute, and tea, there are the flood dangers from the Ganges and Brahmaputra rivers. The natural economic outlets and trading partners for East Pakistan were in the neighboring parts of India. West Pakistan turned naturally for its cultural and commercial exchanges toward the Arab Middle East, and East Pakistan toward India and the Asian Far East. Both the West, with a population of about 55 million at the time of the genocidal conflict, and the East, with about 75 million, were large enough in population and territory to constitute separate states.[5]

The pluralism extended beyond the division between East and West. In the East there were 10 to 12 million Hindus and many Urdu-speaking Muslims who had migrated to East Pakistan and were known as the Biharis, though only a part came from Bihar. In areas with large concentrations of Biharis, hostility and resentment developed between them and the Bengalis.[6] In the West there was the pluralism of the different populations in the constituent provinces— Punjabi, Baluchi, Pathan, and Sindhi.

Given the diversity of peoples and the problems of setting up a new state, it is not surprising that there were difficulties in arriving at a constitutional accommodation. In 1940, seven years before partition, the Muslim League had passed a resolution in terms of which the constituent units would be autonomous and sovereign. But this

3. Levak, 1975:284.
4. Bengali was recognized as an official language only after language riots in 1952.
5. See J. E. Owen, 1972:24, and the International Commission of Jurists, 1972:71.
6. International Commission of Jurists, 1972:9.

was later changed to a commitment in favor of a unified sovereign state. There was delay in framing the constitution and resort to different constitutional arrangements, including the consolidation of the four provinces in the West into a single unit. This seemed to be a solution to problems of parity of representation in the national parliament between the West and the East, but in fact it contributed to polarization.

The main source of polarization lay, however, in a relationship between West and East that the Bengalis saw as colonialism and that indeed bore many of the marks of a colonial domination. The West wing became increasingly more industrialized and prosperous, while conditions in the East deteriorated. On partition, the per capita income of the West exceeded that of East Pakistan by 10%; this disparity had risen to 30% by 1960, to 40% by 1965, and to 60% by 1969.[7] The bulk of Pakistan's foreign exchange was earned in the East but largely expended on industrial development in the West. So, too, a disproportionate share of foreign aid went to the West. Economic domination was secured by political domination, the senior military personnel, the senior civil servants, and the central government bureaucracy as a whole, being overwhelmingly West Pakistani. The effect of this wide-ranging discrimination was to nurture the movement for greater regional autonomy in East Pakistan.

The long periods of military dictatorship and of martial law give some measure of the tensions in the creation of the new state. These tensions reached their apocalypse after the Legal Framework Order introduced in 1970 by the then military dictator (or chief martial law administrator). This laid down the conditions and procedure for the framing of a new constitution. It reaffirmed an earlier pledge to restore democratic institutions, it promised elections in October 1970 with a distribution of seats in the National Assembly proportionate to population, and it defined the constitutional relations between the federal government and the provinces as maximum autonomy for the provinces, but with adequate powers for the federal government "to discharge its responsibilities in relation to external and internal affairs and to preserve the independence and territorial integrity of the Country." By another order, the province of West Pakistan was dissolved into the four provincial divisions of the Punjab, the Northwest Frontier, Sind, and Baluchistan.

7. J. E. Owen, 1972:25.

In the elections the Awami League campaigned on a six-point program for almost the maximum possible autonomy for the East, short of total separation. It gained 167 of the 169 seats allocated to East Pakistan in the National Assembly, thus becoming the majority party, and in the East Pakistan Assembly it won 288 of the 300 seats. There followed negotiations and a campaign of noncooperation in the East, accompanied by violence when the president (and chief marital law administrator) postponed the convening of the National Assembly sine die. Negotiations were resumed and seemed to be moving cordially toward a resolution of conflict. But during the course of the negotiations, the government was in fact mobilizing its military forces in the East, and on 25 March 1971 it struck with devastating force.[8]

It seems that the government intended to eradicate dissidence in the East by admonitory massacres and massive terror. The International Commission of Jurists[9] describes the principal features of this ruthless repression as "the indiscriminate killing of civilians, including women and children and the poorest and weakest members of the community; the attempt to exterminate or drive out of the country a large part of the Hindu population; the arrest, torture and killing of Awami League activists, students, professional and business men and other potential leaders among the Bengalis; the raping of women; the destruction of villages and towns; and the looting of property. All this was done on a scale which is difficult to comprehend." It was carried out, I should add, with unspeakable brutality, and with the additional horror of torture and extermination centers. As the resistance of the Bengalis mounted, the army responded with massive collective reprisals in the annihilation of Bengali villages. Where non-Bengalis were in a majority, the Biharis attacked the Bengalis, and many Biharis served in the auxiliary forces of the West Pakistan Army.[10] Bengalis too engaged in massacre and atrocity against Hindus and Biharis.

8. In these brief comments on the constitutional difficulties and the discrimination against the East, I have drawn on the following sources: J. E. Owen, 1972:23–28; International Commission of Jurists, 1972; Mascarenhas, 1971:6–33; Levak, 1974:203–21, and 1975:281–308; Morris-Jones, 1972:187–200; and Indian Ministry of External Affairs, 1971.

9. 1972:26–27.

10. For accounts of the war, see International Commission of Jurists, 1972; Chaudhuri, 1972; Mascarenhas, 1971; Payne, 1973; and Indian Ministry of External Affairs, 1971. See also Nafziger and Richter (1976) for an analysis of the role of economic forces

On 16 December 1971 the war ended after the intervention of the Indian Army, which sealed the successful secession of the now independent state of Bangladesh. Estimates of the Bengalis killed in Bangladesh vary greatly, with an upper limit of perhaps 3 million. Chaudhuri[11] presents a chart—incomplete, however—of the worst affected places in 18 districts, giving figures for property damaged, slaughterhouses and mass graves discovered, women ravished, skulls and skeletons found, and total killed (in all, 1,247,000). A separate chart (on page 148), prepared by the United Nations Relief Committee in February 1972, gave a total of more than 1.5 million houses destroyed (with an allowed error of ± 25%). In addition, there were some 10 million refugees in India, largely Hindu, living under conditions of extreme hardship and with an appalling death rate.

The International Commission of Jurists expressed the view that there was "a strong prima facie case that the crime of genocide was committed against the group comprising the Hindu population of East Bengal." It viewed the army atrocities as part of a deliberate policy by a disciplined force. As to the killing of non-Bengalis by Bengalis, the commission found it "difficult to accept that spontaneous and frenzied mob violence against a particular section of the community from whom the mob senses danger and hostility is to be regarded as possessing the necessary element of conscious intent to constitute the crime of genocide." Throughout this massive catastrophe "the United Nations failed to use its available machinery to deal with the situation either with a view to terminating the gross violations of human rights which were occurring or to deal with the threat to international peace which they constituted."[12]

After the first massacres on 25 March 1971 the secretary-general of the United Nations acted promptly. On 1 April a U.N. spokesman stated, in reply to questions, that if the government of Pakistan were to request the secretary-general to assist in humanitarian efforts, he would be happy to do everything in his power in that regard. On 19 May the secretary-general launched an emergency appeal for the refugees, largely women and children, who had fled to India from East Pakistan; and on 16 June, in a further appeal, he announced the co-

and social classes in the conflict. A discussion by Young (1976, chap. 12) deals with the politics of secession in Biafra, Bangladesh, and Southern Sudan from the perspective of cultural pluralism. Nordlinger (1975) discusses the same conflicts from the perspective of the role of military governments in communally divided societies.

11. 1972:199–202.
12. International Commission of Jurists, 1972:57, 98.

operation of the Pakistan government in the relief operations, and his designation of the United Nations high commissioner for refugees as a focal point in the coordination of U.N. relief activities.[13]

A month later, on 19 July, in an aide-mémoire to the permanent representatives of India and Pakistan, the secretary-general suggested that the appointment of field representatives of the high commissioner for refugees on both sides of the border might facilitate the voluntary repatriation of refugees. At the same time, on 20 July, he presented a memorandum to the president of the Security Council in which he expressed his increasing apprehension at the steady deterioration of the situation. Assistance for refugees was far from sufficient, and the Indian government still faced the appalling and disruptive problem, over an unforseeable period, of caring for millions of refugees, whose numbers were still increasing. Moreover, in East Pakistan itself, international and governmental efforts to cope with the results of two successive disasters, one of them natural, were increasingly hampered by the lack of substantial progress toward political reconciliation; this political reconciliation was also an indispensable prerequisite for the return of any large proportion of the refugees.

These human tragedies, the secretary-general warned, could have wider consequences for the relations between religious and ethnic groups in the subcontinent as a whole, and for the relations between the governments of India and Pakistan. *"The conflict between the principles of the territorial integrity of States and of self-determination has often before in history given rise to fratricidal strife and has provoked in recent years highly emotional reactions in the international community."* In the present case there was the additional danger that the crisis was unfolding in the context of long-standing, and unresolved, differences between India and Pakistan—differences which had given rise to open warfare only six years ago. There was a potential threat to peace and security in the present tragic situation, which presented a challenge that the United Nations as a whole must meet. "If the Organization faces up to such a situation now, it may be able to develop the new skill and the new strength required to face future situations of this kind."[14]

The government of India, in its reply to the secretary-general's

13. *UN Monthly Chronicle*, May 1971, p. 24; June 1971, pp. 49–50; and July 1971, pp. 26–27.
14. Ibid., Aug.–Sept. 1971, 56–59.

aide-mémoire, agreed that the repatriation of the refugees was a matter of the utmost concern and urgency. But it was a matter of even greater concern and urgency to stop the military atrocities in East Pakistan and the daily flow of refugees into India at the rate of 40,000 to 50,000 a day. The root cause of the influx of more than 7 million refugees into India, and the continuing daily exodus, could be explained only by the total absence of conditions in East Pakistan that would encourage the refugees to return to their homes. An improved political atmosphere in the country was the indispensable prerequisite. "The conflict between the principles of territorial integrity of states and self-determination is particularly relevant in the situation prevailing in East Pakistan where the majority of the population is being suppressed by a minority military regime which has refused to recognise the results of the elections held by them only in December last year and has launched a campaign of massacre, genocide and cultural suppression of an ethnic group comprising 75 million people." The time was past when the international community could continue to stand by and watch the situation deteriorate, in the hope that relief programs, humanitarian efforts, the posting of a few people here and there, and good intentions would be enough to turn the tide of human misery and potential disaster.[15]

In contrast to the government of India, the government of Pakistan immediately accepted the proposal to post representatives. It responded to the Indian government's charges by repudiating responsibility for the exodus of refugees. The root cause, it claimed, was armed rebellion designed to bring about the dismemberment of the state of Pakistan. The will of the people of East Pakistan, as expressed in the national elections of December 1970, was for autonomy within Pakistan, and not for secession from Pakistan. The tragic civil strife occurred not because of East Pakistan's demand for autonomy—which was conceded—but because some of the Awami League representatives had betrayed the mandate they had received from the people. And India itself had encouraged the movement for secession by making declarations, by training and directing the rebel forces, and by engaging in direct military operations. It was of the utmost regret to Pakistan that the international community had done little to restrain India from a course of conduct which violated

15. Ibid., 59–62.

"the two most fundamental principles of the Charter of the United Nations—non-interference in internal matters and refraining from the threat or use of force against the territorial integrity or political independence of any state." As for the right of self-determination, it was

the established jurisprudence of the United Nations that, while the principle of self-determination governs the liberation of territories which are under colonial rule or are in dispute between Member States, it cannot be extended to areas that are recognized as integral parts of the territories of Member States. Any such extension on the ground of ethnic, linguistic or racial composition of the people, or of economic disparities within a country, would give rise to such a multiplicity of disputes and cause such anarchy and ceaseless strife as to destroy the present international order. Such a development would be disastrous even from a purely human point of view, particularly for the newly-independent states of Asia and Africa. Pakistan is only one among the many multi-racial, multi-linguistic or multi-religious states which would then be exposed to the dangers of fission and disintegration.[16]

On 27 October, the secretary-general released the texts of identical letters to the prime minister of India and the president of Pakistan, with copies to the president of the Security Council. In these letters he expressed his anxiety over the growing tensions that might give rise, all too easily, to open hostilities between the two countries and also might constitute a major threat to the wider peace; and he tendered his good offices of conciliation. In December, he made a desperate appeal to the parties to the conflict to take every possible measure to spare the lives of innocent civilians, and he announced that arrangements were being made for the evacuation of United Nations and other international personnel from Dacca.

The secretary-general did all in his power to activate the United Nations, and he did succeed in mounting a massive program of humanitarian relief. This was a major contribution. But, for the rest, he failed utterly to involve the United Nations in the resolution of a conflict the course of which he had so clearly predicted.

There had been some activity in U.N. bodies. In discussion of humanitarian relief at the meetings of the Economic and Social Council in May, the Indian ambassador raised the issue of a permanent solution, the creation of conditions that would enable the refugees to return to their homeland. In September both India and

16. Ibid., 59, 62–67.

Pakistan raised the matter in the General Assembly but without substantive outcome.[17]

Earlier, in August, there had been a serious attempt to involve the Sub-Commission on Prevention of Discrimination and Protection of Minorities. Twenty-two nongovernmental organizations, in consultative status with the Economic and Social Council, submitted a statement expressing grave concern that no organ or agency of the United Nations had commented on the implications of the events for the human rights of the affected peoples. They called on the subcommission to examine the allegations of violations of human rights and to recommend to the commission the protective measures that might be taken. The subcommission should also consider the extent to which events in the affected areas might be relevant to its contemplated studies on minorities, indigenous populations, and genocide.[18]

The Pakistan representative replied at great length, traversing much of the same ground as in his government's aide-mémoire. He also challenged the competence of the subcommission, as an expert and nonpolitical body, to concern itself with political issues. There was negligible participation in the debate by members of the subcommission. The observer for India responded briefly and with restraint, and the Pakistan representative exercised his right of reply. Thereupon the chairman commented that the debate seemed to have taken a political turn, and he suggested that the subcommission should consider the matter as having been dealt with. *It was so agreed.*[19]

The appropriate body to deal with the conflict was, of course, the Security Council. It was vested with the necessary authority and power, and it was specially entrusted with the responsibility for ensuring world peace. But it was only "seized" with the matter, on the initiative of nine members of the Security Council, when incidents of armed conflict between Pakistan and India had turned to open warfare, that is to say, almost nine months after the first massacres. In fairness to the Security Council it must be said that members were deeply concerned and that they did, in fact, respond to the memorandum from the secretary-general. In the Security Council debate on 4 December 1971 the Italian representative commented that, during

17. A/PV 1940, pp. 4–9, and A/PV 1941, pp. 22–26. See also Franck and Rodley, 1972:145–50.
18. E/CN.4/Sub.2/NGO 46, dated 23 July 1971.
19. E/CN.4/Sub.2/SP, pp.628, 629, and 633.

his presidency of the council in August, he had held extensive consultations but that "unfortunately, in such a complicated and complex situation, raising, as it does, constitutional and juridical as well as political problems of all sorts, we could not discover one course of action among the several we discussed that would at that time have commanded the full support of the Council."[20]

The French representative explained the delay as a result of the dilemma in responding to the dual nature of the crisis.

> The present situation has two aspects. One is at the root of the crisis and is political in nature. It affects relations between the Government of Islamabad and the population of East Pakistan. It is subject to a political solution susceptible of receiving acceptance by both sides. The second aspect is derived from the first, by reason of the influx of refugees to India. It affects relations between that country and Pakistan. It has created a state of tension which after much violence has eventually reached the stage of open acts of hostility. A civil war has thus been transformed into a war between nations.
>
> This dual aspect of the crisis gives rise to a dilemma. If we were to consider only the first aspect of the crisis, our action risks being considered as interference in internal affairs, and we appreciate the fact that Pakistan is attached both to its sovereignty and its integrity. But if we were to consider only the second aspect, our action risks being considered as partial and as not going to the root of the matter, and we appreciate the fact that India cannot feel satisfied with superficial solutions when it has millions of refugees under its care.
>
> It is this dilemma which explains the difficulties confronting the United Nations, the warnings of the Secretary-General and the hesitation of the Security Council for three months to be seized of the question.[21]

Given this impasse, nations sought to bring their influence to bear through normal diplomatic channels—without success. And so it was that the Security Council debated the issues for the first time on 4 December, when India had already invaded Pakistan. But the same difficulties that had frustrated earlier endeavors now beset their present deliberations.

The positions of the Indian and Pakistani governments remained irreconcilable. The Indian government continued to insist that the cause of the conflict was the refusal of the Pakistan government to accept the results of the general election and to accord the peoples of East Pakistan the autonomy they sought within the state of Pakistan. It was only when the Pakistan government had launched a genocidal

20. S/PV 1606, p. 20.
21. Ibid., 21.

campaign of suppression that the demands for autonomy within Pakistan were transformed into a movement for secession and the establishment of an independent state. And the Indian ambassador quoted the words of the East Pakistan leader, Sheikh Mujibur Rahman: "Pakistan is now dead and buried under a mountain of corpses. The hundreds and thousands of people murdered by the army in Bangla Desh will act as an impenetrable barrier between West Pakistan and the people of Bangla Desh. By resorting to pre-planned genocide Yahya must have known that he was himself digging Pakistan's grave."[22] The Pakistan government, on the other hand, persisted in its claim that the cause of the internal conflict was the escalation of the mandate for autonomy to a movement for secession and the breakup of Pakistan, and that the massacres carried out by the antistate and secessionist elements in East Pakistan had necessitated the intervention of the army.

There was now added to this confrontation on the internal situation the new element of open warfare following the invasion of Pakistan by the Indian Army. The government of Pakistan charged that India had not only launched aggression on the territory of another member state but also had openly demanded that Pakistan dismember itself and give up that part of its territory which contained the majority of its population. This was a situation which involved every state that believed in the principle of the territorial integrity of states, a principle fundamental to the Charter of the United Nations; and it concerned all who were in danger of being overrun by larger, more powerful and predatory neighbors.[23]

India pleaded self-defense against Pakistan's military aggression. It also put forward the plea of humanitarian intervention, though not explicitly in those terms. (See, for example, the speech of the Indian ambassador on 4 December: "We are glad that we have on this particular occasion absolutely nothing but the purest of motives and the purest of intentions: to rescue the people of East Bengal from what they are suffering.")[24]

Perhaps some solution might have been found if the superpowers had not ranged themselves on opposite sides. The United States of America supported Pakistan, or at any rate, it was "tilted" in favor of

22. S/PV 1608, p. 8.
23. S/PV 1606, p. 7.
24. Ibid., 18.

Pakistan. The USSR was bound to India by treaty, while China, also a veto power, added the further complication of enmity toward both the USSR and India.

The representative of the United States opened his statement with unconscious irony.

In the months since last March we have all been witnesses to the unfolding of a major tragedy. Coming on the heels of the cyclone last year, one of the greatest natural disasters of modern times, civil strife in East Pakistan has caused untold suffering to millions of people, has created a new and tragic refugee community in India of unparalleled dimensions and has brought India and Pakistan to open hostilities. It is time for the United Nations to act to bring the great moral authority of this body effectively and quickly to bear to preserve the peace between two of its largest Members.

The United States government, he said, recognized that a fundamental political solution had not been achieved in East Pakistan and that the only proper solution was a political one. But the immediate cessation of hostilities and the withdrawal of forces were essential conditions for progress. He therefore proposed a resolution calling upon the governments of India and of Pakistan to take all steps necessary for an immediate cessation of hostilities and withdrawal of armed personnel to their own sides of the India-Pakistan borders.[25]

The USSR supported its Indian ally in urging the primacy of a political solution. Its representative argued that the inhuman acts of repression and terrorism by the Pakistan government were the main cause of a most serious problem, which was perhaps without parallel in the extent of the personal suffering of millions of people. He therefore called for a political settlement in East Pakistan. This would inevitably put an end to the hostilities. He also called for the cessation of all acts of violence by Pakistani forces in East Pakistan.[26]

The Indian ambassador, in a brief intervention, added the supporting argument that merely to arrest the hostilities between India and Pakistan would not stop continued fighting by the East Pakistan resistance movement, nor would it stop the Pakistani army from continuing its oppression and sending more and more refugees into India. Had the present concern for saving lives been matched by a similar concern during the previous nine months, it would have been a source of some comfort to his government and the Indian people.

25. Ibid., 18–19.
26. Ibid., 25, 32.

"What, indeed, has happened to our conventions on genocide, human rights, self-determination, and so on."[27]

Representatives of the smaller powers struggled strenuously to bridge the gap between these conflicting demands, and during the three days of debate they showed much ingenuity in their search for a compromise resolution acceptable to the parties. The result, as the Saudi Arabian representative commented, was that draft resolutions and tentative texts wafted in the air of the council like autumn leaves while a full-scale war was being waged between two sister states in the Asian subcontinent, perpetrating untold sufferings on the innocent on both sides. No draft resolution, he continued, would be entirely satisfactory to all parties concerned. "The alternative would be a draft resolution with semantic expressions that could be interpreted differently by one party or the other and thereby would resolve nothing." And suppose there were a compromise draft solution: "A compromise is words, not more and not less. And the war will continue on the sub-continent. . . . Resolutions without the collective will to act will bring us to nought. . . . I will say these draft resolutions will come to nought judging by my experience in this very Council which has passed so many resolutions that were not implemented."[28] And indeed the draft resolutions came to nought. The Security Council, under the tyranny of the veto, could not even agree on the form of a resolution.

It was at this stage of paralysis that a group of small powers took the initiative to refer the issue to the General Assembly under the Uniting for Peace resolution. This provides that "if the Security Council, because of lack of unanimity of the permanent members fails to exercise its primary responsibility for the maintenance of international peace and security in any case where there appears to be a threat to the peace, breach of the peace, or act of aggression, the General Assembly shall consider the matter immediately with a view to making appropriate recommendations to Members for collective measures, including in the case of a breach of the peace or act of aggression the use of armed force when necessary, to maintain or restore international peace and security."[29]

The General Assembly, meeting on 7 December, moved with

27. Ibid., 32.
28. S/PV 1607, pp. 9–11.
29. Resolution 377 (V).

great speed to a decision on the same day, although there was still the irreconcilable division on the scale of values between the primacy of a cease-fire or of a political solution. The final resolution, carried by 104 votes to 11, with 10 abstentions, emphasized the call for an immediate cease-fire but with reference in the preamble to the necessity for an early political solution and with a call, in the substantive provisions, for intensified efforts to bring about the conditions necessary for the voluntary return of the refugees to their homes. The abstainers were quite a varied group; the negative votes, in support of the Indian position, came mostly from the East European socialist states.

The explanation for the rapid decision by the General Assembly is to be found, partly, in the frustration and disgust that members felt at the inability of the Security Council to agree on a form of action when confronted with a major conflict. There are repeated references to this failure.

Despite all the appeals made to it and the gravity of the situation, the Security Council once again has demonstrated its impotence, that is, the powerlessness of the United Nations. . . . I should like to declare—and I am aware that this statement is supported by the whole of the United Nations—that, in not adopting any decision, the Security Council has not acted on behalf of the United Nations, has not acted on behalf of all its members, has not acted on behalf of a world public opinion which is troubled and dismayed at the turn of events. . . . Even a decision concerning a mere cease-fire met with a veto. This is a heavy international responsibility, a heavy responsibility to the world.[30]

No one who watched over the week-end the proceedings of the Security Council on the Indo-Pakistan dispute could have left the Security Council chamber without a feeling of sadness, deep disappointment and frustration. I am sure we all recognize that we have before us a human tragedy of very great proportions and therefore the performance of the Security Council in the face of such human tragedy—a performance which we all saw—was nothing short of irresponsibility. This is no time for speech-making; this is a time for action, for speedy action, to arrest the tragedy before it becomes uncontrollable.[31]

I come with a feeling of sadness and anguish—sadness as a member of the Council because of the failure of that main organ of the United Nations to exercise its primary responsibility for the maintenance of peace and security while there was still time to do so even before the last three days and anguish

30. Tunisian representative, A/2002, p. 5.
31. Representative of Ghana, ibid., 5–6.

because, while the world Organization continues its deliberations, people suffer and die in the Hindustan subcontinent.[32]

If power politics makes the Security Council what a few minutes ago was called a private club, with five permanent members and 11 occasional guests, then the General Assembly is under the urgent duty of enforcing compliance with the provisions of the Charter, enshrining the last hopes of mankind, which had hoped that a final end had been put to the scourge of war and to the threat or use of force.[33]

The speed of decision, in reaction to the failure of the Security Council, was of course made possible by an appreciable unanimity among the members of the General Assembly, as the voting indicated. The basis for this wide consensus was the commitment to two general principles of international relations between independent states, namely, respect for their sovereignty and their territorial integrity, and noninterference in their internal affairs. To this must be added the fear of fragmentation as a result of the exercise of the right to self-determination. The Pakistan representative continually emphasized these themes in the earlier debates, and he returned to them when the decision of the General Assembly was referred to the Security Council for action.

So the issue, the basic issue involved today is that a State, a sovereign State, brought into being by the will of its own people, freely, without coercion, without interference, cannot be dismembered by force. It would be a tragic precedent for the world at large, a terrible precedent. Today I speak not only for Pakistan but for a principle; I speak for a basic principle which affects Asia, Africa and Latin America. That is why the third world overwhelmingly supported the cause of Pakistan in the historic resolution adopted by the General Assembly on 7 December.

If I had spoken only for Pakistan, I would have been isolated, because India is a bigger country than Pakistan. Power politics would have come into play. Pakistan's cause succeeded on 7 December because it was based, not on the interests of Pakistan conceived selfishly and subjectively, but on a world principle—universally accepted, universally recognized—that a sovereign State, brought into being by its own blood and toil and sweat, cannot be dismembered by a predatory neighbour wanting to tear it apart limb by limb. Today it is Pakistan; tomorrow it will be other parts of the world. Please realize that position. Please remember, we are not fighting the war for Pakistan alone; we are fighting the war for a cause, for a just cause: the cause that involves a State which came into being by its people's volition and whose establishment was recognized by India.[34]

32. Italian representative, A/2003, p. 6.
33. Representative of Ecuador, ibid., 26.
34. S/PV 1611, pp. 15–16.

He also warned the member states that the pluralistic structure of many of their societies rendered them equally vulnerable to fragmentation.

Today you may rejoice over what is happening to us. But if you think that today you are going to dismember Pakistan and the germs of dismemberment are not going to spread to your country, you are sadly mistaken. And where is this Pandora's box going to be closed? Is it going to be closed in Yugoslavia? Why not Yugoslavia? Why not Czechoslovakia? Why not Wales and Scotland? I shall not mention Northern Ireland because there is the Queen's peace there. There has been no trouble in Northern Ireland, so I shall not mention Northern Ireland but only Wales and Scotland. And Brittany, the Basque country, Morocco, Algeria, all the countries in Africa? Can it not happen in any single country in Africa and in Asia? If there is Bangla Desh in Pakistan, there must be Bangla Desh everywhere. Why should Bangla Desh emerge only in Pakistan by force? The fragmentation that it symbolizes can occur in Europe, Asia, Africa and Latin America, and it cannot leave untouched the great Powers themselves—in Uzbekistan and in other parts of the world. There will not be a Bangla Desh only in Pakistan. There will be a Bangla Desh everywhere. We shall see to it that it is not only in Pakistan. Then there will be Bangla Desh everywhere. Let us open up the floodgates, because if sovereign States are going to be mutated in this fashion, let the deluge come. Why should it affect only my country?[35]

The proceedings of the Security Council from 12 to 21 December were a replay of the earlier meetings. There were the same arguments, the same irreconcilability of the superpowers, and a similar flurry of draft resolutions. The president enumerated them: "the draft resolution submitted by Italy and Japan as contained in document S/10451; the draft resolution submitted by Poland contained in document S/10453/Rev.1; the draft resolution submitted by the Syrian Arab Republic contained in document S/10456; the draft resolution submitted by France and the United Kingdom contained in document S/10455; the draft resolution submitted by the Union of Soviet Socialist Republics contained in document S/10457; in addition there is the draft resolution submitted by China contained in document S/10421 and the draft resolution of the USSR contained in document S/10428, which were not pressed to the vote earlier."[36]

But now there was more urgency, with events moving to a climax. The Pakistan representative reacted to the proceedings of the Security Council with passion, despair, pride, anger, and cynicism;

35. Ibid., 21.
36. S/PV 1616, p. 1.

and he charged filibustering and dilatory tactics, in anticipation of the fall of Dacca, the East Pakistan capital. It may indeed have been as he said. Indian troops were in the ascendancy, and on 16 December the Indian ambassador was able to announce to the Security Council that the Pakistani armed forces had surrendered in Bangladesh and that the Indian government had also ordered a cease-fire in the West. The Indian government had already recognized Bangladesh on 5 December.

Now, with the surrender of the Pakistan forces, the secession was complete. And now, finally, the Security Council was able to agree on a resolution, though with the abstentions of the USSR and Poland. On 21 December, nine months after the first massacres and with Bangla Desh a fait accompli, the Security Council resolved as follows:

Having discussed the grave situation in the subcontinent, which remains a threat to international peace and security,

Noting General Assembly resolution 2793 (XXVI) of 7 December 1971,

Noting the reply of the Government of Pakistan on 9 December 1971,

Noting the reply of the Government of India on 12 December 1971,

Having heard the statements of the Deputy Prime Minister of Pakistan and the Foreign Minister of India,

Noting further the statement made at the 1616th meeting of the Security Council by the Foreign Minister of India containing a unilateral declaration of a cease-fire in the western theatre,

Noting Pakistan's agreement to the cease-fire in the western theatre with effect from 17 December 1971,

Noting that consequently a cease-fire and a cessation of hostilities prevail,

1. *Demands* that a durable cease-fire and cessation of all hostilities in all areas of conflict be strictly observed and remain in effect until withdrawals take place, as soon as practicable, of all armed forces to their respective territories and to positions which fully respect the cease-fire line in Jammu and Kashmir supervised by the United Nations Military Observer Group in India and Pakistan;

2. *Calls upon* all Member States to refrain from any action which may aggravate the situation in the subcontinent or endanger international peace;

3. *Calls upon* all those concerned to take all measures necessary to preserve human life and for the observance of the Geneva Conventions of 1949 and to apply in full their provisions as regards the protection of the wounded and sick, prisoners of war and civilian population;

4. *Calls for* international assistance in the relief of suffering and the rehabilitation of refugees, and their return in safety and dignity to their homes, and for full co-operation with the Secretary General to that effect;

5. *Authorizes* the Secretary-General to appoint if necessary a special rep-

resentative to lend his good offices for the solution of humanitarian problems;

6. *Requests* the Secretary-General to keep the Council informed without delay on developments relating to the implementation of the present resolution;

7. *Decides* to remain seized of the matter and to keep it under active consideration. (Security Council Resolution 307, dd. 21 December 1971)

5

The Issues Raised

Bangladesh confronted the United Nations with many conflicts of values surrounding the exercise of the "right" to self-determination in its most extreme form—that of secession in a postcolonial society. The contradictions between basic principles of international relations were immediately apparent.

I have referred to the secretary-general's comment in his memorandum to the president of the Security Council that the conflict between the principles of the territorial integrity of states and of self-determination had often before given rise to fratricidal strife, and had provoked in recent years highly emotional reactions in the international community. So here was the first contradiction, a contradiction between territorial integrity and self-determination by way of secession.

I referred also to the complaint by the government of Pakistan that the international community had done little to restrain India from a course of conduct which violated the two most fundamental principles of the Charter of the United Nations: noninterference in the internal affairs of a state and the obligation to refrain from the threat or use of force against its territorial integrity or political independence. And to this perfectly valid statement of basic principles, the Pakistan government had added its controversial interpretation of United Nations' jurisprudence to the effect that while the principle of self-determination governed the liberation of territories under colonial rule or in dispute between member states, it could not be extended to areas recognized as integral parts of the territories of member states.

But the Indian government had charged Pakistan with launching a campaign of massacre, genocide, and cultural suppression against the Bengalis. How then could the international community fulfill its obligations to extend protection against gross violations of human rights and against genocidal massacres in the face of a general principle prohibiting intervention in the internal affairs of a sovereign state? And why should a right of self-determination, vigorously asserted in colonial contexts, cease to be relevant in postcolonial successor states? And how could the United Nations take steps to preserve the peace in the Bangladesh crisis when the political solution necessary to arrest the flow of refugees into India and to avert the threat of war might be viewed as an intervention in the internal affairs of a sovereign member state?

So here was a whole series of contradictions to frustrate attempts at arbitration and conciliation. Indeed, the availability of these basic but contradictory principles could serve only to legitimize the intransigence of the contending parties.

Self-determination in its original conception was a liberating revolutionary doctrine, and it has served this function in the decolonizing process. Indeed, it may be viewed as the "Marseillaise" of decolonization. But in other contexts, the doctrine has been domesticated to serve the interests of ruling classes. Its present state, in United Nations practice, is a bewildering complex of radicalism and conservatism.

A vast literature of debates, resolutions, declarations, and reports, "a veritable blizzard,"[1] attests to the significance of the doctrine in the proceedings of the United Nations. It includes two major studies, both under the aegis of the Sub-Commission on Prevention of Discrimination and Protection of Minorities. The first, by Hector Gros Espiell, *The Right to Self-Determination: Implementation of United Nations Resolutions*,[2] is concerned with the implementation of United Nations resolutions relating to the right of peoples under colonial and alien domination to self-determination. It was intended not merely as a theoretical work but as a contribution to the struggle against colonialism in all its forms, and it is essentially a revolution-

1. Phrase used by Buchheit, 1978:34.
2. United Nations Publications, E/CN.4/Sub.2/405/Rev.1.

ary document. Thus the right to self-determination is viewed as extending beyond the original free determination of political status to the maintenance, assurance, and perfection of "full legal, political, economic, social and cultural sovereignty." Moreover, it is conceived as having lasting force: it does not lapse after having been first exercised to secure political self-determination, and it extends to all fields.[3]

At the same time, there is a strong conservative cast to the exposition of the doctrine. The right, we are told, does not apply to peoples already organized in the form of a state that is not under colonial and alien domination, since various U.N. instruments condemn attempts aimed at the partial or total disruption of the national unity and the territorial integrity of a country. So, too, "the right to secession from an existing state member of the United Nations does not exist as such in the instruments or in the practice followed by the Organisation, since to seek to invoke it in order to disrupt the national unity and the territorial integrity of a State would be a misapplication of the principle of self-determination contrary to the purposes of the United Nations Charter." We are warned, however, against accepting surface appearances: colonial and alien domination may persist under the guise of an ostensible national unity. And our attention is drawn to a proviso, in the *Declaration on Principles of International Law concerning Friendly Relations and Co-operation among States*. This ties respect for territorial integrity to the requirement that the State should conduct itself in compliance with the principle of equal rights and self-determination, and thus be "possessed of a government representing the whole people belonging to the territory without distinction as to race, creed or colour."[4]

The second study, by Aureliu Cristescu, *The Right to Self-Determination: Historical and Current Development on the Basis of United Nations Instruments*,[5] deals more broadly with the development of the basic concepts involved in self-determination. The right itself is described in the most glowing terms. It is "a fundamental right, without which other rights cannot be fully enjoyed. It is not only a principle, but the most important subjective right among human rights . . . a prerequisite for the exercise of all individual rights and freedoms."[6]

3. Ibid., para. 47.
4. Ibid., paras. 60, 89, and 90.
5. United Nations Publications, E/CN.4/Sub.2/404/Rev.1.
6. Ibid., para. 228.

The principle of equal rights and self-determination should be understood in its widest sense. It signifies the inalienable right of all peoples to choose their own political, economic and social system and their own international status. The principle of equal rights and self-determination of peoples thus possesses a universal character, recognised by the Charter, as a right of all peoples whether or not they have attained independence and the status of a State. Furthermore, the very concept of the principle of equal rights and self-determination of peoples is extremely wide ... The charter of the United Nations should not be interpreted as confining that right to a particular category of peoples, because, as United Nations practice has made clear, the word "peoples" as used in Article 1, paragraph 2, of the Charter means all peoples.[7]

The statement of the principle could hardly be more radical, and this radical quality is particularly marked in the subsidiary principles that the author derives from the right to self-determination. Thus, in discussing the right of peoples freely to pursue their economic development as an essential element of the right to self-determination, the author raises the issue of social justice at both the national and international levels. At the national level, "public ownership of the means of production, which is practised by an increasing number of countries, remains the decisive factor in achieving equitable distribution of the national income, economic and social democratization and social justice." At the international level, "the principles of law and justice which necessarily derive from the development of the right to self-determination" should "provide for the equalization of the levels of economic development of all countries, as a genuine basis for the democratization of international life."[8]

But again, political conservatism is juxtaposed to revolutionary radicalism. The conservatism is protective of the independent sovereign state. A provision of the Declaration on the Granting of Independence to Colonial Countries and Peoples (1960) is invoked as authority for the proposition that "the principle of equal rights and self-determination is not to be applied to parts of the territory of a sovereign State. Such a provision is needed in order to prevent the principle from being applied in favour of secessionist movements in independent States."[9] In a later passage, we read that

the principle of equal rights and self-determination of peoples should serve to unite peoples on a voluntary and democratic basis, not to break up exist-

7. Ibid., para. 268.
8. Ibid., paras. 346, 715.
9. Ibid., para. 174.

ing national entities. It is necessary to avoid any formulation of the principle which might be interpreted as widening its scope and making it applicable to peoples who already form part of an independent sovereign State. To do otherwise would be to encourage secessionist movements in sovereign States, and might serve as a pretext for endangering the national unity and territorial integrity of sovereign States. . . . The principle of self-determination should not be misused. It should not be invoked to call in question the frontiers established between States.[10]

There are further warnings against the principle being interpreted as an encouragement to secessionist or irredentist movements, and in one passage an admonition against its use to justify "activities aimed at changing a country's system of government."[11] And as if all this were not conservative enough, the author includes a panegyric in favor of nationalism, which, I would have thought, constituted the major contemporary threat to the survival of our species.[12]

The report does not totally exclude the right of secession. It "unquestionably exists . . . in a special, but very important case: that of peoples, territories and entities subjugated in violation of international law."[13] And the rapporteur does introduce some nuances to the conservatism. He links the self-determination of peoples to human rights and comments that "the international community has generally accepted the idea that the principle of non-intervention does not apply in a case of violation of those rights."[14] However, the implications of this exception are not very clear to me, nor are they developed in the report, which emphasizes the general principle of non-intervention in the domestic affairs of sovereign states. There is mention of the proviso, or qualification, to the general obligation to refrain from actions that would dismember or impair the territorial integrity or political unity of a sovereign and independent state, namely, that the State conduct itself in compliance with the principle of equal rights and self-determination of peoples and be representative, without discrimination, of the population as a whole. But in a passage dealing with this qualification, the rapporteur curiously introduces the word *particularly* so as to strengthen the injunction against "any act likely to prejudice the national unity and territorial

10. Para. 209.
11. See para. 268.
12. Paras. 281–86.
13. Para. 173.
14. Para. 180.

integrity of a State—particularly a State" that conducts itself in the manner described above.[15]

These major United Nations reports thus elaborate a radical revolutionary ideology in respect to liberation from colonial and alien subjugation and in the perspectives they offer on external self-determination of the successor sovereign states. By contrast, the perspectives on internal determination in the independent sovereign states are highly conservative, especially in relation to secession. The term itself is pejorative, with connotations of disloyalty, of treachery. Why should the process not be described as "separation" or, in appropriate cases, as "liberation"?

This combination of radical and conservative ideologies should not surprise us. The radical ideologies, both in respect to decolonization and in the extension of self-determination to economic, social, and cultural areas, are ideologies of Third World countries. Indeed, they have a wider basis of support within the United Nations. But as for the conservative ideologies on internal self-determination, they are clearly not the ideologies of many of the peoples of Third World countries, as is indicated by numerous destructive struggles for political restructuring of ethnic relations, for autonomy and for separation. They are essentially ideologies of the ruling classes of these countries, ideologies protective of their power and privilege.

These conservative interpretations are by no means mandatory. They do not flow inescapably from United Nations declarations. Cristescu, in chapter 2 of his study, surveys the development of the right to self-determination in major United Nations instruments, and I have selected the following key references from his survey.

Article 1, paragraph 2, of the United Nations Charter states that one of the purposes of the United Nations is

To develop friendly relations among nations based on respect for the principle of equal rights and self-determination of peoples, and to take other appropriate measures to strengthen universal peace.

In addition, the introductory paragraph to article 55 refers to

the creation of conditions of stability and well-being which are necessary for peaceful and friendly relations among nations based on respect for the principle of equal rights and self-determination of peoples.

15. Para. 228.

The General Assembly's Declaration on the Granting of Independence to Colonial Countries and Peoples mentions self-determination in the preamble and describes it as follows in paragraph 2.

All peoples have the right to self-determination; by virtue of that right they freely determine their political status and freely pursue their economic, social and cultural development.[16]

The right appears again, in the same terms, in both the International Covenant on Economic, Social and Cultural Rights and the International Covenant on Civil and Political Rights.[17] As article 1 in both covenants, it has pride of place, indicating its status as a fundamental human right.

On the occasion of the twenty-fifth anniversary of the United Nations, the General Assembly adopted the Declaration on Principles of International Law concerning Friendly Relations and Co-operation among States in accordance with the Charter of the United Nations.[18]

Cristescu describes this declaration as being "of the greatest importance in the progressive development and codification of the principle of equal rights and self-determination of peoples."[19] The following three paragraphs of the preamble deal with this principle.

Convinced that the subjection of peoples to alien subjugation, domination and exploitation constitutes a major obstacle to the promotion of international peace and security.

Convinced that the principle of equal rights and self-determination of peoples constitutes a significant contribution to contemporary international law, and that its effective application is of paramount importance for the promotion of friendly relations among States, based on respect for the principle of sovereign equality.

Convinced in consequence that any attempt aimed at the partial or total disruption of the national unity and territorial integrity of a State or country or at its political independence is incompatible with the purposes and principles of the Charter.

The substantive provisions regarding self-determination define it as follows:

By virtue of the principle of equal rights and self-determination of peoples enshrined in the Charter of the United Nations, all peoples have the right freely to determine, without external interference, their political status and

16. G.A. Resolution 1514 (XV), dated 14 Dec. 1960.
17. Adopted by G.A. Resolution 2200 A (XXI), dated 16 Dec. 1966.
18. By Resolution 2625 (XXV), dated 24 Oct. 1970.
19. 1981, para. 54.

to pursue their economic, social and cultural development, and every State has the duty to respect this right in accordance with the provisions of the Charter.

Further provisions impose on states the duty to promote the realization of equal rights and self-determination of peoples and the respect for, and the observance of, human rights and fundamental freedoms. There is a duty to refrain from any forcible action that deprives peoples "in the elaboration of the present principle of their right to self-determination and freedom and independence." The political forms of self-determination are described as "the establishment of a sovereign and independent State, the free association or integration with an independent State or the emergence into any other political status freely determined by a people."

The declaration thus expresses the right to self-determination in the widest terms. The right is clearly available to the peoples of independent states (there is a separate paragraph dealing with colonial and other non-self-governing territories). Any injunction against the impairment of the territorial integrity or political unity of sovereign and independent states is in direct conflict with the principle of self-determination as defined above. Yet the declaration includes this prohibition as one of the cardinal principles. Thus, two contradictory cardinal principles are incorporated in the same declaration.

However, the declaration does make a "courageous attempt"[20] to reconcile this contradiction in the following manner

Nothing in the foregoing paragraphs shall be construed as authorizing or encouraging any action which would dismember or impair, totally or in part, the territorial integrity or political unity of sovereign and independent States conducting themselves in compliance with the principle of equal rights and self-determination of peoples as described above and thus possessed of a government representing the whole people belonging to the territory without distinction as to race, creed or colour.

The implication of this provision, to which we have already made reference, is that people of different race, religion, or color enjoy the right to self-determination but in a form that falls short of separation or total independence. However, the limitation on the right to self-determination applies only in the absence of discrimination. Where there is discrimination and the government does not

20. Phrase used by the International Commission of Jurists in an excellent discussion of the problem in the context of the Bangladesh conflict. See *The Events in East Pakistan, 1971*, 1972, part v.

represent all the peoples, self-determination may take the form of the establishment of a sovereign and independent state. This is a far less conservative position than that taken in the Cristescu report, or by the Pakistan representative in his contention that it was "the established jurisprudence of the United Nations that, while the principle of self-determination governs the liberation of territories which are under colonial rule or are in dispute between Member States, it cannot be extended to areas that are recognised as integral parts of the territories of Member States."

The reference in the above quotation is to the *established jurisprudence* of the United Nations, a phrase that presumably incorporates actual practice. So let us turn to this aspect, with primary concern, however, for cases involving secession from member states.

The United Nations has been very actively involved in the whole process of decolonization. This is indeed one of its major contributions. In the report *The Right to Self-Determination: Implementation of United Nations Resolutions*, the rapporteur refers to the very large number of situations in which the United Nations has passed resolutions relating to the right of peoples under colonial and alien domination to self-determination.[21] It is clearly the established jurisprudence of the United Nations that the principle of self-determination governs the liberation of colonial territories.

However, the process of self-determination in colonies has generally taken the form of a self-determination of *populations*, not of *peoples*. That is to say, a territorial criterion has governed the liberation of colonies.[22] Many member states thus inherited the diversity of peoples in former colonial territories and were confronted with the problem of integrating them into a national unity. In the actual process of decolonization, consideration was often given to the relations between these different peoples, or it was a matter of contention. In a few cases, decolonization immediately provoked genocidal massacre, as for example, in India on partition, and in Rwanda. At the present time, the relationship between different ethnic and other groups, racial and religious, continues to be a contentious issue in many of the successor states, raising demands for internal self-determination.

21. 1981, chap. 3.
22. See discussion by Sureda, 1973:355, and Murphy, 1980:44–45. Murphy contrasts the Wilsonian period after World War I with self-determination focused on ethnic groups and with the application of a territorial criterion after World War II.

Indeed, the phenomenon is worldwide and not confined to the recently decolonized societies.[23]

Bangladesh raised in acute form the problem of self-determination by way of secession, in the context of a great destruction of human life. The problem was raised similarly in Nigeria by the secession of Eastern Nigeria (Biafra) and in the Sudan by a movement for the secession of Southern Sudanese African peoples. I propose to refer briefly to these cases as a way of introducing general comment relating to the "established jurisprudence" of the United Nations on the issue of secession from independent sovereign states. But first, mention must be made of the United Nations' response to the secession of Katanga from the newly independent Congo in July 1960.

The events in the Congo during the turbulent period immediately following independence from Belgian colonial rule obliged the United Nations to define its attitude toward secession, and its final opposition may be regarded as setting a precedent against secession. But there were many special circumstances to the secession. Katanga was rich in minerals, and it was clear that the Congo could not easily survive without the revenues to be derived from these mineral resources. Moreover, outside investment in Katangan wealth encouraged the belief that secession was being supported, if not instigated, by certain Western nations to protect business interests in the region. Many members of the United Nations did not believe that the Katangan regime represented the true wishes of the majority of the Katangan population. Then, too, "the Congo showed every indication of being further beset by separatist demands if the legitimacy of the Katanga secession had been recognised." And finally there was a readily available legal justification for opposition to secession in a provision of the constitution that "the Congo constitutes within its present boundaries, an indivisible and democratic State."[24]

The secession of Biafra raised the very different issue of secession as a protection or remedy against gross violations of human rights. The *Proclamation of the Republic of Biafra*, on 30 May 1967, makes many charges of discrimination by the federal government against the Eastern Region, and above all, it describes a series of massacres by Northerners.

23. See the discussions by Connor, 1967:30–53 and 1972:319–55.
24. This discussion of Katanga follows the analysis by Buchheit, 1978:142–43, 152–53.

On May 29, 1966, thousands of Easterners residing in the North, were massacred by Northern civilians. . . . Then on July 29, 1966, . . . the real pogrom against Eastern Nigerians residing in the Federation began. . . . This time Northern soldiers acted in concert with Northern civilians. Defenceless men, women and children were shot down or hacked to death; some were burnt, and some buried alive. Women and young girls were ravished with unprecedented bestiality; unborn children were torn out of the womb of their mothers. . . . Again on September 29, 1966, the pogrom was resumed. Thirty thousand Eastern Nigerians are known to have been killed by Northerners. They were killed in the North, in Western Nigeria, in Lagos; some Eastern soldiers in detention at Benin were forcibly removed from prison by Northern soldiers and murdered.

Easterners had good reason to fear that these events were a grave threat to their survival as a unit, and the Declaration of Independence is a clear exercise of the right to self-determination, justified by the belief that Easterners were no longer protected in their lives and in their property "by any Government based outside Eastern Nigeria," and by their unwillingness "to be unfree partners in any association of a political or economic nature."

There were other major differences from Katanga. Like Katanga, Eastern Nigeria had important economic resources, but its secession would not have threatened the economic viability of the federation.[25] There was certainly the danger of other secessions following upon the Biafran secession, but, as Buchheit argues, "the common currency of secessionist talk in all of the Nigerian regions right up to the actual separation of the East in 1967 gave the Biafrans a reasonable ground for believing that secession was recognised in Nigeria as a legitimate method of altering one region's relationship to the others, or at least that it would not be strenuously opposed."[26] And finally, there was strong support for secession in the Eastern Region, as shown by the decisions of the Consultative Assembly and the Advisory Committee of Chiefs and Elders, and by the sustained resistance of the general population over a long period.[27]

In the two and a half years of civil war, which followed the Declaration of Independence, between 600,000 and 1 million Easterners

25. Buchheit, 1978:173.

26. Ibid., 174. Nixon (1972:476) comments to similar effect that "the belief in the legitimacy of secession had deep roots in Nigerian political thought."

27. The Eastern Region included a number of minority groups, the Ibo representing only some 64 percent of the population. This led Panter-Brick (1968:262–65) to question the legitimacy of the claim for self-determination for the Eastern Region as a whole. Nixon (1972:480–82) argues persuasively to contrary effect.

were killed in battle or massacre or died of famine and disease. Immense publicity was given to the heartbreaking anguish of the conflict, with charges of genocide, reports of massacres, and agonizing pictures of a starving people. The circumstances were such that one could surely have anticipated action by the United Nations. There was some humanitarian relief by United Nations agencies, but apart from that the United Nations did not at any time consider the events in Nigeria during this period of highly destructive conflict. The secretary-general explained, defensively, that not one single member state out of 126 had raised the issue in the United Nations, because member states knew that the United Nations would refuse to discuss the matter.[28] A United States Foreign Staff Report commented that both the United Nations and the secretary-general took the position that a civil war fell completely outside the competence of the organization in terms of its Charter.[29]

The United States decided against bringing the dispute to the United Nations due to African opposition to such action, a policy decision reinforced by lack of unity in Congress concerning the appropriate U.S. role.[30] One of the cardinal principles of the Organization of African Unity (OAU) was indeed the rejection of secession in independent African states. The organization's charter safeguards the independence, sovereignty, and territorial integrity of African states, members proclaiming their adherence to the principle of respect for the sovereignty and territorial integrity of each state. In accordance with this principle, the OAU passed the following resolution in September 1967.

The Assembly of Heads of State and Government meeting in its Fourth Ordinary Session, at Kinshasa, Congo, from 11 to 14 September 1967,

Solemnly reaffirming their adherence to the principle of respect for the sovereignty and territorial integrity of Member states;

Reiterating their condemnation of secession in any Member States;

Concerned at the tragic and serious situation in Nigeria;

Recognizing that situation as an internal affair, the solution of which is primarily the responsibility of Nigerians themselves;

Reposing their trust and confidence in the Federal Government of Nigeria;

28. See the discussion by Buchheit, 1978:168–69.

29. *International Protection of Human Rights,* Hearings before the Sub-Committee on International Organizations and Movements of the House Committee on Foreign Affairs, 93d Congress, 1st sess., 1973, p. 890.

30. Ibid., 888.

Desirous of exploring the possibilities of placing the services of the Assembly at the disposal of the Federal Government of Nigeria;

Resolves to send a consultative mission of 6 Heads of State (Cameroon, Congo (Kinshasa), Ethiopia, Ghana, Liberia and Niger) to the Head of the Federal Government of Nigeria to assure him of the Assembly's desire for the territorial integrity, unity and peace of Nigeria.

The Ethiopian emperor Haile Selassie, a member of the consultative mission, declared that "the national unity and territorial integrity of Member States is not negotiable. It must be fully protected and preserved.[31]

The only countries that accorded recognition to Biafra were Tanzania, Gabon, the Ivory Coast, Zambia, and Haiti. The first country to do so was Tanzania, whose foreign minister explained that Easterners had genuine and deep-seated fears after the murder of 30,000 of their number in two major pogroms. Biafrans, he said, had suffered the same fate of rejection within their state that the Jews of Germany had experienced.[32] The Tanzanian president commented that "it is foolish for Africans to stand by idly while millions of Africans are being killed by other Africans in the name of 'territorial integrity.' . . . You cannot kill thousands of people and keep on killing more in the name of 'unity.' There is no unity between the dead and those who killed them, and there is no unity in slavery and those who dominate them."[33]

In the United States Congress there were similar attacks on the inhumanity of diplomatic support for "one Nigeria." It was time "to reexamine our policy of 'one Nigeria,' which has resulted in our accepting the deaths of a million people as the price for preserving a nation that never existed. . . . Political preconceptions have kept us from recognising that the boundaries of Nigeria . . . are not so sacred as to justify the deaths of several million people. The price of unity is too high."[34]

Whatever the established jurisprudence and whatever the national interests and geopolitical concerns of member states, the inaction of the United Nations was profoundly dehumanized. Meanwhile there was a civil war in the Sudan, which also raised issues of

31. Ijalaye, 1971:556.
32. Ibid., 553.
33. Mojekwu, 1980:230.
34. Statement by Senator McCarthy in *International Protection of Human Rights* (1973:886).

self-determination and secession, and the integrity of the territorial area formerly administered as a colony.

The Sudan was a peculiarly artificial state, bringing together quite disparate peoples. The North is largely Muslim, peopled by Arabs and also by non-Arab Islamicized groups. The South is African, divided into different ethnic units, mostly animist by religion but with appreciable numbers of Christians and a small number of Muslims. Communication between the two areas was, and remains, difficult. North and South had been joined together by the British "for no significantly better reason than the colonial convenience of having a single regime for this long stretch of the Nile and the vast surrounding countryside."[35] The British had administered the South as a separate entity and had contemplated a different postcolonial destiny for it but reversed this policy in 1946.

In addition to the ethnic and religious differences, and the geographical and administrative separation, there was hostility based on historical relationships and on differential development and discrimination. A Government Commission of Inquiry into disturbances in the Southern Sudan during August 1955, in the year preceding independence, referred to the persistence of the great feeling of hatred, and of fear, toward the Northern Sudanese inspired by the slave trade. The Southerners regarded the Northerners as their "traditional enemies." Northern attitudes, too, were affected by this past history. Many Northern Sudanese, "especially from amongst the uneducated class," saw the Southerners as being of an inferior race, and traders in the South often referred to and addressed them as *abeed*, a constant and contemptuous reminder of the old days of the slave trade.[36]

The South was educationally backward and economically undeveloped. Inevitably, given the greater economic, educational, and political development of the much more populous North, independence in 1956 meant domination by the North. The Commission of Inquiry in 1955 had commented that "the Northern administration in Southern Sudan is not colonial, but the great majority of Southerners unhappily regard it as such." And three of the Southern leaders, in books published in 1963 and 1970, analyzed the relationship of North to South in terms of colonial subjugation.[37]

35. See the discussion by Emerson, 1964:45.
36. See my book *Genocide*, 1981:70–73.
37. Ibid.

It would seem that Southerners had a legitimate claim to exercise their right to self-determination by way of secession from a regime of alien subjugation. But this was not the view of Northerners, who suppressed the Southern rebellion in a civil war that lasted until 1972, when a measure of regional autonomy was granted to the South. The North thereby protected the "territorial integrity" and the "unity" of the conglomeration of peoples inherited from the colonial rulers. The number of deaths in the South in the course of the war, in reprisals against and massacres of civilians, and from famine and disease is often estimated at 500,000 or more. Estimates of refugees seem more reliable: more than 1 million from a southern population of some 3 million.[38] It was a high price to pay for the preservation of "unity" and of "territorial integrity."

The response of the United Nations and of the Organization of African Unity can best be described as *absention*. The destruction of human life was allowed to take its uninhibited course. There was humanitarian relief, however, and the U.N. high commissioner for refugees, Haile Selassie, observers from neighboring territories, and others helped to facilitate the final peace settlement.[39]

United Nations reaction to these major conflicts gives some support for the contention of the Pakistan ambassador that self-determination is not applicable to the territories of member states. There is further supportive evidence in a number of surveys of U.N. practice both prior to and after the Bangladesh crisis. Rupert Emerson deals with this problem in two influential papers. In *Self-Determination Revisited in the Era of Decolonization* he writes that

if its primary purpose is the right to overthrow alien rule, its secondary and almost equally important purpose is very close to being the reverse of this. Self-determination has been proclaimed as the inalienable right of all dependent peoples and has in fact been applied to the great bulk of them; but in the eyes of most of those who have been asserting the immediate and unchallengeable validity of self-determination, it has, once exercised, no justification for a reappearance on the scene. It represents in other words, no continuing process, but has only the function of bringing independence to people under alien colonial rule. As colonialism is held to be incompatible with the Charter, so is any attempt to appeal to self-determination in such fashion as to disrupt "the national unity and the territorial integrity" of a country which is achieving or has already achieved independence. Laid out in these terms, self-determination safeguards the maintenance and advance-

38. Ibid., 69–70, n. 28.
39. O'Ballance, 1977, chap. 12.

ment of the state-nations as they have been delimited by the colonial powers but denies the right to existence of nations within, or cutting across, the states which have been so formed.[40]

In a later paper, "The Fate of Human Rights in the Third World," he comments that despite the broader language embracing "all peoples," the doctrine of "self-determination in its contemporary manifestation can for almost all practical purposes be defined as the UN-sanctioned right of every colonial people (assumed to constitute a single and indivisible whole) to achieve its independence as speedily and completely as possible."[41] A second meaning is the right of peoples to determine the internal structure and functioning of their societies without interference.

In a major study entitled *Secession: The Legitimacy of Self-Determination*, Buchheit analyzes seven cases of secessionist attempts backed by armed force and covering a period starting in 1960. In addition, he refers throughout his work to other examples of the attempted exercise of self-determination.

The seven cases of attempted secession were selected to illustrate the complexity of historic, ethnic, and political factors involved. They serve

to point up the problems surrounding active United Nations involvement in a dispute of this nature (the Congo); ineffective United Nations action (Bangla Desh); and the total absence of such involvement (Biafra). They exemplify the peculiar difficulties presented when ethnic regions overlap national frontiers (the Kurds, Somalis, Nagas); when the desire for secession amounts to an irredentist demand for unification with an ethnically similar State (Somalia); when the basis for secession is largely conditioned by the wealth of the seceding province (Katanga), or is a direct result of its impoverishment (Bangla Desh).[42]

The case of Somalia presents some unique features. The most unyielding opposition to secessionist self-determination has come from those states that have themselves only recently emerged from the process of colonial self-determination.[43] The reason is clear enough. They are polyethnic states still engaged in integrating their disparate peoples, and the secession of any group carries the threat of a more general fragmentation. By contrast, Somalia is probably

40. 1964:29–30.
41. 1975:204.
42. 1978:141.
43. Ibid., 102.

the most ethnically homogeneous country in Africa. It enjoys "the rare luxury of being able to advocate a right of secessionist self-determination for cohesive minority groups without having to fear that it might itself become the victim of such claims."[44] But Somalis also populate neighboring areas in Kenya and Ethiopia. The irredentist wishes of these Somalis to amalgamate with the Republic of Somalia are in effect demands for secession from Kenya and Ethiopia.

Though these demands would seem to accord with a perfectly legitimate exercise of the right to self-determination, they are of course resisted by the governments of Kenya and Ethiopia on the grounds that the regions involved are part of their territory and that the principle of self-determination is completely inapplicable because self-determination has no function in an independent state. It has relevance only to foreign domination and not to territorial disintegration by dissident citizens. In the final analysis, it is "only the respect for territorial integrity and the arguable effect of a secession on other dissident groups within Kenya and Ethiopia which undermines the theoretical soundness of the Somali claim."[45] The Ethiopian suppression of Somalis in the Ogaden area was accompanied by heavy destruction of human life and horrifying atrocity.

The conclusions reached regarding United Nations' practice are strongly supported by the documentation offered. Buchheit establishes that "the history of United Nations' practice lends substantial support to the thesis that the principle of self-determination, as interpreted by that body, is primarily a vehicle for decolonisation, not an authorisation of secession. The reactions of the organisation to the situations in (among others) the Congo, Tibet, Biafra, and Bangla Desh ... evidence a lack of sympathy for separatist demands that conflict with the principle of the territorial integrity of established States." And he refers to the secretary-general's reply at a press conference in 1970 to the question whether there was a deep contradiction between a people's right to self-determination and the attitude of the federal government of Nigeria toward Biafra. The secretary-general reminded his listeners that the United Nations had spent over $500 million in the Congo primarily to prevent the secession of Katanga from the Congo. "So, as far as the question of secession of a particular section of a Member State is concerned, the United Na-

44. Ibid., 184.
45. This account of Somali self-determination summarizes some of the material in Buchheit, 1978:176–89.

tions' attitude is unequivocable [*sic*]. As an international organiza-tion, the United Nations has never accepted and does not accept and I do not believe it will ever accept the principle of secession of a part of its Member State." Shortly thereafter, the secretary-general reit-erated his view on the scope of self-determination, explaining that "when a State applies to be a Member of the United Nations, and when the United Nations accepts that Member, then the implication is that the rest of the membership of the United Nations recognises the territorial integrity, independence and sovereignty of this partic-ular Member State."[46] (There is a further implication in the secre-tary-general's interpretation, namely, that the United Nations is a club of member states for the protection and advancement of their interests, not an organization of, and for, the peoples of the world. The clarion call of the United Nations Charter, WE THE PEOPLES OF THE UNITED NATIONS, would seem to be pure illusion).

In practice, then, "the doctrine of self-determination as such has been of negligible value in contributing to the international com-munity's collective response to these secessionist attempts." Buchheit argues that this situation may be remedied (I would suppose in part) by basic agreement on the boundaries of the doctrine. Its application "as a theoretical tool facilitating the international community's en-dorsement of certain behavior, is noticeably impaired only when the community cannot determine whether it is confronted with a legiti-mate claim to the principle." In general, the world community "seems to prefer that the grievance of a particular group be remedied by means which stop short of secession." But claims for the redress of grievances by means of political restructuring, not involving seces-sion, "will almost certainly be viewed as an 'internal affair' beyond the realm of legitimate international concern."[47] International sup-port for secessionary self-determination conflicts with respect for ter-ritorial integrity, while support for redress of grievances by means short of secession may conflict with respect for sovereignty over in-ternal affairs.

Many other studies present a similar view of United Nations practice on self-determination. Thornberry sums it up concisely in a discussion of international law and minority rights. "The main ben-eficiaries of self-determination, the newly independent states of Af-rica, Asia, the Caribbean and the Pacific, have advanced a version of

46. Ibid., 87–88.
47. Ibid., 214–15.

the doctrine which dominates United Nations practice. The principal elements are: (a) Self-determination applies in situations of 'salt-water colonialism'; (b) it is fully realised when a colony achieves independence; and (c) it can only be exercised once by a majority in a colony, so that, for example, Biafra had no right to secede from Nigeria."[48] The phrase "salt-water colonialism" is of interest. It refers to external colonialism as distinct from the internal colonialism of, say, the Sudan, but it also has a connotation of "pigmentational self-determination" because the overseas colonizers were European, while the peoples they colonized were of different race.[49] In U.N. practice, self-determination applies to decolonization, to liberation from white domination in southern Africa, and, in some cases, to liberation from alien subjugation through conquest or annexation, as in the West Bank and Gaza.

From a United Nations point of view, resistance to secession may be explained by the anxiety over the disruption of interstate relations that would follow a proliferation of secessions from multiethnic states.[50] Then, too, the United Nations expresses on secessionary movements, and on self-determination in general, the perspectives of the majority of its members. Many of the Third World countries, particularly in Africa, need a period of stability in which to establish their independence, develop their economies, and integrate their peoples. They have good reason to fear secessionary conflict and Balkanization, with increased vulnerability to outside intervention and neocolonial domination.[51]

United Nations practice, however, is not to be equated with established jurisprudence. Declarations by the United Nations, embodying international norms, repeatedly reaffirm the right of *all* peoples to self-determination. Certainly, the free exercise of the right may conflict with international norms governing respect for unity and territorial integrity. But there are many political and social forms of self-determination that do not challenge unity and territorial integrity. Indeed, even a federative type of political solution may enhance the unity of a state by removing a source of continuing griev-

48. 1980:452.
49. Confirmatory comment will be found also in Franck and Rodley, 1972:163; Sureda, 1973:215, 237–38; and Friedlander, 1980:320.
50. Buchheit, 1978:13–19.
51. A somewhat different view of the African perspective is given by Mojekwu, 1980:230–31, who argues that, in accepting the colonial boundaries, African leaders condemn themselves to live under the spell of colonialism.

ance and disruption. It is only secession that by its very nature frag-
ments territorial integrity. Whether it disrupts the unity of the
peoples of a state should be a matter for investigation. There is no
reason to accept an a priori assumption of unity. But leaving this
aside, the *Declaration on Friendly Relations* regulates the ordering of
these basic norms. Respect for territorial integrity and political unity
have primacy where states conduct themselves in compliance with
the principle of equal rights and self-determination of peoples and
are thus possessed of a representative government. The clear implication must surely be that secession is available when these conditions are not met. It is certainly not compatible with any conception
of international justice that a people should be obliged to submit to
extreme oppression and to massacre in the interests of preserving
"unity" and territorial integrity.

There is a further doctrine of relevance for the jurisprudence of
self-determination. This is described by the secretariat of the International Commission of Jurists in *The Events in East Pakistan, 1971*
as a "widely held view among international lawyers that the right of
self-determination is a right which can be exercised once only."[52] It
has been mentioned in some of the quoted comments cited above.
The effect would be a radical limitation of the scope of self-
determination in postcolonial society, much along the lines of U.N.
practice. Claims to self-determination might still be based on the
failure to implement the conditions referred to in the *Declaration on
Friendly Relations*. And there would also remain the possibility of establishing that, appearances notwithstanding, the right of self-
determination had not been exercised but that, quite to the contrary,
the constitutional arrangements had been imposed. This was the position taken by the secretary-general of the International Commission of Jurists in "Self-Determination and the 'Independent' Bantustans."[53] Clearly, the Bantustans in South Africa are not an expression
of self-determination by African peoples but an imposition by an
oppressive government pursuing a highly elaborated policy of systematic racial discrimination. However, in discussing whether the
different Bantustan groups constitute peoples entitled to self-
determination, the secretary-general concluded that "the 'peoples' in

52. 1972:69. See, in general, the discussion in this report of the right of self-
determination in international law (part V). See also the ICJ's discussion of Eritrea's
claim to self-determination (1981:8–14).
53. *ICJ Newsletter—No. 8*, Quarterly Report, Jan.–Mar. 1981, pp. 25–38.

South Africa who are entitled to self-determination are the whole of the disenfranchised African, Asian and coloured population, and not each of the somewhat artificial tribal groupings of which the Africans are said to be composed."[54] This falls back on the territorial population test, applied to colonial territories, with the bizarre consequence that a group like the Zulus, for example, are not deemed to be a people. Yet they have a political organization as a kingdom going back to the early nineteenth century, a distinctive history, culture, language, and literature, and a well-defined territory, however reduced and fragmented as a result of conquest.

But the doctrine of a once-and-for-all exercise of the right of self-determination is questionable. The rationale for it must be the pragmatic consideration that the free exercise of self-determination would render relations within and between states unpredictable and disorderly. But self-determination is exercised in the context of, and in relation to, a specific social situation, and it would seem unreasonable to demand that it be binding in perpetuity, notwithstanding totally changed circumstances following the first exercise of the right. To take the example of decolonization, the widespread support for the Algerian revolution was a clear exercise of the right of self-determination in the form of independence from French colonial rule. But it was not a self-determination regulating the relations between Arabs and Berbers. Indeed, tensions between the two groups almost erupted into civil war at the moment of independence, and they continue to threaten the stability of Algerian society. In Nigeria, on the other hand, the relations between the major ethnic groups were in the forefront of concern during the negotiations preceding independence. The constitutional arrangements were specially designed to forestall the fratricidal conflicts that later overtook the country. Surely, radically changed circumstances should allow a group to renew its right to self-determination.[55] Of course, in many cases, perhaps in most cases, these radically changed circumstances would involve the breach of the principles of equal rights and representative government, referred to in the *Declaration on Friendly Relations*.

In the light of the above discussion of self-determination, I turn now to some of the conclusions that can be drawn from the U.N. proceedings on Bangladesh as they relate to the conflicts of norms. Of

54. Ibid., 33–34.
55. See the discussion by Buchheit, 1978:22.

course, it is misleading to place too strong an emphasis on the vote and on the arguments advanced in support of the vote as an indication of normative concern. The exercise of the veto by the USSR in the Security Council debates is hardly to be explained as reflecting an overriding concern for human rights. The USSR was pursuing its political self-interest in the promotion of its alliance with India, and the delaying tactics it employed gave the Indian armies time to consolidate their victories on the battlefields. But nevertheless, where there is a consistent overwhelming vote in one or other direction and the vote runs contrary to ordinary conceptions of reason and morality, it may be taken as a fair indication of the normative priorities of member states.

Bangladesh stirred up a great confrontation of norms, with respect for territorial integrity, unity, domestic sovereignty, and nonintervention ranged against concern for human rights, including the right to self-determination, and above all, the right to protection against large-scale massacre and genocidal assault. At a different level, the confrontation of norms may be seen as a conflict between law and morality, and between peace and justice.[56]

The Indian government sought to establish the equality of the norms of respect for sovereignty, territorial integrity, and nonintervention on the one hand and the protection of human rights or self-determination on the other. Not only were these norms to be considered as having equal importance, but they were to be regarded as reciprocal. A failure to abide by one would stop a state from invoking the others.[57] This is in accord with the provisions of the Declaration on Friendly Relations.

The refusal or failure of the United Nations to deal with the conflict, save by way of relief operations, had the effect of asserting the primacy of the norms protective of the status quo while relegating the human rights issues, including large-scale massacres, devastation, and genocide, to a secondary role. This is perhaps not altogether surprising, given the fact that the United Nations is an organization of the ruling classes of member states or, as Franck and Rodley express it, "a professional association of governments, which cannot be counted upon to act in any way likely to undermine the authority of one (and, by implication, all) of the member regimes."[58]

The outbreak of war between India and Pakistan, and the inva-

56. See the discussion by Franck and Rodley, 1973:275.
57. Frank and Rodley, 1972:165.
58. Ibid., 151.

sion of East Pakistan by the Indian Army, compelled the highest organs of the United Nations, the Security Council and the General Assembly, to be "seized" of the matter. These events raised new issues affecting fundamental United Nations norms, namely, the duty to preserve the peace, to respect the territorial inviolability of member states, and to refrain from armed intervention. They also raised the issue of the normative justification of intervention as necessitated by humanitarian concern, that is to say, the according of primacy to protection against gross violations of human rights.

The doctrine of forceful humanitarian intervention is in considerable disrepute, on the grounds (a) that, in the past, it was invariably, or almost invariably, motivated by political self-interest; (b) that in the absence of this political self-interest, states refrained from intervention, even in response to the grossest and most odious violations of human rights; and (c) that the possibility of invoking humanitarian concern is an invitation to powerful states to interfere in the internal affairs of weaker states. It was no doubt for this reason that the Indian government justified its armed action as self-defense, and not explicitly as humanitarian intervention. But the humanitarian concern was consistently emphasized by the government in its memoranda to the secretary-general and in the debates. And this humanitarian concern was also the basis for the government's insistence on the need for a political solution, a human rights solution, as a first priority.

Indeed, it seems to me that it was quite contrary to reason and morality to have called for a cease-fire without a political solution, thereby leaving the Pakistan government in a position to continue its extreme repression of the Bengali people. Yet this was the decision taken by an overwhelming majority in the General Assembly, with only a preambular reference to the need for a political solution. Member states thereby expressed their rejection of humanitarian intervention and their overriding commitment to norms protective of state sovereignty and territorial integrity and noninterference in the internal affairs of member states.

As for the Security Council, its final resolution was quite meaningless, even as a face-saving device. Paralysis by superpower intransigence is almost certain to be a continuing feature of the Security Council response to large-scale massacres and genocide. Given this paralysis of the United Nations body supremely vested with sanctions for the enforcement of international obligations, one must ask whether member states are to stand idly by as spectators of genocidal massacres threatening the survival of whole groups. Or should they not singly, or preferably in combination, assert a right to humanitarian intervention?

PART THREE

UNITED NATIONS PERFORMANCE

6

Problems of Implementation within the United Nations

There are many difficulties in assessing the significance of norms and values in the performance of states on matters affecting human rights. At the internal domestic level, a constitutional commitment by states to the Universal Declaration of Human Rights, and the ratification of the major human rights conventions, is no guarantee against the grossest violations of such elementary human rights as the right to life and to protection against genocide. So, too, at the international level, the separation between practice and norms and values frustrates the implementation of human rights covenants and denies to many victims even the most minimal protection against the most massive violation of their human rights.

Paradoxically, however, human rights enjoy so high a prestige in the deliberations of the United Nations that their violation is routinely defended in the rhetoric of human rights. The same rhetoric serves also to frustrate attempts to devise effective procedures for protection against violations of human rights. And the most vigorous denunciations of violations often proceed from governments guilty of the very violations they castigate. The impact on the outside observer, in such organs of the United Nations as the Commission on Human Rights, is of an overwhelming hypocrisy.

The cliché-ridden, and often unctuous, style of debate heightens the impression of hypocrisy. There are the interminably repetitive routines of elaborate congratulations to the chairman and members of the bureau and the ritualized politesse of the replies. Delegates are distinguished, no matter how wretched their performance, or that of their governments, or both. Determination is categorical. So too is opposition. Support is unreserved. Floods are veritable. Declarations are historic. Rights are enshrined in constitutions (in the sense of dead and buried?). And authoritarian or totalitarian or fascist governments are democratic.

Quite apart from the difficulty in assessing the sincerity and strength of the commitment to particular norms or human rights policies, the expression of this commitment may also be variable. Thus, the Russian delegation strongly opposes, as a general policy, any interference in the internal affairs of member states. Yet, as we have seen in the case of Bangladesh, its delegation urged the primacy of a political solution. And it does not hesitate to campaign for political interference in the internal affairs of South Africa, Israel, Chile, and a number of other member states within the orbit of U.S. influence. Nor does it draw back from direct intervention.

Then, too, there is no general agreement on a scale of values, and situations juxtapose different values in new relationships, raising problems of their ordering. This was the dilemma in the recognition of the Pol Pot government as the accredited representative of Cambodia (Democratic Kampuchea) in the United Nations. The problem was that the Pol Pot government had imposed a most brutal and murderous regime from the time it assumed power in April 1975 until it was overthrown in January 1979 by an invasion of Vietnamese and rebel Cambodian troops. In March 1979 the chairman of the Sub-Commission on Prevention of Discrimination and Protection of Minorities had reported to the commission that the situation under the Pol Pot regime constituted "nothing less than auto-genocide" and that the events described in the documents were "the most serious that had occurred anywhere in the world since nazism."

The governments of Canada, Norway, the United Kingdom, the United States, and Australia had taken a lead in denouncing the Pol Pot regime before the commission and in urging the commission to initiate action. Yet in the General Assembly, in September 1979, these same governments, with the exception of Norway, voted for the continued assignment of the Cambodian seat to the ousted government. The dilemma was, of course, that the Vietnamese invasion had introduced a new element which posed a Hobson's choice between recognizing the government installed by the Vietnamese (and, supposedly, thereby legitimizing intervention by force) and continuing to recognize the Pol Pot regime (and thereby affirming that mass murder on the most lavish scale was no bar to participation as a "distinguished" delegation in the United Nations). Incredibly, the governments in question chose the latter alternative—to my mind a thoroughly disreputable choice.

There were doubtless other considerations involved, considerations of geopolitical strategy. These again introduce variability, often taking the form of a double standard. The relevant norms are applied in some cases. In other, comparable cases, their relevance is denied or evaded, as protection is extended to offending governments by their patrons or by regional or ideological alliances of member states. Contradictory norms and disagreement on the scale of values permit these denials and evasions to be justified in the name of concern for human rights, lending the color of legitimacy to unprincipled expediency.

At a less grandiose level than geopolitical strategy, account must be taken of the maneuvers of states to advance their perceived interests. These often have the effect of weakening both the definition of the human rights violation in question and the procedures proposed for protective action. Julius Stone, in the course of a devastating analysis of the highly acclaimed, but in his view quite meaningless, definition of *aggression* arrived at by the United Nations after many years of agonized debate, comments that "manoeuvering for a definitional text which will advance the proponent State's self interests, and strike at its adversary's, is thus a central, socio-political reality." To this he adds the qualification, a little generous perhaps, that this competitive type of self-interest acts "side by side with noble aspiration for a text which will move States towards a more peaceful world in which there is a juster distribution among States and peoples."[1]

The self-interest extends also to protection against vulnerability. In cases where a state judges that it may be vulnerable to attack, its interests would suggest undermining the effectiveness of proposed procedures for implementation.

In each concrete situation then, the influence of norms, values, and ideologies is an empirical question related to conceptions of state interests and of geopolitical strategy in the particular situation, and to perceptions of the state's own vulnerability, since the action proposed may set a threatening precedent. Nevertheless, there is a

1. 1977:113.

general ideological influence on the position taken by member states on human rights, lending a certain predictability in broad outline to their deliberations in the United Nations. And this influence is especially marked in relation to the procedures for the handling of human rights violations. These procedures are the gateway to implementation and to control over the process of implementation. There is in consequence a continuous struggle to harmonize these procedures with ideological orientations and state interests.

At the present time, the major confrontation in the United Nations is between a states rights orientation and a liberal orientation to procedures for the implementation of human rights. The states rights orientation rests on two major premises, to which I have already referred in chapter 3. The first concerns the relationship between the state and the individual. The state is viewed as the source of human rights, there being no entitlement to these rights prior to, and independent of, the state. The state does not *recognize* rights—it *grants* them. Only states are subjects of international law. The second premise relates to the scale of values. Primacy is accorded the collectivity, which is to say, the state as the representative of the collectivity. And the emphasis, in relation to the exercise of human rights, is on the structural conditions, more particularly the economic foundations, for their enjoyment.

From this orientation, it follows that the protection of human rights is viewed as essentially a function of the state. In the internal affairs of a state, it is regarded as the exclusive concern of the state itself; that is to say, a highly restrictive interpretation is given article 2, paragraph 7, of the Charter, which excludes intervention in matters essentially within the jurisdiction of any state. Externally, in international relations within the United Nations, the protection of human rights is to be achieved by cooperation between member states. There is no role for such supranational institutions as the proposed high commissioner for human rights, nor is there a role for the individual, who must seek redress from the authorities in his own state.

Ideally, information on human rights practices should be sought from the states themselves, the preferred procedure being the submission of reports by states to the appropriate United Nations bodies. While petitions from individuals are to be excluded, participation by nongovernmental organizations may be tolerated, but under close restraint, and not extending to criticism of member states.

Such criticism is to be confined to member states meeting in closed sessions and under strictly confidential procedures.

The scale of values regulates the salience of different human rights issues and the significance to be accorded their violation. In principle, such matters as the imprisonment, exile, or confinement to a psychiatric hospital of a political dissident should not be the concern of the Commission on Human Rights. The raising of such issues is likely to be interpreted as a pretext for interference in the domestic affairs of sovereign states. Instead the commission, and other U.N. bodies, should be concerned rather with violations of human rights affecting large numbers, especially such violations as flow from the imposition of structural conditions inimical to the enjoyment of human rights, for example, colonization, conquest and annexation, apartheid and similar systems of racial and ethnic oppression, and economic exploitation.

In rough outline, this approximates the theoretical orientation of the East European socialist states to procedures for the protection of human rights. In practice, there are many deviations from this orientation.

The liberal orientation to human rights is identified primarily with the Western approach, as described in chapter 3. Human rights are conceived as inherent in the very nature of man, not tied to citizenship in a particular society. Historically, these individual rights, wrested from despotic rulers, served as a protection against the tyranny of the state, and this remains a central element in the liberal orientation. Though the functions of the state have changed profoundly, as notably in the welfare states, it is nevertheless mostly states that systematically violate human rights; this is especially true of genocide, which is, with few exceptions, essentially a state crime.

In the scale of values, civil and political rights are viewed as primary, the indispensable foundations of human freedom. There is, however, increasing receptivity to the role of structural factors and recognition of the need for, or the right to, economic development.

The procedural implications of this liberal orientation are an acceptance, and indeed an appreciation, of the contributions of nongovernmental organizations to the protection of human rights. So too, individual petitions are accepted as a source of information and as a means for activating United Nations consideration of human rights violations. Protection of human rights extends also to the rights of an individual, or of a few individuals, as where punitive measures are taken against political dissidents. But, of course, these measures are often the individual manifestation of a societal problem, namely, the suppression of political opposition in the society as a whole.

Since the state is actually, or potentially, the major violator of human rights, it cannot be entrusted with the sole protection of these rights. Hence the liberal interpretation is associated with attempts to strengthen the existing procedures within the United Nations and to establish such new supranational institutions as the office of a high commissioner for human rights. The provisions of article 2, paragraph 7, of the Charter are not interpreted so restrictively as to exclude action relating to the internal affairs of member states. On the contrary, the many covenants and resolutions of the United Nations for the protection of human rights are deemed to render their violation a matter of international concern.

The West opposed the inclusion of economic, social, and cultural rights in the same covenant as civil and political, arguing that they were of a different order, attainable progressively, in contrast to the immediately enforceable civil and political rights. Derogation from civil and political rights was to be permitted only in exceptional, and clearly defined, circumstances, and then only within prescribed limits. The West rejects the contention that there is, in many developing societies, an inherent incompatibility between the urgent needs of economic development and civil and political rights, which justifies the suspension of these rights.[2] Moreover, it does not view economic development in a country as automatically advancing the promotion of human rights. Indeed, in many countries, the proceeds of economic development, or the funds provided by international aid for such development, are appropriated by a small, oppressive ruling elite, without benefit to the general population but with an increasing, rather than diminishing, maldistribution of resources and denial of civil and political rights. And though the West is now more receptive to the need for the restructuring of international economic relations, it resists the large-scale transfer of resources and the radical revision of the conditions of exchange, which the Third World de-

2. An interesting discussion of the issues from a Western perspective is presented by the American Association for the International Commission of Jurists in *Toward an Integrated Human Rights Policy* (1979).

mands as necessary for the establishment of a new international economic order, based on social justice, on equal rights, and on reparation for past exploitation.

The orientation of the Third World is toward an emphasis on states rights. But this does not derive from any common philosophy of human rights. There is too great a diversity of tradition, of political ideology, and of state and social structure for any such basic consensus. However, many of the states share similar problems deriving from past colonization and from present foreign and neocolonialist exploitation, poverty, illness, illiteracy, and the instability of administrative and institutional structures.[3] To this should be added their very realistic fears of intervention by powerful states. These shared elements provide, at the level of "practical ideology," the basis for a Third World orientation to the protection of human rights.

The main elements of this orientation appear clearly in two "historic" documents. The first is the *Proclamation of Teheran* of 13 May 1968, which reviewed the progress made in the 20 years since the adoption of the Universal Declaration of Human Rights and formulated a program for the future. The second is General Assembly Resolution 32/130 of December 1977, *Alternative Approaches and Ways and Means within the United Nations System for Improving the Effective Enjoyment of Human Rights and Fundamental Freedoms*. Both these documents bear the stamp of the Third World approach to human rights and their protection and reflect the numerical dominance of these states within the United Nations.

The *Proclamation of Teheran* opens with a reaffirmation of the major human rights documents and a call on members of the international community to fulfill their solemn obligations to promote and encourage respect for human rights and fundamental freedoms. Then follow many of the central preoccupations of the Third World: "gross denials under the repugnant policy of *apartheid*," "the evils of racial discrimination," continuing "problems of colonialism," "massive denials of human rights, arising out of aggression or any armed conflict," "gross denials of human rights arising from discrimination on grounds of race (religion, belief or expressions of opinion),"[4] and

3. See Espiell, 1979:60–61.
4. I have put the phrase in parentheses in order to indicate that, in my view, it is discrimination on grounds of race that is a preoccupation of Third World countries, and not particularly discrimination on grounds of religion, belief, and expression of opinion.

"the widening gap between the economically developed and developing countries," which "impedes the realization of human rights in the international community."

The relationship of civil and political rights to economic, social, and cultural rights is defined in paragraph 13 in the following terms:

Since human rights and fundamental freedoms are indivisible, the full realization of civil and political rights without the enjoyment of economic, social and cultural rights is impossible. The achievement of lasting progress in the implementation of human rights is dependent upon sound and effective national and international policies of economic and social development.

The proclamation concludes with references to a number of specific problems and to general and complete disarmament as "one of the highest aspirations of all peoples."

The later document expresses more explicitly and with greater clarity the preoccupations and priorities of the Third World. Paragraphs 1 (e) and (f) provide as follows:

(e) In approaching human rights questions within the United Nations system, the international community should accord, or continue to accord, priority to the search for solutions to the mass and flagrant violations of human rights of peoples and persons affected by situations such as those resulting from *apartheid*, from all forms of racial discrimination, from colonialism, from foreign domination and occupation, from aggression and threats against national sovereignty, national unity and territorial integrity, as well as from the refusal to recognize the fundamental rights of peoples to self-determination and of every nation to the exercise of full sovereignty over its wealth and natural resources;

(f) The realization of the new international economic order is an essential element for the effective promotion of human rights and fundamental freedoms and should also be accorded priority.

The above resolution, and somewhat similar formulations in the past, readily provide argument that interference in the internal affairs of member states for the protection of human rights is restricted to the listed violations; the phrase "such as those resulting from *apartheid*" is given a limitative interpretation. And, indeed, these formulations have been used in this way to obstruct consideration of other violations. Moreover, in practice, the inordinate amount of time accorded to the debates on the priority items has somewhat the effect of a filibuster, leaving little time for the consideration of other gross violations. Thus the Third World orientation effectively limits the scope of implementation.

From the above discussion of orientations, one might readily conclude that the West had always been active in promoting the protection of civil and political rights and in strengthening the capacity of the United Nations to respond more effectively to gross violations of these rights. But, in fact, this is a recent development. The period of Western domination in the United Nations was devoted to standard setting and to promotion by persuasion and education. It was remarkable for the neglect of protective action against violations and for its contemptuous treatment of complaints. Indeed, one of the first decisions of the Commission on Human Rights was that it had "no power to take any action in regard to any complaints concerning human rights," and this decision was approved by the Economic and Social Council. As a former director of the Division of Human Rights commented, "The system established by the United Nations for dealing with appeals directed to it by 'the peoples' in whose name the Charter had been adopted had become the world's most elaborate waste-paper basket."[5]

Conversely, my earlier discussion might suggest consistent obstruction by the East European socialist states and the Third World to the implementation of commitments for the protection of civil and political rights. But, quite to the contrary, it was the campaign waged by the Soviet Union and by Third World countries to accelerate the process of decolonization that launched the United Nations on an action-oriented course and forced the West into a defensive position.[6] However, the extension of this campaign from the decolonization of dependent countries to action against the independent sovereign state of South Africa represented a departure from the commitment of the East European socialist states to the inviolability of sovereignty in domestic affairs. And this in turn provided an opening for the West to insist that consideration be extended to violations in all countries.[7] So the modest Western initiative in the protection of human rights can hardly be attributed to a direct expression of the liberal orientation.

There are other ambiguities in the manifestations of the liberal orientation within the United Nations. For example, the United States, which initially played so prominent a role in the human rights program of the United Nations and is currently pressing for more effective implementation, signed, but failed to ratify, such key covenants and conventions as those on economic, social, and cultural

5. Humphrey, 1971:470.
6. See the discussion by Gonzales, 1981:443–55.
7. Ibid., 450.

rights, civil and political rights, the prevention and punishment of the crime of genocide, and the elimination of all forms of racial discrimination. In the debates of the United States Senate on the ratification of the Genocide Convention, recommended by the president in 1949 and by succeeding administrations, the main objections were on constitutional grounds. It seems that these objections were quite invalid.[8] There were also well-grounded criticisms of the text of the convention. But underlying these objections was a sentiment that ratification of the conventions and covenants would expose the United States to external interference in its domestic affairs. A report by the Senate Foreign Relations Committee on the ratification of the Genocide Convention makes the highly revealing comment that "there is a note of fear behind most arguments—as if genocide were rampant in the United States and this Nation could not afford to have its actions examined by international organs."[9] At a different level, there is the anomaly of United States support for some of the most tyrannical governments in the world today.

The right of individual petition may be taken as a further example of ambiguity in the liberal orientation. I have commented on the significance of this right, given the fact that the state itself is the main violator of human rights and hardly to be entrusted with their protection. Consistent with the liberal orientation, the West campaigned for the inclusion of the right of individual petition in the Convention on Civil and Political Rights, but it failed to win the necessary support. However, as a compromise solution, provision was made in an optional protocol for a state to recognize the competence of the Human Rights Committee, appointed under the convention, to receive and consider communications from individuals falling under its jurisdiction. Yet in the years that have elapsed since its adoption in December 1966, only nine of the Western industrialized states— the five Scandinavian countries, Canada, Italy, the Netherlands, and Portugal—have ratified the protocol. The remainder of the 29 ratifications and accessions are by Caribbean and Latin American states (strongly represented) and by a sprinkling of African states.[10] In ef-

8. See Richard Lillich, ed., *U.S. Ratification of the Human Rights Treaties*, 1981, for a discussion of this issue, and especially Nigel Rodley, in ibid., 3–19, and Louis Henkin, in ibid., 20–26.

9. United States Congress, 1971, 17. See also Sohn and Buergenthal, 1973:913– 92, for a general discussion of the objections raised to ratification of the Genocide Convention.

10. As of May 1983.

fect, the Protocol came into force as a result of ratifications by Third World states.

The introduction of a right of individual petition is a remarkable innovation in international law, so hesitation in accepting the right was to be expected.[11] In the American Convention on Human Rights, the acceptance of individual petitions is obligatory, not optional, the right of individual petition following automatically from ratification.[12] This may explain the ratification of the U.N. Optional Protocol by so many of the Latin American states. In the European Convention for the Protection of Human Rights and Fundamental Freedoms (which preceded the U.N convention by 16 years), the European Commission of Human Rights is empowered to receive petitions by any person, nongovernmental organization, or group of individuals claiming to be the victim of a violation by a state party to the convention (article 25). But this is subject to the condition that the state party in question has recognized the competence of the commission to receive such petitions. So acceptance of the right of individual petition is optional. But in contrast to the response within the United Nations, the great majority of the member states in the Council of Europe have accepted the procedure.[13] There is obviously an additional element of trust involved. What is acceptable within a regional organization whose members have many traditions in common is likely to be fraught with apprehension in the United Nations. Notwithstanding the many rhetorical references in U.N. debates to the organization's moral stature, it is precisely this quality that is highly suspect—and for good reason.

Clearly, the expression of the states rights and liberal orientations is most complex. East and West do not operate as "two solitudes."[14] The state of human rights and the procedures for their protection are appreciably the product of many years of antagonistic interaction.

The conflicts of perspective and interest that attended the formulation of the Genocide Convention were restrained by a common determination to liberate mankind from the scourge of genocide.

11. See Robertson, 1972:73.
12. Ibid., 128–29.
13. Robertson, 1977:149–53.
14. Phrase used by French Canadians with reference to their own situation vis-à-vis English Canadians.

But, nevertheless, as discussed in chapter 2, the divergences and confrontations in the debates gave rise to many compromises, which jeopardize implementation.

Ambiguities are embedded in the very definition of the crime as one of a number of acts "committed with *intent* to destroy, in whole or *in part*, a national, ethnical, racial or religious group, *as such*." Of course, these ambiguities could have been clarified by the judicial interpretations of a functioning international penal tribunal. But this is possible too, under the present convention, even in the absence of such a tribunal, since article IX provides that:

Disputes between the Contracting Parties, relating to the interpretation, application or fulfilment of the present Convention, including those related to the responsibility of a State for genocide or any of the other acts enumerated in article III, shall be submitted to the International Court of Justice at the request of any of the parties to the dispute.

However, the effectiveness of this article is severely limited by the reservations entered by the members of the Soviet bloc and a number of other states, which declared that they did not consider themselves bound by its provisions and that agreement of all the parties to a dispute was an essential condition for submissions to the International Court. Still, despite these definitional ambiguities, there is a sufficient and workable specification of the acts that constitute genocide, and this is rendered more comprehensive by the extension (in article III) of the punishable acts to include conspiracy to commit genocide, direct and public incitement to genocide, attempted genocide, and complicity in genocide.

A much more serious defect restricts the scope of the convention. This is the exclusion of political groups. Quite apart from the historical circumstances of the Nazi annihilation of religious, national, ethnic, *and* political groups, which inspired United Nations action against genocide, and the original unanimous United Nations resolution in December 1946, it seems logical to include these categories in a single convention. In many cases, they tend to merge, and it is impossible to disentangle the political component from the ethnic, racial, or religious. Often, too, the processes of mass murder are quite similar.

I suggested in chapter 2 that the real issue in the exclusion of political groups was the freedom to dispose of political opposition without interference from the outside world. I do not mean to imply that, in eliminating political groups in the convention, any member state necessarily contemplated eliminating political groups in the flesh. But some governments may have wished to keep that option open. And I can well understand that the protection of political groups might not be acceptable to many governments, since it strikes at the very roots of political power. Besides, it could lend the color of legitimacy, or provide the pretext of legitimacy, for the most unwarranted interference in the political affairs of other countries.

Since the adoption of the convention, ideological divisions within the United Nations have grown sharper, and there has been a great proliferation of totalitarian and militaristic regimes freely practicing the torture, and the murder, of political opponents. In these circumstances, opposition to the inclusion of political groups would be even more intense than in 1948, when the convention was adopted. But the addition of a protocol or supplementary convention may become feasible at a later date.

The major casualties during the debates on the convention were the procedures proposed for implementation. The convention is described as the Convention on the Prevention and Punishment of the Crime of Genocide. However, there are only two perfunctory references to prevention. But one of these (article VIII) opens up the possibility of taking such preventive measures as are within the competence of the United Nations. It provides that:

Any Contracting Party may call upon the competent organs of the United Nations to take such action under the Charter of the United Nations as they consider appropriate for the prevention and suppression of acts of genocide or any of the other acts enumerated in article III.

For the rest, the convention is directed to the punishment of the crime. The model is that of municipal criminal law, which specifies the nature of the crime and the available sanctions. Since this was, presumably, a common element in the legal systems of the parties framing the convention, it would have provided a basis for agreement at a pragmatic level. There was also the precedent of the Nuremberg trials. Underlying this approach, however, is the assumption that, in a manner comparable to sanctions under municipal law, the fear of punishment would be an effective deterrent. However, one cannot easily transpose assumptions in regard to the fear of punishment *within* a society to presumed similar effects in an *international setting*: those who commit genocide are likely to be protected within the confines of their own societies, unless there is a revolutionary change in government. In the case of "domestic" genocides (that is to say, genocides internal to a society and arising out of divisions between its racial, ethnic, or religious groups), once the genocidal process is under way, the perpetrators are not likely to be accessible to moral or reasoned appeals or readily deterred by the threat of punishment; indeed, they may no longer be in control of the forces they have unleashed. But in the early stages, the fear of punishment may very well act as somewhat of a deterrent for the leaders, and with greater effect at all times on subordinates, since a plea of superior orders is not a valid defense.

Given the fact that genocide is generally committed by governments, any effective system of punishment would require supranational institutions and procedures; and the original draft by the secretariat made the necessary provision for an international penal court. It also provided for universal enforcement, permitting the state whose authorities had arrested those charged with the crime to exercise jurisdiction regardless of the nationality of the accused or of the place where the offense was committed. But with the elimination of the principle of universal enforcement and the failure to establish an international penal court, it is only the governments of states, in the territories of which the crime was committed, that can institute proceedings for its punishment.

The consequences are particularly absurd in the case of domestic genocides. The effect of the present procedures is that in most cases of domestic genocide, governments would be required to prosecute themselves. In actual practice, of course, the mass murderers are protected by their governments, save in those cases where governments have been overthrown, as in Equatorial Guinea and Kampuchea.[15] In some cases, however, government action is conceivable, as for example where vulnerable indigenous groups are being annihilated by invading economic forces, but in these cases too there is generally government involvement or condonation.

Where genocides are perpetrated in the course of international warfare, the state in whose territory the crime was committed has jurisdiction and can apply to the offending government for extradition of the mass murderers. Or if the mass murderers have found refuge in other countries, the application can be made to the govern-

15. Hannah Arendt, 1969: chap. 1, has an interesting discussion of the dilatory, reluctant, and lenient prosecution of Nazi war criminals under the jurisdiction of the German government.

ments of those countries. The same procedure is available in domestic genocides when the mass murderers have fled their own countries. But applications for extradition are often denied or evaded. And some of the most murderous of the Nazi genocidal criminals found sanctuary in Argentina, Paraguay, Bolivia, and indeed also in the United States though in contravention of the law. One thinks of Dr. Josef Mengele, perhaps the most horrifying of torturers and mass murderers in recorded history, protected by the government of Paraguay. And the Israeli trial of Adolf Eichmann, who had organized the deportation of Jews to the death camps of the German Reich, was made possible only by the Israeli kidnapping of Eichmann in the streets of Buenos Aires. If the present regime in Uganda had not also committed gross violations of human rights, it might perhaps apply for the extradition of Amin. But the application would have to be made to Saudi Arabia, where Amin enjoys sanctuary and where it would seem that the bonds of Islam are strong enough to embrace mass murderers. Indeed, the most horrendous mass murderers are almost certain to find refuge and sustenance in one or another of the member states of the United Nations.

The present position, then, is that the United Nations is not responsible for punishment of the crime of genocide. But within the United Nations there are other procedures for action against genocide, both under the convention and under the general provisions relating to gross and consistent violations of human rights.

The main channels for implementation of the Genocide Convention are the Commission on Human Rights, the Sub-Commission on Prevention of Discrimination and Protection of Minorities, and the Security Council. Of course, member states can raise complaints of genocide in the General Assembly and in other bodies, such as the Economic and Social Council, and the Social and Humanitarian Committee (since genocidal conflict always raises humanitarian issues calling for immediate action). And, as noted above, article VIII of the convention specifically empowers any of the contracting powers to call upon the competent organs of the United Nations to take appropriate action under the Charter for the prevention and suppression of acts of genocide.

The most effective sanctions are those within the competence of the Security Council in situations that constitute a threat to the peace or a breach of the peace. These include the interruption of eco-

nomic relations and communications, severance of diplomatic relations, recommendations to the General Assembly for the suspension
or expulsion of the offending member state, and the use of armed
force. They are clearly available for action against genocides committed in the course of international war. But they could also be
available in what would appear to be purely internal domestic genocides. The Division of Human Rights (now Center for Human
Rights) has been seeking to establish the perspective that, peace
being indivisible, gross violations of human rights internal to a society may reach such an intensity that they can be seen as constituting
a threat to peace;[16] this argument appeared in 1982 and 1983 on the
agenda of the sub-commission under the heading "The Effects of
Gross Violations of Human Rights on International Peace and Security" and was to be discussed further at the next session in 1984, after
a review of the comments of member states.

There are cogent arguments for this point of view. The gross violations of human rights incite external intervention; and they also
encourage the rulers in the offending countries to find external diver-
sion for internal misery or chaos, thus increasing the likelihood of
international conflict.[17] Moreover, neighboring states are almost inevitably involved by reason of their having to provide for refugees,
and by reason of their possible involvement in the military operations taken by the offending state against resistance movements
mounted in the territories of refuge. In the case of Bangladesh (East
Pakistan), it was clear to members of the Security Council at an early
date that the internal conflict constituted a threat to peace, but the
Security Council was paralyzed by the superpowers' irresponsible
use of the veto and failed to act. It is difficult to see a solution to the
problem. One can only hope that the increasing threat to world
peace, and indeed to survival, posed by the superpowers themselves
may set in motion the search for an effective counterpoise to the
abuse of the veto.

There are other possibilities of action within the United Nations,
such as intercessions by the secretary-general. Or, again, the system
of reporting by states parties to the Covenant on Civil and Political
Rights offers the Human Rights Committee, appointed under the
covenant, the opportunity to probe threatening situations in the relations between ethnic, racial, and religious groups. In addition,

16. Information from a staff member.
17. See Hoffmann, 1981.

under article 41 of the covenant, states parties may recognize the competence of the committee to receive and consider complaints against other states parties who have similarly accepted the competence of the committee. But as of the end of 1981, the committee's competence had been recognized by only 14 states, all within the Western orbit, with the exception of Senegal and Sri Lanka. In any event, states are reluctant to enter formal complaints against other states. Finally, as discussed earlier, a state party to the optional protocol accepts the competence of the committee, under carefully defined conditions, to receive complaints from individuals under the state's jurisdiction that their rights under the covenant have been violated.

Action may also be initiated in organizations within the U.N. orbit, such as the International Labour Organisation, World Health, Children's Fund, and various aid programs, through which may be raised specific issues that flow from the genocidal massacres and are relevant to the organization's goals. Action is also possible through regional intergovernmental organizations. The effectiveness of action through these organizations will of course vary with the organization and the issue. The Organization of American States has the institutions and procedures for relatively effective action in the protection of human rights, but it has not been able to restrain the many regimes practicing atrocity on the American continent. And as for the Organization of African Unity, it has in the past rendered Africans a great disservice by its protective stance toward African governments engaged in mass murder; perhaps this may change with the adoption of the African Charter on Human and Peoples' Rights.

In addition, there are the procedures within the United Nations for protection against gross and consistent violations of human rights. B. G. Ramcharan, a senior U.N. Human Rights official, drew my attention to the psychological reluctance within the United Nations to use the term *genocide*, even when dealing with it. He explained that there were also substantive reasons for this reluctance. Charges of genocide immediately close off the possibility of discourse. If the objective is to arrive at a solution in cooperation with the government concerned, this is more readily achieved by handling the complaint under the procedures for dealing with gross violations of human rights. So, too, if the issue is dealt with under other nongenocidal categories, such as a threat to the peace, or as raising humanitarian considerations, much of the emotive sting is removed.

The bodies seized with initial jurisdiction on complaints of violations of human rights, including genocide, are the Commission on Human Rights and the Sub-Commission on Prevention of Discrimination and Protection of Minorities. In the 1960s, under pressure from the decolonized member states, the commission began to concern itself with the implementation of human rights and with protection against violations. In 1967, by Resolution 1235 (XLII), the Economic and Social Council authorized the Commission on Human Rights to make "a thorough study of situations which reveal a consistent pattern of violations of human rights, as exemplified by the policy of *apartheid* as practised in the Republic of South Africa . . . and racial discrimination as practised notably in Southern Rhodesia, and report, with recommendations thereon, to the Economic and Social Council." From 1967, the committee carried out "a series of operational fact-finding activities which reflected the political and human rights preoccupations with the situations in Southern Africa, the occupied territories in the Middle East, and in more recent years, the situation in Chile."[18]

These inquiries are carried out openly and with full publicity. In 1970

the Economic and Social Council approved, in Resolution 1503 (XLVIII), a procedure whereby a complex machinery was set up for the screening of communications and the further examination of those communications which "appear to reveal a consistent pattern of gross and reliably attested violations of human rights and fundamental freedoms." The resolution provides for a multi-stage procedure, in which a working group of the Sub-Commission on Prevention of Discrimination, the Sub-Commission itself, the Commission on Human Rights and eventually (theoretically) an *ad hoc* investigatory committee appointed by the Commission serve successively as organs of implementation.[19]

Complaints (communications) of genocide under the 1503 procedure would generally be made by individuals and organizations. The complaints are sent to the governments concerned for comment; and they are referred, together with the replies, to the 1503 working group of the sub-commission, which meets, however, only once a year. These communications are handled under confidential procedures. If action is recommended, the nature of the action is not dis-

18. Van Boven in Cassese, ed., 1979:123.
19. Ibid., 124.

closed, nor do the confidential communications become available for public scrutiny. Information surfaces, however, in a variety of ways. The complaints may be referred to in parliamentary debate or in congressional reports, or there may be leakages by representatives. But it is necessary to bear in mind that one is dealing with what are in many ways secret procedures, and that one cannot hope for full information.

In the past there was little to encourage a complainant to make use of the commission's procedures for the handling of gross violations. These procedures are slow and cumbersome, with their various stages and annual postponements, whereas the genocidal conflicts call for the most immediately urgent action. And quite apart from the tortuous delays, there is the problem of the protective attitude taken by the commission, with the majority of its members according primacy to the political concerns for national self-interest and for regional and ideological alliances. Moreover, the main sanction the commission can apply is that of public exposure. As a result, the genocidal process has usually pursued a course uninhibited by actions of the commission.

The commission's performance for the protection of human rights is discussed in the three chapters that follow. It could hardly be more negative. And yet in recent years, under the dedicated and courageous leadership of the former director of the Division of Human Rights, there have been signs of constructive change.

The sub-commission, which consists of experts appointed in their own right and not as representatives of member states, has become increasingly militant in its public denunciations of gross violations of human rights and in its attempts to establish more effective procedures for their protection. Of course, there are counterpressures of the states rights orientation within the sub-commission itself, and the sub-commission is somewhat politicized and responsive to political pressures from member states. But the main frustration of its initiatives comes from the parent body, the commission.

The commission, in contrast to the sub-commission, is composed of the official representatives of state members. It is a highly politicized body. Human rights are politics because they affect the distribution of power; and it is pure U.N. fiction that they can be discussed in a nonpolitical way. Nevertheless, it should be possible in a commission entrusted with the promotion and protection of human rights to transcend the narrow political self-interest of member states in cases of mass murder and genocide and to strengthen the procedures for responding to the massive annihilation of groups.

The tension between the sub-commission and the commission, and the negation of its efforts by the commission, was such that the sub-commission had been seeking by various means to secure some measure of autonomy or a more supportive affiliation.[20] But even in the commission there was an increasing willingness, under van Boven's directorship, to deal with violations of human rights by other than a small group of pariah states. Moreover, the sanction of public exposure is not without effect. Most governments are sensitive to international opprobrium, as shown by the pains they take to defend themselves against complaints of gross violations. And as for the procedural deficiencies, they can certainly be surmounted, and the commission has concerned itself with this issue.

A disquieting augury for human rights under the regime of the new secretary general of the United Nations, Javier Pérez de Cuéllar, is that one of his first acts was to dismiss the director of the division under pressure from member states with a poor record on human rights. Still, given indications of the commission's greater concern for the protection of human rights, it seems conceivable that under pressure of international public opinion, the commission may be moved to a proper sense of its responsibilities as a U.N. body specifically designed for the advancement of human rights. However, there are many other U.N. channels, procedures, and institutional devices for action against genocide and mass murder.[21] The problem is how to make use of these procedures and how to render them more effective.

But first it is necessary to analyze the barriers to effective action by the United Nations. The following three chapters deal with United Nations performance in relation to slavery, political mass murder, and genocide. Slavery was selected in the expectation that there would be maximum consensus among member states and that United Nations action to suppress the crime would be at its most effective. There was the added interest of a significant institutional innovation.

20. See E/CN4/SR 1592, 1594, 1595, for attacks on and defense of the sub-commission in the commission's meetings on 9–11 February 1981, and E/CN.4/Sub.2/896–98, for strategies of the sub-commission.
21. See an excellent paper by Ramcharan, 1981.

7

Implementation of the Anti-Slavery Conventions

Contrary to expectations, it was only after many years of campaigning, with the Anti-Slavery Society as the main protagonist, that the United Nations was finally prevailed upon to provide for implementation of the Anti-Slavery Conventions. And even then, the provision made could hardly have been more grudging or more minimal. Analysis of the course of this campaign throws some light on the inhibitions of the United Nations when discourse moves from declaratory idealism to practical action.

In July 1966 the Social Committee of the United Nations Economic and Social Council (ECOSOC) debated a proposal to appoint a standing committee of experts on slavery that would assist ECOSOC "in the eradication of slavery, the slave trade and institutions and practices similar to slavery." The measure had been proposed by the special rapporteur, Mohamed Awad, in his report on slavery and was designed to render the Anti-Slavery Conventions more effective. There were historic precedents for the proposal. In 1933 the League of Nations had established the Standing Advisory Committee of Experts on Slavery, which functioned effectively for some years. In the United Nations, following a request by the General Assembly that ECOSOC study the problem of slavery, an Ad Hoc Committee of Experts met in 1950 and 1951. It reported that the creation of international supervisory machinery for the abolition of slavery and other forms of servitude was urgent and should be undertaken immediately and that a standing body of experts would be the most practical type of organization for the task envisaged.

The Anti-Slavery Society for the Protection of Human Rights had consistently advocated this course. The society is a nongovernmental body, based in England and enjoying second-class consultative status to ECOSOC. It has a distinguished record in the struggle against the slave trade and for the emancipation of slaves, with a history reaching back to 1823 (and indeed earlier, into the late eighteenth century). In 1909 it merged with the Aborigines Protection Society. It was instrumental in the setting up of a Slavery Bureau under the General Act of Brussels for the Repression of the Slave Trade (1890). When the League of Nations proved to be lethargic on the subject of slavery, the society continually lobbied for a slavery convention; and this was finally framed in 1926 with assistance from the society. On its recommendation, the League of Nations established the Standing Advisory Committee of Experts on Slavery in 1933.

The founding of the United Nations opened a new chapter. Charles Greenidge, the secretary of the society in the early years of the United Nations, comments in his book *Slavery* that the U.N. Charter made no specific reference to slavery and that its abolition could be inferred only from the commitment to the promotion of human rights and fundamental freedoms.[1] This was remedied, however, in the Universal Declaration of Human Rights, which declares in article 4 that no one shall be held in slavery or servitude and that slavery and the slave trade shall be prohibited in all their forms. But there was no provision for implementation; indeed, originally the declaration was not regarded as imposing binding obligations on member states.

The society lobbied for more effective action, and this resulted in December 1949 in the appointment of the Ad Hoc Committee of Experts, with a mandate to survey the field of slavery and customs resembling slavery, to assess its present nature and extent and to suggest methods for attacking the problem. The secretary of the society served as a member of this committee. There was an unfortunate setback in its deliberations. A memorandum prepared for the committee on forms of servitude in Latin America named Peru among the countries in which these practices still existed. This so incensed the delegate from Peru that he launched an attack on the committee's

1. 1958, chap. 16.

procedure and program and prevailed on ECOSOC to curtail sessions. As a result of these and other difficulties, the committee could not attempt an assessment of contemporary slavery. But the society's secretary remained behind at U.N. Headquarters and filed a minority report that contained information on this subject.

The committee made three main proposals: (1) that the United Nations should assume the powers and functions of the League of Nations under the Slavery Convention of 1926; (2) that a supplementary convention be made covering institutions and practices similar to slavery; and (3) that a Standing Committee of Experts on Slavery should be set up by the United Nations to supervise the application of the conventions on slavery and to recommend measures for its abolition. This last recommendation was essential, in the society's view, for implementation of the convention. It argued cogently, in the words of Charles Greenidge, that of the hundreds of instruments made in the past for the suppression of slavery, the General Act of Brussels of 1890 was the most successful, for it alone provided for the establishment of a permanent bureau, and that the convention of 1926 made scarcely any headway until the League of Nations set up its Permanent Committee of Experts on Slavery. He recommended that the supervisory task be carried out by independent experts, and not by international civil servants who are naturally loath to say anything derogatory about their employers. "But the battle against slavery cannot be fought in a vacuum. Unless people can be found sufficiently courageous to say that slavery exists wherever it does exist, the struggle might as well be abandoned."[2]

The first two recommendations of the Ad Hoc Committee were acted upon with remarkable expedition, if one bears in mind the inevitable complexity of the composition, structure, and procedures of the United Nations. By a protocol that came into force in July 1955, the United Nations assumed the powers and functions of the League of Nations under the Slavery Convention of 1926, while the Supplementary Convention on the Abolition of Slavery, the Slave Trade, and Institutions and Practices Similar to Slavery came into force in April 1957. It was some indication of the commitment of ECOSOC that it had followed the procedure of submitting the draft of the supplementary convention to a conference of plenipotentiaries of nations, a procedure designed to hasten adoption. The Soviet Union was the first

2. Ibid., 198–200.

nation to ratify the convention. However, the third recommendation, for a standing committee of experts, failed to gain acceptance.

Some of the explanations for this failure emerge in a speech by Lord Winster, one of the presidents of the society, to the British House of Lords. He stated that slavery was an accepted practice in the Arab world, with Africa as the chief source of supply and with traffic in slaves openly carried on. He referred to slavery in other countries and to related practices (peonage in Latin American countries, forced labor in the Portuguese colonies) and then observed that, between 1951 and 1954, the secretary-general of the United Nations had made four reports on slavery, but in not one of them had he mentioned the countries where slavery exists. "That is an interesting fact and explains why so little progress is made." The subject of forced labor, he said, seemed to arouse peculiar bitterness at the United Nations. "The guilty States are vigorous in denials or in opposition to reform, so that only completely innocuous Resolutions are passed on the subject."[3] To this, we must add the comment of Greenidge that "opposition to the idea today comes mostly from some of the colonial powers who argue that if such a Committee was set up by the United Nations it would constitute another forum for attacks on them by the anticolonial powers."[4]

But, in 1966, the issue was again raised sharply in the United Nations. The special rapporteur on slavery, appointed by the secretary-general, had recommended in his report, and in a draft resolution for ECOSOC, the establishment of a committee of experts on slavery; and the matter was now before the Social Committee of ECOSOC for consideration. The situation had changed radically in the ten years that had passed. These were years of rapid decolonization, in which the easy domination of the United Nations by the Western powers had dissolved before the mounting representation of Third World countries and their alliance on many issues with the socialist bloc. Of the 118 member states at the time of the meeting, 35 (excluding South Africa) were from the African continent, a continent that had suffered most grievously from the extreme depredations of the slave trade. There was a new militance on human rights, and because slavery was the total negation of the Universal Declaration of Human Rights, the special rapporteur's recommendation should have received overwhelming support. But alas, the issue

3. *The Anti-Slavery Reporter and Aborigines' Friend*, June 1956, pp. 88–90.
4. 1958:200.

proved most complex, and the debate pursued a course that could have been devised only by Kafka.

The delegation from the Anti-Slavery Society had gone to Geneva full of enthusiasm. The policy of the British government was in general agreement with that of the society, although its representatives were instructed *not* to table a resolution in the first instance: and a disturbing feature was that the society could not find a single delegation to sponsor the rapporteur's recommendation. But the meeting of the Social Committee, on 6 July 1966, opened smoothly enough. The special rapporteur, Mohamed Awad, presented his report on slavery and referred the committee to the resolution he had drafted. There were a new chairman of the Social Committee and a new director of the Division of Human Rights, and the meeting followed the conventional course of delegates rising seriatim to praise the chairman, the director, and the rapporteur and to present their country's position and achievements, not without some suggestion of the braggadocio of wrestlers. This type of proceeding makes tedious reading and conveys an impression of fulsome and insincere diplomacy. But I think it is to be regarded rather as a ritual or as a stage play, in a situation that encourages delusions of grandeur and invites the players to transform minor roles into star performances.

The attack on the rapporteur's resolution was launched by the Soviet representative. It should be remembered, she said, that slavery was not limited exclusively to the facts mentioned in the report. Apartheid and certain forms of colonial exploitation still to be found in South Africa and in the territories administered by Portugal contributed perhaps one of the most insidious forms of slavery with which the United Nations had to contend. Although she supported in principle the conclusions and suggestions of the special rapporteur, she had reservations about the establishment of a committee of experts, which would contribute little and would constitute an additional financial burden on the United Nations. The struggle aginst slavery and similar practices was part of the work of ECOSOC and the Commission on Human Rights, and it was hardly likely that a new committee of experts would be able to take really positive action in this field.

The United States delegate also did not support the appointment of a Committee of Experts on Slavery on the ground that ECOSOC was not in a position to undertake further tasks in this field. It seems that the United States representative was concerned about the additional financial cost which would be incurred by the appointment of a committee of experts. This was a concern to which the secretary of the society had reacted, at a preliminary meeting of the NGO (Non-Governmental Organization) Committee of ECOSOC, with the comment: "The thought that posterity might one day read that the United Nations with its 20th century standards of living could refuse on grounds of expense to pay the cost of seven part-time experts to cure a 10th century disease, is too grotesque for words."[5]

The attack was pressed home by the Tanzanian delegate, Waldron-Ramsey, on the following day, 7 July. In a 70-minute speech the Tanzanian delegate moved a resolution to send the special rapporteur's proposal to the Commission on Human Rights and to incorporate the words *apartheid and colonialism* (which he equated with slavery) in both preambular and operative paragraphs. Since Waldron-Ramsey's views prevailed, I quote the brief summary report of his speech as it appears in the official record of the proceedings.

MR. WALDRON-RAMSEY (United Republic of Tanzania) said that it was necessary to begin by defining the term "slavery." In the view of his delegation the policy of *apartheid* followed by South Africa in its own territory and in South West Africa, and by the racist, traitorous and illegal regime in the Colony of Rhodesia and the colonialist methods applied by the Portuguese Government in the so-called Portuguese territories of Mozambique, Angola and Portuguese Guinea, were flagrant examples of slavery. The fact that the Special Rapporteur had not taken such evidence into account meant that he had not fully carried out his duties, and the report suffered as a consequence.

It was manifest that the methods traditionally used by the colonialists must be regarded as practices similar to slavery. In Rhodesia, 220,000 whites imposed their rule and slavery on 4 million Africans; in South Africa two million privileged persons exploited 10 million Africans who were the rightful owners of South Africa. Various forms of forced labour existed in Mozambique and Angola, and the methods applied by President Salazar's regime could not be considered as being other than a form of slavery. Refusal to recognize that fact would render all efforts deployed in that sphere completely futile.

As to the establishment of a committee of experts, suggested by the Special Rapporteur, he felt that there were already sufficient competent bodies which could take more effective action than a committee of experts appointed in an individual capacity and not representing Governments. Of the bodies competent to deal with the question, examples were the Commission on Human Rights, the Council, the Third Committee of the General As-

5. See his report on the July meetings to the Committee of the Anti-Slavery Society.

sembly, and the General Assembly itself. All those bodies were fully qualified to deal with the type of slavery that was cloaked by the convenient term of colonialism and which had now taken on a far more insidious and hypocritical form than previously—in the time of the Romans, for example, who had not been afraid to say that all inhabitants of the lands conquered by them became their slaves.

There was therefore no point in setting up a committee of experts or any other new body unless the endeavour was first made to widen the actual definition of slavery. That question should be tackled frankly and realistically, and any relevant action undertaken should lead to a forthright condemnation of the action of the colonial powers in those African countries which still remained under the yoke of certain privileged minorities.[6]

To this I add the following extracts from the very extensive comments made by the Tanzanian delegate on 11 July.

The definition of slavery should not give rise to any difficulty. Slavery obviously meant the domination of one individual or group of individuals by another. What better example of slavery could be found than the situation at present prevailing on the African continent, in South Africa, Rhodesia and the Portuguese colonies of Mozambique, Angola and Guinea, not to mention the territory of South-West Africa? Any failure to recognize that would clearly be a denial of the classic definition of slavery.

The Committee was not asked to go back to the 1926 or 1956 Conventions, to which the Greek representative had referred, but to deal with slavery in 1966. Some delegations interpreted the notion of slavery in a limited technical sense and were endeavouring to restrict its definition to suit their own ends; he was not fooled by their humbug. They drew attention to the slavery alleged to exist in India and Pakistan where it was supposed to result from traditional debtor-creditor relationships, or in the High Andes of Peru and Bolivia, where it was said to stem from landlord-tenant relationships. In point of fact there was no slavery either in those Asian countries or in Latin America, but slavery undoubtedly existed in the African countries he had mentioned.

Similarly, it had been claimed that forms of slavery were to be found in certain Islamic customs, particularly polygamy. He protested against such allegations which were designed purely to camouflage other motives. Forms of bondage similar to slavery might be said to exist in certain European and American countries, particularly in the Anglo-Saxon countries where prostitution and drug-addiction were rife, as he well remembered from the time when he had practiced as a barrister in London. Nor could the question of racialism be excluded, for it was the direct corollary of slavery. In his opinion, the classic definition of slavery he had given should either be accepted or extended to include all related manifestations of it without exception. . . . How could it be asserted that colonialism and apartheid were not absolutely

6. E/AC.7/SR. 536.

identical with slavery? It was impossible to discuss slavery without considering those two phenomena which were so closely bound up with it.[7]

There were two main issues in the debate: first, the nature of the committee that should be vested with authority to act, and second, the coupling of slavery with apartheid and colonialism. On the first issue, three possibilities were canvassed: a special committee of experts, the Sub-Commission on Prevention of Discrimination and Protection of Minorities, and the Commission on Human Rights. I have listed these in diminishing order of independence and expert qualification. The sub-commission is, in theory, a body in which expert knowledge on human rights is a qualification for membership, whereas the commission consists solely of government representatives. The British representative at the meeting of the Social Committee, Sir Samuel Hoare, argued for the appointment of a committee of experts. If that was not accepted, the next best thing would be for the rapporteur's report to be referred to the sub-commission, which "comprised at least some experts who took on particular questions a line not laid down by their respective governments." As for the Commission on Human Rights, he did not consider it the proper body to undertake the task. I may add that one hears the Commission on Human Rights described as "the graveyard of human rights." But this did not seem to be Sir Samuel Hoare's objection. There was a need, he said, for a committee of experts, whereas the members of the commission were government representatives, and the commission was engaged, moreover, on urgent work for the General Assembly and the council. To refer the question to the commission "was therefore a good way of burying the question of slavery and the slave trade in the Special Rapporteur's report."

The counterargument was that the commission would be able to take more effective action precisely because it consisted of government representatives, and that there need not be undue delay. In the end the Tanzanian view prevailed, and the council decided to refer the question of slavery to the commission, with the request that it make specific proposals to the council, not later than its session, in two years' time, for effective measures to end slavery.

On the second issue Sir Samuel Hoare questioned the coupling of apartheid and colonialism with slavery in a resolution that origi-

7. E/AC.7/SR. 538.

nated from inquiries into the question of slavery in the classical sense, including those practices defined in the 1956 Supplementary Convention as being similar to slavery. Moreover, although it might be true that there were aspects of apartheid and colonialism that partook of the nature of slavery and should properly be considered by whatever body considered the question of slavery, it was difficult to see how consideration of those aspects could add anything to the work of the Special Committee on the Policies of *Apartheid* of the Government of the Republic of South Africa, and of the Special Committee on the Implementation of the Declaration on the Granting of Independence to Colonial Countries and Peoples. In introducing his comments, he was careful to point out, however, that his delegation was on record as having said, in a United Nations body, that apartheid was economic slavery.[8] Indeed, other representatives, who spoke against the introduction of reference to apartheid and colonialism in the resolution, also took pains to make clear their opposition to apartheid.

Here, too, the Tanzanian view prevailed. The final resolution (1126, XLI) contains the following references:

in the preamble:

Believing that slavery in all its forms, the trade in persons, *apartheid* and colonialism should be eradicated, *Believing* that action should be taken to put an end to slavery and the slave trade in all their practices and manifestations, including the slavery-like practices and aspects of *apartheid* and colonialism,

and in the substantive paragraphs:

5. *Decides* to refer the question of slavery and the slave trade in all their practices and manifestations, including the slavery-like practices of *apartheid* and colonialism, to the Commission on Human Rights.

In the course of the debate, many of the delegates changed sides. This was due in part to pressure (to use a euphemistic term) brought to bear on delegates. The Tanzanian spokesman worked on the vulnerabilities of some countries to the discussion of their slavery-like practices, and on the fears of other countries that opposition to the inclusion of apartheid in the category of slavery-like practices would be represented as support for apartheid: and he heightened the pressure by asking for two roll-call votes, one on paragraph 5, and the

8. E/AC.7/SR. 541.

other on the resolution as a whole. This was a challenge to stand and be counted, a challenge that many delegations clearly found inhibiting. The vote on the words "including the slavery-like practices of *apartheid* and colonialism" in paragraph 5 was carried by the overwhelming majority of 20 for and 5 (the United States, France, Greece, Luxembourg, and the United Kingdom) against. Canada took the courageous, independent stand of abstaining. The final resolution was adopted by 22 votes to 0, with 4 abstentions (France, Greece, Luxembourg, and the United Kingdom).

The resolution seemed to be a strategy for shelving the Slavery Conventions. And indeed, at the conclusion of the debate, the Tanzanian representative declared that the only surviving manifestations of slavery in the world consisted of the slavery-like practices and aspects of apartheid and colonialism in South Africa, Rhodesia, South-West Africa, Angola, Guinea, and Mozambique.

I will not linger on events during the next decade in the marathon struggle for effective measures to implement the Slavery Conventions. In March 1967 the members of the United Nations Commission on Human Rights met to consider the agenda item "Question of Slavery and the Slave Trade in all their Practices and Manifestations, including the Slavery-like Practices of Apartheid and Colonialism."

Again, the debate was most convoluted, with draft resolutions, amendments, and subamendments. The major wrangle seemed to be on the emphasis to be given to apartheid and colonialism. Predictably, the commission resolved that it was unable, because of lack of time, to submit specific proposals for effective and immediate measures to end slavery in all its practices and manifestations, and it passed the problem to the Sub-Commission on Prevention of Discrimination and Protection of Minorities, with instructions to report its recommendations to the commission.

At the meeting of the sub-commission in October 1967, the response was encouraging. The special rapporteur on slavery was present and spoke of there being "some two million slaves in the world," adding . . . "or three million—or four million." It was, of course, impossible to give a reliable estimate. As the secretary of the Anti-Slavery Society, Colonel Montgomery, pointed out, "In some countries where slavery persists, there has not yet been a census taken of the free, let alone of the slave populations," and "if governments did know they could not tell us because slavery is illegal in their countries."[9] Still, it was clear that slavery continued to be a massive, and urgent, problem. One of the delegates expressed his incredulity that the sub-commission should be considering the question of slavery for the first time, despite the fact that millions of human beings throughout the world were still the victims of slavery and slavery-like practices.

In 1971 the special rapporteur submitted a further report to the sub-commission under the heading "Question of Slavery and the Slave Trade in all their Practices and Manifestations, including the Slavery-Like Practices of Apartheid and Colonialism." There is a strange misstatement in it. Paragraph 110 states: "The Anti-Slavery Society has reason to believe that chattel slavery, serfdom, debt bondage, the sale of children and servile forms of marriage survive today to the extent that they constitute a recognizable element in the pattern of society in some African countries."[10] In fact, the statement that the Anti-Slavery Society submitted in response to an invitation from the secretary-general reads as follows: "The Anti-Slavery Society has reason to believe that either chattel slavery or serfdom or debt bondage or the sale of children or servile forms of marriage survive today to the extent that they constitute a recognizable element in the pattern of society in seventeen African countries, fifteen Asian countries and six Latin American countries." The rapporteur was strongly committed to the antislavery cause, and the episode is rendered all the more puzzling by the fact that the United Nations omitted to print the report.

In 1974 ECOSOC approved the appointment of a committee of five experts, not seven, to meet for three days in the year, later extended to five days. I would have been shattered by this decision; not so, the society's secretary, who is made of sterner stuff and who had persisted, most persuasively over the years, with a variety of appeals. And in 1980 an excellent staff member was appointed.

Thus were the labors of Sisyphus rewarded after 25 years of dedicated and courageous persistence.

9. Society's statement to the commission, 7 Mar. 1968.
10. E/CN.4/Sub.2/322.

SOME REFLECTIONS

From the experiences of the Anti-Slavery Society, recounted above, we can draw a number of comments of relevance to United Nations action on human rights in general.

1. There was appreciable achievement on the normative side. The protocol, by which the United Nations assumed the powers and functions of the League of Nations under the Slavery Convention of 1926, came into force in 1955, and the Supplementary Convention in 1957. This relatively prompt reaction is to be explained by a strong revulsion of many member states for slavery as the very symbol of the negation of the Universal Declaration of Human Rights. To be sure, the reaction was not as speedy as in the case of genocide, with the adoption of the Genocide Convention as early as December 1948. But the experience of genocide in the Second World War was immediately present and overwhelming.

2. The achievement on the normative side was accompanied by a reluctance to provide machinery for enforcement. There was a willingness to establish norms but not to provide measures for implementation. As we have seen, after a generation of struggle by the Anti-Slavery Society for the creation of international supervisory machinery, the response was almost derisory; and this, notwithstanding the persistence of slavery and of institutions and practices similar to slavery. In its annual report for 1965 the society referred to the great increase in slavery and slave-trading during the fifteen years after the Second World War as a result of the ready cash available in the Near East from the oil market. It added that there had been encouraging legislation against slavery in Saudi Arabia and in Republican Yemen. In a report entitled *Its Task Today*, dated November 1966, the society listed many countries in which there was reliable information of slavery and of similar practices, and I have already mentioned its memorandum to the special rapporteur to the effect that one or more forms of slavery survived significantly in 17 African, 15 Asian, and 6 Latin American countries (*Annual Report*, 1970–1971).

This gap between norms and machinery for implementation (or between norms and performance) raises questions about the significance of the norms. Do the covenants and declarations secure consent because there is no serious intention to implement them? And are they reduced then to empty rhetoric, with noble, ego-inflating resonance for the actors, but devoid of meaning for the victims? And why is there machinery for implementation in some cases and not others? Why, for example, were governments willing to cooperate on the establishment of an International Narcotics Board but not on supervision by an International Slavery Board? What considerations govern the acceptance or evasion of responsibility?

3. The reluctance to provide for supervision, or other measures for implementation, lies partly in the vulnerability of member states to the very practices they condemn. It was this vulnerability that the representative for Tanzania manipulated in his campaign to reduce contemporary slavery to apartheid. But the vulnerable states are involved in regional and ideological alliances and often too in patron-client relations, and receive protective support from their regional and ideological partners and patrons, even when the latter themselves are in no way on the defensive. This protective complicity appears also in other contexts. Thus, in a communication dated 30 August 1979 to the Sub-Commission on Prevention of Discrimination and Protection of Minorities, the society complained of silence and complicity, for commercial or strategic reasons, by representatives of governments, multinational corporations, and a United Nations Development Programme in Equatorial Guinea, where a tyrant had been engaged for some years in the massive slaughter and ruination of his people.

4. Effective protection of offending states calls for control of the sources, and of the processing, of information. Ideally, in terms of protection, the only source of information should be the offending state itself. Some of the bizarre consequences of such an approach can be seen in the sort of hagiography that often emanates from member states reporting on their own activities. But since present procedures permit other sources of information, there is a continuous struggle to block, canalize, or otherwise control them.[11]

---

11. See the following comment by van Boven, 1977:69: "It is regrettably clear that by and large the position of the non-governmental sector in inter-governmental organizations is frail, particularly if matters concerning human rights are at stake directly relating to particular countries. An exception to this is the involvement in human rights situations which have been publicly declared by the inter-governmental community as areas of public concern (South Africa, Namibia, Rhodesia, Chile, occupied territories in the Middle East). In other instances non-governmental organizations are not considered as partners in the cause of human rights; but some governments and inter-governmental circles are inclined to look upon them as opponents

Against this background, we can readily understand the reluctance to appoint a body of experts who would introduce the wayward
element of independence, integrity, and commitment.

5. As if all these protective devices did not already provide sufficiently massive defense, there is the further device of the specific focus. We have seen this in the attempt to reduce slavery to the specific
localized situation of Southern African apartheid. This would have
the effect of extending immunity to other states, while enabling their
representatives to indulge in the moral fervor of condemning slavery
and similar practices in other countries that are institutionalized in
their own. Moreover, it provides protection for other systematic violations of human rights, first by preempting the time that might be
given to their consideration, and second, by a form of blackmail, in
that the raising of these issues is a stratagem designed to deflect attention from apartheid; and we have seen how effective the imputa-
tion of support for apartheid can be in winning support for the narrow focus.

6. There are a number of suggestions to be derived from the deliberations described.

(a) With vulnerability protected, the way is opened for the framing of the most exalted norms: and this accounts in part for the wide
gap between declaration and enforcement. Moreover, the free indulgence in the condemnation of the pariah nation strengthens the sen-
timents of moral righteousness at the same time that this sentiment
is corrupted by the refusal to consider equally gross violations in
other countries.

(b) Where there is controversy, as in the present case, and the
majority is reluctant to impose its will crudely on the minority, compromise may be sought in the creation of norms by incorporating the
conflicting views in a compromise resolution. Thus, the final resolution coupled slavery and the slave trade with apartheid and colonialism but did not exclude other manifestations of slavery and related
practices. This leaves open the precise emphasis to be given in the

'engaging in unsubstantiated and politically motivated acts against States Members
of the UN contrary to and incompatible with the principles of the Charter.'" See also
ECOSOC Resolution 1296 (XLIV), para. 36 (b); Shestack, 1978:89–123 (particularly
115–17); and Liskofsky, 1975:883–914 (particularly 896–900 and 911–14). At the 1982
meetings of the commission the Argentinian ambassador almost succeeded in excluding the representative of the International Commission of Jurists, who was seeking to
submit a statement on disappearances in Argentina.

implementation of the resolution as an issue for future political struggles in the relevant committees.

7. Nevertheless, notwithstanding the many obstacles, the Working Group on Slavery has been able to make an appreciable contribution. It views slavery as an evolving phenomenon, an extreme form of exploitation, with many different and changing manifestations. Meeting annually, the working group has been able to shape the concept so as to respond to its contemporary forms and so as to reflect an increasing sensitivity to its manifestations. Thus, it has dealt with chattel slavery, serfdom, the exploitation of labor under apartheid and colonialism, slavery-like practices affecting women (involuntary marriage and forced abortion, traffic in women, exploitation of prostitution, genital mutilation), debt bondage, forced labor, illicit traffic in migrant workers, and exploitation of children. A startling extension of child exploitation was revealed by the Anti-Slavery Society at the meetings of the sub-commission in 1983. This was the engagement of child soldiers by the Iranian government in the war against Iraq. Trained to martyrdom, with the Imam's special authorization to enter paradise, they are sacrificed in the most dangerous of military tasks.[12]

The sub-commission is certainly the most democratic organ of the United Nations. In contrast to many other sections, which are almost exclusively the domain of the ruling cliques of member states, the sub-commission provides a ready forum for the peoples of the world. There is ease of access to the working group, and through the working group, to the sub-commission and upward in the U.N. hierarchical structures. As a result, complaints and recommendations are more likely to receive consideration by sections of the United Nations with the power to implement some form of remedial action.

The working group and the sub-commission also provide the opportunity for cooperative relationships with some of the U.N. Specialized Agencies. The International Labour Organisation is centrally concerned with the protection of labor against exploitation, but other agencies also have objectives relevant to the suppression of slavery or are in a position to offer technical assistance programs. Some of these agencies may actually participate in the meetings of

12. See the submission by Irandokhte on behalf of the Anti-Slavery Society, August 1983.

the working group, or the sub-commission may transmit decisions to the relevant agency. This area of cooperation between the Working Group on Slavery and the Specialized Agencies is one that needs to be institutionalized and strengthened.

The potentialities for effective action on complaints of slavery and slavery-like practices in particular countries are quite varied. The preferred procedure is to notify affected member states in advance so that they can reply to the complaints. In the case of Mauritania, the government made an ideally cooperative response to an initial complaint by the Anti-Slavery Society in 1981, and in 1983 it sent a strong delegation to take part in the proceedings of the working group and to report also to the sub-commission. The report was remarkable for the integrity of the analysis of the historical roots of slavery in Mauritania and of the difficulties in absorbing the slaves into a free economy, given the extreme poverty of the country. The present projected solution, arrived at in cooperation with the government, was for a visit by a U.N. mission to advise on the steps to be taken and on the necessary international aid that would be indispensable if an effective program against slavery is to be mounted.

Unfortunately, the more usual response to complaints is defensive aggression. In some cases, a veritable barrage of vituperation is directed against the complainants, with attacks on their bona fides. The facts cited may be dismissed contemptuously or rebutted by fabricated evidence. Or the government may be quite intransigent. The Iranian government frankly and proudly acknowledged the role of child martyrs in the Iran-Iraq war. They had volunteered to sacrifice their lives for the honor and dignity and human values of Iran's Islamic Revolution, and the country was grateful to them. Martyrdom was an Islamic ideology, which materialist-minded people were incapable of understanding.

A major problem, then, at the level of the working group and the sub-commission, is that the effectiveness of the procedures depends significantly on the cooperation of the offending government. But the airing of the complaints in the meetings does exert some pressure, and, as we have seen, the issue may be taken up at higher levels or by one of the Specialized Agencies.

In 1980 the formation of the Working Group on Slavery was followed by the establishment, on an annual basis, of a Working Group on Enforced or Involuntary Disappearances, which includes, euphemistically, the institutionalization of torture and murder as instruments of government in many member states. It has been able to make some contribution to a most intractable problem. Finally, in 1982, the sub-commission was authorized to establish a Working Group on Indigenous Populations.

There have long been special committees on decolonization, racial discrimination, and apartheid, and ad hoc working groups on the human rights situation in Africa, on Israeli practices in the Occupied Territories, and on Chile. But the recent developments in the Center for Human Rights extend the scope of protection and invite a more balanced approach to gross violations by member states. They constitute an innovative, if modest, addition to the available procedures for the protection of human rights.[13]

13. In my comments on the working group, I have drawn on the "Updating of the Report on Slavery Submitted to the Sub-Commission in 1966," prepared by Ben Whitaker (1982).

8

Political Mass Murder

The original United Nations resolution on genocide, passed unanimously in December 1946, referred to the many instances of genocide in which racial, religious, political, and other groups were destroyed; and it declared genocide to be a crime under international law, whether committed on religious, racial, political, or any other grounds. Pursuant to this resolution, the Ad Hoc Committee, appointed to prepare a draft convention, defined genocide as one of a number of "deliberate acts committed with intent to destroy a national, racial, religious or political group, on grounds of the national or racial origin, religious belief, or political opinion of its members." In the course of the debates, reference to the protection of political groups was eliminated from the convention. And yet, I am now reinstating political mass murder, though somewhat marginally, as a special category in a book devoted essentially to the problem of international protection against genocide. This is partly for the reason that political mass murder at the present time almost certainly takes an even greater toll of lives than genocide. But, more cogently, the German atrocities in the 1930s and during the Second World War, which provided the stimulus for the Genocide Convention, combined political mass murder with ethnic and religious massacres. And the interweaving of the political with the racial, ethnic, or religious massacres persists in many of the contemporary genocides.

The interweaving is especially marked in plural societies, that is to say, societies comprising people of different racial, ethnic, and/or religious groups and characterized by past violent conflicts and present pervasive cleavages. These plural societies are the social arena for domestic genocides. In situations of group conflict, the internal divisions become politicized, and political division tends more and more to coincide with ethnic (or racial or religious) origin. Thus political mass murders and the ethnic factor become interwoven, raising difficult problems of classification.

In the chapter on genocide (9), for example, I include the massacres of Hutu by Tutsi in Burundi in 1972 and the years immediately following. These massacres are conventionally described as genocide, and correctly so. Hutu were being murdered as Hutu, the massacres reaching down to Hutu children in the schools. But in the struggles for power after independence, the society had become polarized along ethnic lines, with political division and ethnic affiliation tending to coincide. In these circumstances, how is it possible to disentangle the ethnic component from the political? Conversely, in the present chapter on political mass murder, I deal with the massacres in Uganda under Amin's rule. But Amin's rule was ethnically based in a society characterized by past ethnic conflicts and current pervasive cleavages. Moreover, certain ethnic groups were special targets for massacre. Here again, though the large-scale murders were perpetrated in the consolidation of political power, the political component is not easily disentangled from the ethnic.

Moreover, the methods of persecution in genocide and political mass murder are not all that different, though there is less of a tendency for political mass murders to extend to whole families. But there were many executions of families in the Indonesian anticommunist massacres and in other political mass murders, such as in Soviet Russia under the Stalinist regime, in Democratic Kampuchea under the Pol Pot regime, and in Equatorial Guinea under Macías. And past political affiliation can be as ineradicable a stigma, and as irrevocable a warrant for murder, as racial or ethnic origin.

Given this interweaving of political mass murder and genocide in plural societies, the difficulties of classification in the absence of authoritative decisions by international tribunals, and the comparability of the phenomena in many respects, it seems advisable to include the category of political mass murder. Other analysts may prefer to assign a particular case I have described as genocide to the category of political mass murder or vice versa. The inclusion of mass murders should help to avoid some of the controversies over classification. Moreover, the problem of international action against political mass murder is at least as acute as that of action against genocide, and many of the same protective remedies are available.

A final consideration for the inclusion of political mass murder is that the response of the United Nations throws light on many of the obstacles to implementation of human rights and supplements the argument in the last chapter. As I have commented earlier, political murder is an instrument for the consolidation of the power of many of the governments represented in the United Nations. The practice is certainly more widespread than slavery, and since action against political murder strikes at the very roots of power, it is to be expected that protection of vulnerability will operate with even greater force. Its characteristic expression is the invocation of article 2, paragraph 7, of the United Nations Charter, which provides that nothing contained in the Charter shall authorize the United Nations to intervene in matters that are essentially within the domestic jurisdiction of any state.

The four case studies in this chapter are of political murders on a massive scale, arising on the basis of political divisions within a society and comparable in many respects to the domestic genocides against racial, ethnic, and religious groups. I am excluding political mass murder in the course of international warfare, as for example in the military interventions by the United States in Southeast Asia. And I do not attempt a general survey of domestic political mass murder. Indeed, the major domestic political mass murders of the twentieth century (in the Soviet Union and in Nazi Germany) are not discussed. I have referred to these in my book *Genocide*. In the present chapter, I deal only with the period since the founding of the United Nations; and the case studies presented here were selected for the light they throw on United Nations performance in situations of the grossest violations of human rights.

Political murders on a massive scale are generally a prerogative of governments. Three of the cases selected for discussion deal with mass murder by governments. In the fourth case, that of Indonesia, the Indonesian army was the active initiating and organizing force. In all four cases, United Nations performance was totally ineffectual. But because there have been recent encouraging developments in U.N. protective action, more particularly against political murders in some of the Latin American countries, I close with brief comment on the decisions taken.

Two of the cases are complementary. These are the massacres of communists in Indonesia and the massacres of the real and assumed political opponents of the communist regime in Democratic Kampuchea. In both cases the massacres were legitimized by a political formula: in one case by the fear of a communist putsch and domination, and in the other by the threat of capitalist and imperialist domination and the commitment to the establishment of a communist state. In both cases the political formula was intimately associated with the conquest and maintenance of political power. The two remaining cases, Uganda and Equatorial Guinea, are of similar regimes, in which there was a more naked expression of the thrust for power, though also with the license of legitimizing formulas: anticolonialism-neocolonialism-imperialism, and the creation of a socialist state in Equatorial Guinea, and in Uganda, anticolonialism, including theatrical rituals of degradation of the old colonial masters, and the colorful assertion of African and Muslim identity.

In Indonesia, members of the Communist party and affiliated organizations were massacred in large numbers after an attempted coup in October 1965. There is controversy on the question of whether the Indonesian Communist party was involved in the planning of the coup and, if so, in what measure. The events themselves had all the appearance of a revolt by middle-ranking officers against the supreme military command, that is to say, of an internal army conflict. In any event, the Indonesian Communist party was compromised in a number of ways, and the army, in repressing the coup, imposed its own judgment of Communist party guilt.

The background to the massacres was largely a struggle for power between the Communist party and the army. There was also conflict between the Communists and a powerful religious group, religious and ideological opposition being interwoven with class conflict. The army engaged actively in the massacres, participating directly, or indirectly by organizing and arming civilian killers. Communists were sufficiently stable and sufficiently identifiable to serve as the target for slaughter. They were readily identified from party lists of members, and, particularly in the villages, by intimate knowledge of political affiliation. Of course, the massacres extended beyond known affiliation and provided the opportunity to settle private scores, and to draw in other categories, as in the killing of

Chinese merchants and their families in North Sumatra. Estimates of the number of Communists and their affiliates killed range from 200,000 to more than 1 million. Amnesty International, in a controversy with a former United States ambassador to Indonesia, wrote that "Admiral Sudomo, the chief of Indonesian State Security, has openly admitted that 'during the bloody "people's revenge" after the unsuccessful coup, an estimated half a million actual or suspected Communists were killed.'"[1] In addition, there were great waves of arrest, and detention for many years without trial.[2]

In Cambodia (Democratic Kampuchea), the country had been devastated by many years of civil war, and by massive American bombing designed to root out Vietcong bases. When the revolutionary forces of the Khmer Rouge finally prevailed in April 1975, they faced a desperate food crisis and great uncertainty in the consolidation of their power; they proceeded ruthlessly with the liquidation of selected social strata and with a most radical restructuring of the society. They immediately evacuated the capital, Phnom Penh, which had been swollen by refugees to perhaps as many as 3 million. Its inhabitants, and those of other towns, were driven out in a gigantic mass migration and exposed, with much loss of life, to extreme hardship, accompanied by summary executions, in the journey to their new work sites.

Persons associated with the previous regime were special targets for liquidation. In many cases the executions included wives and children. There were summary executions, too, of intellectuals, such as doctors, engineers, professors, teachers, and students, leaving the country denuded of professional skills. Vietnamese in Cambodia, and Cambodians trained in Vietnam as revolutionaries also came under attack. There was a systematic campaign to eradicate the national religion, Buddhism; and members of a Muslim tribal group, the Cham, were victims of genocidal massacres. Later, struggles for power between the different revolutionary factions added greatly to the vast destruction of human life.[3]

The revolution itself was most radical in its objectives. On 2 November 1978, *Izvestia*, in a full-scale attack on Kampuchea, charged that a special course, aimed at the construction of a historically un-

1. Amnesty International, 1978.
2. For further discussion of the Indonesian massacres, see Anderson and McVey, 1971; Budiardjo, 1975–76; Palmier, 1973; and Wertheim, 1966. See also my discussion in *Genocide*, 1981:150–54.
3. See Kiernan and Boua, eds., 1982.

precedented society, had been proclaimed—a society without cities, without property, without commodity-money relations, without markets and without money, without families. Those who were dissatisfied with the new regime were being "eradicated," along with their families, by disembowelment, by beating to death with hoes, by hammering nails into the backs of their heads, and by other cruel means of economizing on bullets. Responsibility for this "monstrous situation," according to *Izvestia*, and for a cultural revolution that had destroyed the old intelligentsia and the student class, eliminated doctors and technical specialists, and completely wrecked the educational system, stemmed from the importation of the wild ideas of Mao-Tse-Tung.[4]

The whole country had indeed been turned into an agricultural work site, where the people labored ceaselessly on irrigation works, on the cultivation of rice, and on other agricultural pursuits. Here their rulers subjected them to what the Sub-Commission on Prevention of Discrimination and Protection of Minorities described as "draconian discipline" in both work and private life. Sentimental ties were dissolved in the separation of families, the indoctrination of children, the continuous surveillance, and the ubiquitous presence of spies in a system of collectivized labor and communal living. Exhaustion from the extremely arduous work, malnutrition from minimal diets, starvation, and disease took a heavy toll of lives; and to this must be added the ravages of the revolutionary terror, with its purges of prescribed categories and of party cadres and with the easy resort to executions, carried out most brutally for slight infringements of discipline or for complaints or criticism. This was a regimented setting in which it was nearly impossible to escape the "guilt" of social origin or of past affiliation.

There are no reliable statistics of the deaths. Perhaps as many as 2 million or more of a population of 7 million may have died as a result of starvation, disease, and massacre during the rule of the Khmer Rouge from 1975 to 1979, when the government was overthrown by an invading Vietnamese army and rebel Cambodian troops.[5]

4. *Current Digest of the Soviet Press*, 30, no. 34 (20 Sept. 1978), 17, and no. 44 (29 Nov. 1978), 12.
5. For discussion of the background to the conflict and the massacres, see Debré, 1976; Ponchaud, 1978; Barron and Paul, 1977; Hildebrand and Porter, 1976; Shawcross, 1978 and 1979; Chomsky and Herman, 1979; and Kiernan and Boua, 1982. See also Amnesty International's 1982 report *Mass Political Killings in Indonesia (1965–1966) and Kampuchea (1975–1979)*.

According to a report of the former United Nations high commissioner for refugees, about 35,000 refugees had succeeded in
fleeing Kampuchea during the Pol Pot regime, "despite violent deter-
rents to escape which gave rise to estimates that only one in 10 actually managed to cross to Thailand." In the months following the
Vietnamese invasion, an estimated 650,000 people, "mostly in a state
of more or less advanced emaciation" took refuge in makeshift camps
on the border, or in "holding centres" administered by the Thai military.[6]

In Uganda the political murders started immediately after a successful coup by Amin in January 1971 but did not become internationally notorious for a few years. The first issue that evoked international involvement was the decision by Amin in August 1972 to
expel Ugandan Asians on 90 days' notice. They numbered about
75,000, one-third of whom were Ugandan citizens. Some exemption
was accorded the citizens, who might choose between expulsion or
banishment to remote and arid areas, where they could occupy
themselves as farmers. The expulsions took their course, uninhibited
by outside concern. The victims were brutally treated, a few were
killed, and they were stripped of their possessions, which were dis-
tributed to, or seized as booty by, soldiers and other supporters of the
regime.

In the meantime, the slaughter of Ugandans by a military
usurper was becoming more widely known. It was carried out mainly
in the consolidation of despotic power, and it extended to almost
every conceivable category of victim—ethnic, as in the massacre of
Acholi and Lango soldiers in the Ugandan army, of Acholi and Lango
civilians, and of Karamajong; political, in the annihilation of the
supporters of the ousted president and of political opponents in general; the educated elite; and religious leaders and their followers too,
notably Catholic. There was also much indiscriminate killing, random, whimsical, impulsive, including massacres of entire villages.
The killers came from sections of the army and from security forces
consisting mostly of Southern Sudanese mercenaries, of members of
Amin's own ethnic group, the Kakwa, and generally of Nubians inside Uganda. Godfrey Lule, who had been minister of justice under
Amin, described the Nubians and the newly recruited Sudanese as
exercising "a foreign tyranny more vicious than anything dreamed of
by European imperialists or modern white minority governments in

6. U.N. Commission on Human Rights (CHR), 1981, E/CN.4/1503, annex II, pp.
20–23.

Africa."[7] Amin's regime continued until he invaded Tanzania and was overthrown in a counterinvasion.[8]

The director of the Division of Human Rights gave an estimate of one-quarter of a million murders under Amin's regime.[9] Amnesty International commented that extralegal executions were constant and systematic; between 100,000 and 500,000 were killed by the security forces.[10] The former high commissioner for refugees, in his report on massive exoduses, referred to the discovery, at the end of Amin's rule, of an estimated 1 million widows and orphans of civilians eliminated in one way or another, an "infinitely tragic proof of atrocities perpetrated upon the defenceless population by the armed forces and State Research Bureau."[11] In the civil strife that accompanied and followed the overthrow of Amin, it was estimated that more than 170,000 Ugandans found refuge in neighboring territories.

At about the same time in Equatorial Guinea, political mass murder also pursued its uninhibited course. In October 1968, shortly after Equatorial Guinea attained its independence, the newly elected president, Macías Nguema, assumed dictatorial powers. He appointed himself President for Life, Major General of the Armed Forces, Grand Maestro of Popular Education, Science and Traditional Culture, President of the Unique National Workers' Party, and the only Miracle of Equatorial Guinea; and he assumed the portfolios of defense, foreign affairs, and trade.[12]

Political persecution rapidly expanded into a vast campaign of torture and murder on the pretext, or the reality, of an attempted coup. Torture and murder became institutionalized as instruments of a despotism that engaged also in the pillaging of the resources of the country and in the destruction of its educational system and its economy. Political opponents, political leaders generally, members of the assembly and the cabinet, the intellectual and the economic elite, the Bubi ethnic group, and the Roman Catholic church were the special targets for attack. Often the wives and children of victims were also murdered. Perhaps as many as 50,000 in a population of 400,000 were murdered, and 100,000 took refuge in other countries.

The devastation of the people and the country continued until

7. Kyemba, 1977:7.

8. For discussion of Amin's rule, see International Commission of Jurists, 1974 and 1977; Amnesty International, 1977; and Martin, 1974.

9. Opening address, Commission on Human Rights, 1 Feb. 1982.

10. Amnesty International Conference, *Extra-Legal Executions in Uganda*, 1982:1.

11. U.N. CHR, 1981, E/CN.4/1503, annex 1, pp. 28–29.

12. International Commission of Jurists, 1978:1.

1979, when Macías was overthrown in an army coup. He was tried on a number of charges, including genocide, found guilty, and executed.[13]

The international response to the mass murders in these countries was negligible and totally ineffective. In Indonesia the massacres ceased with the annihilation of communist supporters and the imprisonment of large numbers of political suspects. In Uganda and Kampuchea they ceased when the tyrannical regimes were overthrown by the invading armies of neighboring countries in a context of escalating conflict, and in Equatorial Guinea when the dictator was deposed by an internal coup.

The Indonesian massacres erupted explosively, and they ran their course rapidly, leaving little time for protective action by the United Nations. And there were many other complicating factors. The destruction of the powerful Indonesian Communist party could not have been altogether displeasing to the United States. Furthermore, the USSR must have derived some consolation from the reflection that the party was closely associated with the People's Republic of China. The Third World states would have felt ambivalence in acting against Indonesia, given the country's early struggle for independence and its leadership in the Bandung Conference and the nonaligned movement.

There were further complications. There was the threat of armed conflict between Indonesia and Malaysia. Moreover, Indonesia had withdrawn from the United Nations in January 1965, resuming its membership only in September 1966, when it had completed the destruction of the Communist party. No objections were then raised to its readmission. Perhaps all this explains, but it does not excuse, the failure of the United Nations to take resolute action to restrain the massacres. This neglect is one of the most startling failures of the United Nations in the protection of human rights.

In the case of Cambodia (Democratic Kampuchea), there was ample time for action by the United Nations. The atrocities committed during the forced evacuation of the capital in April 1975 were immediately known to the outside world, and refugees' accounts soon gave abundant testimony to the harshness of the regime and its brutal destruction of human life. Nevertheless, it was only in March

13. See the following references on the regime of Macias: International Commission of Jurists, 1974:10–13; 1978:1–5; 1979: U.N. CHR, 1980, E/CN.4/1371; and Fegley, 1981:34–47.

1978, under pressure by Western governments, that the commission decided to take action, but in the most minimal way conceivable.

There had been submissions by the governments of Canada, Norway, the United Kingdom, the United States, and Australia, and by Amnesty International and the International Commission of Jurists, with supporting documentation, including a unanimous resolution by the Canadian Parliament expressing horror at the genocide committed by the government of Democratic Kampuchea. This evidence could not be easily dismissed. Yet the majority rejected a resolution proposed by the United Kingdom that a study be made of the human rights situation in Democratic Kampuchea with the cooperation of the government of that country. Instead, the commission passed a resolution to invite the government's comments, to be considered, together with other available information, at its next annual session. *The commission, that is to say, decided to defer consideration of the ongoing massacres for a whole year.*[14]

The Kampuchean government responded by rejecting the charges as calumny by traitors to their country and by American imperialists and their partisans, who were seeking to whitewash their own crimes. "As in the past people and government of Democratic Kampuchea will make mincemeat of any criminal manoeuvres of the imperialists and their partisans. They will not tolerate any affront to the sovereignty of Kampuchea."

The initiative was thus returned to the commission. In March 1979, during the annual meetings of the commission, Boudhiba, chairman of the sub-commission, presented a report on Kampuchea that the commission had requested. He concluded that the situation constituted "nothing less than autogenocide," and that the events described in the documents were "the most serious that had occurred anywhere in the world since nazism." The representatives of Australia, Canada, Sweden, and the United Kingdom tabled a motion, which in its revised form would record the commission's view that, on the basis of the evidence available, gross and flagrant violations of human rights had occurred in Democratic Kampuchea, and which would note the commission's decision to keep the situation under review at the next meeting (in 1980) as a matter of priority.

Neither the original nor the revised resolution, though deliberately moderate in tone, was debated. Yugoslavia, acting on behalf of

14. See the summary records of the proceedings of the Commission on Human Rights in March 1979, especially E/CN.4/SR.1510, 1515–17, and 1519.

the sponsors (Benin, Egypt, Pakistan, Senegal, Syria, and Yugoslavia), tabled a draft decision to postpone consideration of the report to the next session in 1980. This was carried by a large majority. As for the revised resolution, which carefully refrained from reference to the sub-commission's report, it was guillotined on a motion by the chairman of the commission, carried by an overwhelming majority, that the commission should decide not to vote on the resolution. Only Australia, Austria, Canada, France, West Germany, Sweden, and the United States opposed this motion.[15]

The issue was not controversy over the facts. There seemed to be fairly general agreement that the government of Democratic Kampuchea had committed gross violations of human rights. The issue was rather one of realpolitik. The commission had been so dilatory that the Vietnamese had already invaded Kampuchea. As already noted, it was left to the new regime, installed by the Vietnamese, to prosecute Pol Pot and the former deputy prime minister on charges of genocide. As for the United Nations, it continues to accept the ousted and murderous government as the accredited representative of Kampuchea.

The mass political murders in Equatorial Guinea and Uganda extended over roughly the same protracted period, giving ample time for protective action. The commission did in fact seek to restrain the Macias regime, although belatedly and in a benignly innocuous way. By contrast, the commission's response to the political mass murders in Uganda can only be described as protective of the regime, with seeming disregard for the sufferings of its persecuted peoples.

The general international reaction to the Macías regime was one of apathy. In some ways this was not surprising. Equatorial Guinea is after all a small, remote, and isolated country, and there is a certain banality at the present time in mass murder by yet another dictator in yet another U.N. member state. But a number of countries, as well as U.N. agencies, were involved in one way or another in the affairs of Equatorial Guinea, and they must have been well informed on the atrocities of the regime. In an article published in 1981, Randall Fegley comments as follows on this international involvement.

Spain, Equatorial Guinea's major trading partner and the supplier of much economic aid and technical assistance, did not wish to change the situation

15. Reports of the discussions are in the proceedings of the commission in March 1979, particularly E/CN.4/SR.1510, 1515–17, and 1519.

to its disfavor. Until 1976, the Spanish government classified all information leaving Equatorial Guinea *materia reservada*. . . . Spanish relations with the Macías government grew steadily worse as atrocities increased, but Spain did little to improve conditions in Equatorial Guinea. When the news of the 3 August 1979 coup was released, the Spanish government admitted foreknowledge of the plot but denied complicity.

The French have a ten-year forestry concession in the country and contracts for the port of Bata and the luxurious $2.8 million administrative palace. In 1976, the United States broke diplomatic relations with the Macías regime under mysterious circumstances, but the U.S. government has provided aid to the country and conducted uranium exploration surveys in Equatorial Guinea since the break. In addition, Continental Oil and Standard Oil have offshore exploration rights. . . . The People's Republic of China has loaned money and donated health and road maintenance aid to Equatorial Guinea. The Soviet Union, which had a most-favored-nation trade pact with Equatorial Guinea, had unlimited fishing rights in Equatorial Guinean waters until the agreement was allowed to lapse this January. A large number of Cuban military, forestry, and educational advisers also worked with the Macías regime. . . . Other nations as varied as North Korea, Sweden, and Germany have conducted trade, aid, and other business with the Macías regime. . . . Macías was an expert at survival on the international scene by keeping his administration flexible to foreign aid and investment. . . .

United Nations agencies said little about the human rights situation under the Macías regime in spite of the restriction and the harassment of their personnel and the interruption of their projects. The U.N. Development Programme, UNESCO, WHO, FAO, and the ILO have all operated or still operate in Equatorial Guinea. . . . The Organization for African Unity provides aid to Equatorial Guinea, but refused to act on any allegations of gross human rights violations claiming that they do not wish to interfere with their members' domestic affairs. Few diplomats, technicians, advisory officials, and businessmen have claimed to recognize anything unusual in Equatorial Guinea even while other diplomats, members of Parliament, and government officials continued to "commit suicide" or "disappear" and refugees increased daily. . . . Under Macías a protective wall of silence was built by ensuring that all major powers, neighboring nations, and potentially concerned parties had vested interests in his regime, irrespective of the terror fostered by his rule.[16]

However, by the mid-1970s, the commission and the subcommission were becoming marginally involved. At its session in 1976 the commission had before it two denunciations of the regime of oppression "said to prevail" in Equatorial Guinea. The government of Equatorial Guinea rejected the allegations in the first denunciation as based on lies by a "few small groups of unsuccessful individuals who are being paid by colonialists and imperialists with the sole

16. 1981:41–42.

object of restoring in Equatorial Guinea the hateful and repugnant colonial past," and it was of the opinion that the second denunciation had been instigated by Spain in order to divide a "political unit which is a free and independent African State, a member of the United Nations and a member of the Organization of African Unity." The government indicated, moreover, that it opposed any action by the commission on the allegations, pursuant to article 2, paragraph 7, of the Charter (against intervention in matters within domestic jurisdiction). The commission's response was to endorse the finding of its working group that the information submitted did not seem sufficient to justify the conclusion that flagrant and systematic violations had been committed. It therefore decided that there was no need to take action on the basis of the documents before it.[17]

At the next session of the commission, in the following year, there was a further documented communication, which included a list of hundreds of political murders and charged that the population of Equatorial Guinea had been subjected to institutionalized genocide by its government for the previous six years. In its replies, the government of Equatorial Guinea continued to play the anticolonial gambit and to fall back on the protection accorded by article 2, paragraph 7, of the Charter. The commission thereupon "adopted a confidential decision . . . by which it requested the Secretary-General of the United Nations to establish direct contact on a confidential basis with the Government of Equatorial Guinea in order to clarify points raised in that Government's observations on documentary material relating to the human rights situation in Equatorial Guinea and with a view to finding ways in which the United Nations might, if necessary, provide assistance to that country."[18]

However, the secretary-general was not able to secure the cooperation of the Macías regime, and in March 1979 the commission decided to remove consideration of the human rights situation in Equatorial Guinea from the confidential to the public procedures and to institute a study by a special rapporteur.[19] But at this stage the Macías regime was already on its way out, and it was the successor regime that authorized the visit of the special rapporteur in November 1979. The commission had, however, acted more expeditiously than the heads of state of the Organization of African Unity (OAU), who,

17. E/CN.4/1371, dated 12 Feb. 1980, pp. 1–2.
18. Ibid., 4, para. 15.
19. Ibid., 1, and annex 1.

"after a decade of pressure," condemned the Macías regime in July 1979.[20]

By contrast with Equatorial Guinea, the atrocities of the Amin regime were an international cause célèbre. Amin was, of course, newsworthy, and the mass media seemed to respond to him with particular affection. Besides, there was early international involvement as a result of Amin's decision in August 1972 to expel the Ugandan Indians. If the United Nations had acted firmly at this stage, perhaps some of the later atrocities might have been prevented. As it is, though the issue of the Indian expulsions was raised immediately in the sub-commission, its members rejected even the modest proposal that it send a telegram of concern to the president of Uganda, on the ground that it had no mandate to send telegrams to heads of state. Instead, it resolved to recommend that the commission consider the applicability to noncitizens of the present international legal protection of human rights, and the measures that would be desirable in this field. The sub-commission thus resorted to one of the techniques for denying help to the victims while extending protection to the executioners—the technique of transforming a concrete and urgent practical issue into a problem of general principles for abstract consideration, the transformation of an issue of protective action into a norm-setting exercise.[21] Unfortunately, this was only the first of a long series of evasions by the United Nations.

At about this time, charges of mass murder and of genocide were beginning to be made. Early in 1973, a former minister of education, who had served for two years under Amin, sent a long memorandum to heads of state in the Organization of African Unity, giving details of the atrocities of mass murder and concluding with the complaint that too many nations regarded what was happening in Uganda as an internal matter. "Is systematic genocide," he asked, "an internal matter or a matter for all mankind?"[22] In May 1973 the ousted president of Uganda wrote to the OAU at Addis Ababa charging that the massacres of Acholi and Lango soldiers and civilians were in fact genocide. Later, in 1974, there appeared David Martin's full-scale study

20. Fegley, 1981:42–43. There had been earlier condemnations by the Algiers International Conference for the Rights of Peoples in July 1976, at the Pan-African Conference on African Refugees in May 1979, and also by the Pan-African Youth Movement in May 1979.

21. This is more fully discussed in my book *Genocide*, pp. 165–66, 215–18.

22. The text of the memorandum is given in the report of the International Commission of Jurists, 1977:109–220.

of the regime, and in May 1974 the International Commission of Jurists submitted a report to the secretary-general of the United Nations *Violations of Human Rights and the Rule of Law in Uganda*, in which it charged the suspension or violation of most of the fundamental human rights, the breakdown of the rule of law, the placing in abeyance of basic freedoms, the arrest, detention, torture, and killing of thousands of civilians, and the establishment of a reign of terror. The submissions included a deposition by a former Ugandan foreign minister. Between 1974 and 1976 the commission submitted, in all, five complaints of human rights violations to the secretary-general of the United Nations, and in January 1977 Amnesty International submitted to the commission similar charges of grave violations.

The secretary-general did call on Amin to conduct an investigation, but as for the Commission on Human Rights, it successfully parried the charges against the Ugandan regime, notwithstanding the wealth of incriminating testimony submitted by the International Commission of Jurists. At its meetings in 1977 the need for action became even more critical, since its sub-commission had recommended that the commission institute an inquiry under open procedure into the violations of human righs in Uganda. However, on the urging of the Ugandan representative,[23] who had been appointed a member of the commission in 1976, the commission decided to keep the matter under review, that is, *it decided to defer consideration to its meetings in the following year.* It seems that it was only as a result of a démarche by the five Nordic governments that the commission finally decided, in March 1978, to undertake an investigation. As for the Organization of African Unity, it was even more reticent and protective. Mass murder did not disqualify Amin from presiding as chairman of the OAU for 1975–76 at its twelfth annual summit meeting in the Ugandan capital. There were a few dissenting voices, and three African countries boycotted the meetings. The Tanzanian government declared that by meeting in Kampala, the heads of state of the OAU were giving respectability to one of the most murderous administrations in Africa; it could not accept "the responsibility for participating in the mockery of condemning colonialism, *apartheid* and fascism in the headquarters of a murderer, a black fas-

23. When this Ugandan member broke with Amin and recanted, he wrote to members of the sub-commission urging them to take action.

cist and a self-confessed admirer of fascism."[24] However, for all practical purposes, Amin continued under the protection of the OAU and of the commission until he was overthrown by external intervention.

Against this background of United Nations negation, I referred earlier to encouraging developments relating to protection against political murder. This was a response, in part, to the mounting pressure of international public opinion, which was outraged by the increasing numbers of political murders, the summary executions after a perfunctory parody of a trial, the institutionalization of torture, with horrifying and obscene mutilation, and the terrorizing anguish of "disappearances." It would seem that, in contrast to the reaction of recoil from the large-scale genocidal massacres, members of the general public readily identify with the victims of political murder and with their families; and the pressure of this international reaction was exerted directly on the Commission on Human Rights through the participating nongovernmental organizations, as in the campaigns by Amnesty International against extralegal executions and by the International Commission of Jurists against torture.

A further and crucial factor in the surprising militance of the United Nations was a change in the policy of the United States under President Carter toward a greater emphasis on the salience of human rights in the country's international relations. This had strong support within the country following revelations of secret CIA involvement in the internal affairs of other countries and of U.S. complicity in the overthrow of the democratically elected government of Allende in Chile. The new policy reduced the element of superpower confrontation in areas within the sphere of U.S. influence; and under pressure by the United States, West European states, and Latin American democracies, U.N. protective action was greatly extended beyond the traditional pariah states of South Africa, Israel, and Chile.

At the meetings of the Commission on Human Rights in 1982, members considered complaints of gross violations of human rights in a wide range of countries, especially in Latin America. It was as if an international alert had been sounded against political murder in Argentina, El Salvador, and Guatemala, with denunciations pouring in on all sides, reports by the commission's special representative on

24. International Commission of Jurists, 1977:106–107.

El Salvador,[25] a collation by the secretary-general of information collected on the human rights situation in Guatemala,[26] the Annual Report of the Inter-American Commission on Human Rights, 1980–1981,[27] and the report of the Working Group on Enforced or Involuntary Disappearances, which contained a general survey, with a substantial section on Argentina.[28] There was a full-scale report too on Bolivia, quoting many supporting submissions.[29]

The political murders take many different forms: outright murder in the streets and other public places or in homes, massacre, summary execution after the travesty of a trial, detention followed by murder and the public display of the tortured and mutilated bodies, or their secret disposal, and disappearances, not to be fully equated with murder. Inevitably, the murders extend beyond the political opponents of the regime.

The victims are to be found in all sectors of the society. In Guatemala the sectors most affected have been political leaders of opposition parties, trade unionists, lawyers, journalists, professors, teachers, and peasants and Indians assassinated in the thousands.[30] In El Salvador the pattern has been much the same, with mass killings of peasants and murders of opposition political leaders, trade unionists, human rights advocates, primary, secondary, and university teachers, students, priests, and journalists.[31] In Bolivia the victims have been political opponents of the regime, trade union leaders, and miners. In Argentina the campaign of "disappearances" against "subversives" has ranged widely over the society, with the victims including children.

Estimates of the numbers murdered are unreliable and vary greatly, as is to be expected in the circumstances.[32] For Argentina, Amnesty International cited an admission in March 1981 by General Roberto Viola, the commander in chief of the army during the worst

25. E/CN.4/1502, dated 18 Jan. 1982.

26. E/CN.4/1501, dated 31 Dec. 1981.

27. E/CN.4/1982/2, dated 25 Jan. 1982.

28. E/CN.4/1492 and Add. 1, dated 31 Dec. 1981, and 22 Feb. 1982.

29. E/CN.4/1500, dated 31 Dec. 1981.

30. Organization of American States, 1981:132. Accounts of the massacres of peasants and Indians are given in the same report (pp. 27–34) and in E/CN.4/1501 (pp. 6–17).

31. E/CN.4/1502, pp. 26–31.

32. See, for example, E/CN.4/1501, pp. 6–17, on Guatemala, and E/CN.4/1502, pp. 24–31, on El Salvador.

period of the repression and later president, that there were between 7,000 and 10,000 dead and "disappeared"; and the organization noted that "within a year of the coup (of 1976) overtly terroristic methods were superseded by silent kidnappings. While several hundred people are known to have been unlawfully killed, at least 6,000 have "disappeared.'"[33]

In 1976 Amnesty International gave an estimate for Guatemala of 20,000 murdered or "disappeared" after being detained during the previous 10 years, and a further estimate of 5,000 seized and killed from the time that General Lucas García became president in 1978.[34] In El Salvador, according to the Legal Aid Service of the Archdiocese of San Salvador, the security forces murdered 1,030 persons for political reasons in 1979, and in 1980 there were a further 8,062 political murders. For the first eleven months of 1981 the acting archbishop of San Salvador gave the number of political murders as 11,723, mostly involving noncombatant peasants.[35] This would make, all told, more than 20,000 political murders in three years. And to this vast destruction of human life in El Salvador and Guatemala must be added the tragic deprivations of displacement of population. In El Salvador, with a population of about four-and-a-half million, the government estimated the number of internally displaced persons as 250,000. In addition, between 180,000 and 300,000 had taken refuge in neighboring countries during 1980 and 1981.[36] In Guatemala there had been a mass exodus of people, with an estimated 200,000 refugees in southern Mexico alone.[37]

The evidence of political mass murder, submitted to the commission in 1982 by many different sources, was overwhelming, and the offending governments responded seriously to the charges against them. There was none of the contemptuous dismissal, or arrogant self-righteousness in mass murder, of the Pol Pot regime in Democratic Kampuchea or the Khomeini regime in Iran. Of course, governments invariably deny responsibility. They may claim that only persons guilty of crimes have been executed. And they may even ac-

33. See 1982:2.
34. E/CN.4/1501, p. 9. See also the figures given in Amnesty International, 1981:4ff.
35. E/CN.4/1502, pp. 24–33. See also Navarro, 1981:8–9.
36. See E/CN.4/1503, p. 37.
37. World Council of Churches, oral presentation, Commission on Human Rights, 9 Mar. 1982.

knowledge that some regrettable excesses were committed, as the government of Burundi conceded in its defense against charges of genocide.

At the present time, a common defense is the attribution of responsibility to terrorist groups. Guatemala and El Salvador laid the blame on guerrilla warfare. Guatemala charged a deterioration in international relations throughout the world and the formation of terrorist fighter groups, which had exalted violence and armed action as a means of attacking democracy and the right of peoples to choose by suffrage the authorities who were to govern them. Communist aggression and internal intervention, designed to force a communist dictatorship on the people of Guatemala, with international support from countries in the Marxist-Leninist camp, had created internal rifts and fratricidal shock.[38]

The representative of El Salvador cited the injustices of past military and oligarchic regimes, which had blocked much needed change in a socially rigid and densely populated society. As a result of the denial of legitimate channels for reform, guerrilla movements had developed in the 1970s; these in turn had provoked a proliferation of extreme right-wing groups, with increasing violence in response to the recent structural reforms introduced by the present government.[39]

The Argentinian government specialized in disappearances. The clandestine nature of these operations readily provides a protective screen for atrocities, which can then be attributed to nongovernmental terrorists. This was the line of defense (or offense) pursued by the Argentinian government.[40] Only the Bolivian government could not fall back on the defense of terrorist activity. The special envoy of the Commission on Human Rights affirmed quite positively that "there was no serious or intensive terrorist activity in Bolivia" at the time of the military coup in July 1980, and that after that date "grave, massive and persistent violations of human rights were committed." The justification put forward by the Bolivian government for the events of July 1980, namely, "political and trade union unrest, general lack of security, electoral fraud, etc.," could not "excuse viola-

38. E/CN.3/1501, pp. 2–3, 36.
39. E/CN.4/1492, annex XI, pp. 2–3.
40. Ibid. 18–21. Annex VII, which contains excerpts of statements made by the permanent representative of Argentina to the U.N. Office of Geneva, is remarkable for its high moral tone.

tions of the most fundamental and inalienable rights and freedoms of the individual."[41]

Quite apart from these denials of responsibility, governments seek to camouflage political mass murder with the color of legality. A common device is the regime of exception. It appears under different rubrics—"state of siege," "state of emergency," "state of internal war," "state of the disturbance of the peace or internal security," "martial law," or "prompt security measures."[42] The effect is to expose subjects more directly to the tyranny of the state by a derogation of human rights, though in international law the permissible derogations do not extend to the denial of the right to life or to the infliction of torture. Argentina relied on a state of siege, El Salvador on a state of siege and a state of emergency,[43] Guatemala reintroduced a state of siege in July 1982, and Bolivia relied on an extensive militarization of the regime.[44]

United Nations action relating to Argentina and Bolivia has been surprisingly effective. "Disappearances" declined dramatically in Argentina. During the debate in the commission in 1980 on the appropriate action against "disappearances," the government of Argentina sought to delay consideration of the problem. Not surprisingly, it feared that the proposed resolution would result in an inquiry into its own practices.[45] But when the working group was established, the government cooperated with it in the detailed investigation of individual cases. The relations between the working group and the Argentinian government seemed very cordial, the inquiries proceeding for all the world as if the government were not the primary agent of the "disappearances." Of course, other external pressures were brought to bear on the Argentinian government, and the ruling military junta was also under the extreme internal pressure of popular outrage against the "disappearances."

In his report on Bolivia, the commission's special envoy concluded that the situation had improved in recent months and that the most serious and grave violations, committed after 17 July 1980, had not recurred with the same intensity. He hoped that the positive trend, which was the result of the decision adopted by the present

41. E/CN.4/1500, p. 51.
42. Organization of American States, 1981:114
43. E/CN.4/1502, p. 12.
44. E/CN.4/1500, p. 17.
45. Kramer and Weisbrodt, 1981:18–33.

government on 4 September 1981, would continue, intensify, and succeed in overcoming the obvious difficulties that restrict, hinder, and
affect it.[46] In its reply the Bolivian government expressed its firm and
sincere desire to cooperate with the commission at all levels and in
every way, and declared its readiness to receive all positive suggestions from the international family of which it formed a part. Expressing regret for some of the inevitable acts of violence that had
occurred in the past, it drew attention to recent reforms and reiter-
ated its decision to ensure progressively full respect for human
rights. The government's memorandum also referred to the sufferings
of the Bolivian people that resulted from the international isolation
of which it was the object.[47].

In El Salvador there appeared to be little abatement in political
murder. In 1982 the Guatemalan government engaged in a massive
antiguerrilla campaign, accompanied by widespread terrorism in
the countryside. According to Amnesty International, peace was imposed at a cost of some 2,600 lives, including women and children.[48]
United Nations action seems to have been quite ineffective, but continued pressure and surveillance have been maintained against these
two governments. The United States Congress has also exerted its
influence on El Salvador, and in 1984 there were indications of serious effort by the government to negotiate with the rebel leaders.

While the more positive response of the United Nations to political mass murder is to be attributed appreciably to the strength of
international public opinion, it also seems to reflect some change in
attitudes and policy.[49] In the past, the United Nations seemed content
to establish norms that were often disregarded in practice or applied
only in condemnation of politically selected targets, thereby undermining the norms and corrupting the organization. However, the
new development in the approach to political mass murder is a potentially effective interweaving of normative regulation and protective action.

Governments that engage in political mass murder are likely to
respond to public outcry and international pressure by resorting to
other techniques of murder, which conceal their involvement—such

46. E/CN.4/1500, 31 Dec. 1981, 53.
47. E/CN.4/1500/Add.1.
48. *Los Angeles Times*, 22 Dec. 1982, p. 8.
49. See the discussion of the significance of the international community in the
exposure and prevention of disappearances (U.N. CHR, E/CN.4/1492, p. 70).

as "disappearances" or the use of organizations of torturers and murderers secretly linked to the government. Then too, there are the techniques that camouflage murder in the guise of legality—states of siege and other emergency assaults on human rights, perfunctory trials and summary executions, trials by tribunals of the people rapidly processing predetermined murder, "suicides" in detention, and so on. As governments respond with the many devices their ingenuity suggests, the United Nations and, more particularly, the commission and sub-commission are able to relate the setting of standards and of procedures for implementation in a more effective and comprehensive strategy for protection against political mass murder.

In the working groups on enforced disappearances and on detention, procedures have been devised for urgent action. Following a report on summary executions, including extralegal executions, the commission decided to accord high priority to consideration of the issue at its session in 1984,[50] and at this session, the commission made a series of recommendations to ECOSOC for action against summary executions. In 1982 the sub-commission adopted the conclusions and recommendations of a report on states of siege or exception, which contained comprehensive proposals to restrain the abuse of powers of detention and imprisonment and to prevent extrajudicial and summary executions, and work continues on this problem.[51]

All these are promising developments in United Nations action against political mass murder. At the very least, there is a narrowing of the field of acceptable or tolerated criminal behavior by member states.

50. See Resolution 1983/36.
51. See the report E/CN.4/Sub.2/1982/15, and Resolutions 1982/32 of the sub-commission and 1982/18 of the commission.

9

Genocide

The major genocides of this century were the Turkish genocides against Armenians in 1915–17 and the holocaust against Jews in the Second World War. These are described in chapters 5 and 6 of my book *Genocide*, which also gives some of the main bibliographic references.[1]

The two genocides are often described as being closely related in their characteristics and significance. Thus Dawidowicz, in a book devoted to the Holocaust and preoccupied with the unique experience of Jews as a people chosen for total extinction, comments that the Turkish massacres of Armenians "in their extent and horror most closely approximated the murder of the European Jews. The once unthinkable 'Armenian solution' became, in our time, the achievable 'Final Solution,' the Nazi code name for the annihilation of the European Jews."[2]

Toynbee had earlier referred to the view that the twentieth century had initiated a new process in genocide, committed in cold

This chapter deals with United Nations performance in cases of genocide, but I also include some brief reference to the twentieth-century genocides that preceded the founding of the United Nations.

1. On the Turkish genocide against Armenians, see Bryce and Toynbee, 1916; Carzou, 1975; Chaliand and Ternon, 1980; Hovannisian, 1967, 1971, and 1978; Lang and Walker, 1981; Lepsius, 1918; Morgenthau, 1918; and Shaw and Shaw, 1976–77 and 1978. On the German genocide against Jews, see Bauer, 1982; Dawidowicz, 1975 and 1981; Fein, 1979; Hilberg, 1961; and Manvell and Fraenkel, 1967.

2. Dawidowicz, 1981:20.

blood by the deliberate fiat of the holders of despotic political powers with the utilization of modern technology and organization, and exemplified by the massacres of Armenians and more effectively by the massacres of the European Jews.[3] A similar conception is to be found in Arlen.[4] Fein, in an influential book, devoted essentially to the Holocaust, includes the massacres of Armenians with those of Jews and Gypsies in her category of "modern premeditated genocide."[5] Melson describes the destruction of Armenians in 1915 and of Jews during the Second World War as the quintessential genocides of our era.[6] And other authors might also be cited as advancing a conception of forms of genocide in which the massacres of Armenians, Jews, and Gypsies are closely related.

I had seen the link between these two genocides as flowing from the role of Armenians and Jews as hostages to the fortunes of their host societies and thus available for sacrifice in times of crisis. This had been a marked feature of the history of Jews in Europe, massacred during the Black Plague, or in periods of religious effervescence or of economic hardship, or in the trauma of international war, and it seemed also to characterize the vulnerability of Armenians in Turkish society. However, a more persuasive interpretation of the Turkish genocide of Armenians has recently been offered by Melson, who emphasizes the role of an exclusivist nationalist ideology, operating in a context of political and military disaster, in which the Armenians, differentiated and discriminated against in the past, were perceived increasingly as alien and threatening.[7]

The genocide of Armenians had been preceded in 1905 by the massacres of the Hereros in what was then South-West Africa. These acts were in reprisal for a revolt, but they were carried out by the commanding officer of the German army with such annihilatory intensity that the Hereros were reduced from a population of 80,000 to some 15,000 starving refugees.

Periods of war or their immediate aftermath seem to encourage, or provide the opportunity for, large-scale massacres of civilian populations and genocide. After the First World War and the Turkish genocide of Armenians, various warring groups in the Russian civil war

3. Toynbee, 1969:241–42.
4. Arlen, 1975:243–44.
5. Fein, 1979:7.
6. Melson, 1983:2.
7. Ibid., 1983.

freely massacred Jews in the Ukraine. Sachar writes that nearly 2,000 pogroms were perpetrated, in which, by conservative estimates, more than 100,000 Jews were destroyed and, by other estimates, nearly a quarter of a million.[8]

In the Second World War, at about the same time that Jews and Gypsies were being annihilated, the Soviets deported whole nations from the northern Caucasus, Kalmykia, and the Crimea in an operation reminiscent of the German deportations. In the inhospitable areas of their exile, under conditions inimical to survival, the exiles died in the hundreds of thousands. The total number of the deported exceeded 1 million, of whom about a quarter of a million or more perished from hunger, cold, and epidemics.[9]

Mention should also be made in this brief review of the many millions who died in the Soviet manmade famine of 1932–33. This has been described as the largest artificial famine in human history. It was particularly severe in the Ukraine, the Soviet Union's major grain-producing area, which had been specially selected for rapid collectivization. Perhaps as many as 6 million Ukrainians died in the famine that resulted from this collectivization, brutally enforced against the resistance of the peasants, and from the seizure of their marketable grain to provide the necessary capital for industrialization. Currently, it is being argued that this artificially induced famine was in fact an act of genocide, designed not only to crush peasant resistance to collectivization but also to undermine the social basis of a Ukrainian national renaissance.[10]

It is clear from these introductory comments that genocides take varied forms. The Genocide Convention, however, draws no distinction between types of genocide, because it seeks to define the elements they share in common: it differentiates only the means. But the different types of genocide raise different problems of prevention and protective action, and it is necessary to distinguish among them.

I have drawn a first distinction between the domestic genocides, arising on the basis of internal divisions within a society, and genocides arising in the course of international warfare. The domestic genocides may be further differentiated by the nature of the group that becomes the victim of genocide and by the social context within which the massacres are perpetrated.

8. Sachar, 1967:382.
9. See my discussion in *Genocide*, 1982:142–46.
10. See Carynnyk, 1983:32–40, and Krawchenko, 1982:17–23.

GENOCIDES AGAINST INDIGENOUS PEOPLES

In the course of conquest, or of later pacification, genocides against indigenous peoples were all too frequent in the colonization of the Americas, Australia, and Africa. Now it is mostly small surviving groups of hunters and gatherers who face the threat of extinction. These minority groups are the so-called victims of progress, victims, that is, of predatory economic development.

Several cases have been brought to the attention of the United Nations (see pp. 11–13).[11] In March 1974 the government of Paraguay was charged with complicity in genocide against the Aché (Guayaki) Indians. The complaint alleged that the following violations led to the wholesale disappearance of the group: enslavement, torture, killing, massacre, withholding of food and medicine, and destruction of cultural traditions. The response of the Paraguayan minister of defense was to deny intent. There had been victims and victimizers but not the intent: hence one could not speak of genocide. The admission that there had been a group destructive process was coupled with the assertion that the process had been launched quite innocently.[12]

A somewhat similar defense was made by the permanent representative of Brazil at the United Nations in response to charges of genocide against Indians in the Amazon River region of Brazil. This was an admission that Indians had been "eliminated" but with reliance on the ambiguity in the U.N. definition of genocide. In other words, Indians had not been eliminated "as such" but "for exclusively economic reasons, the perpetrators having acted solely to take possession of the lands of their victims."[13]

This argument seems to have a Gilbert and Sullivan touch to it. All the genocides of colonization would dissolve as undertaken in the interests of colonization, but not with any special animus against the victims "as such." The same issue arises in different form in the mass annihilation of civilian populations in times of war, when the argument is advanced that they are being annihilated, not because they are members of the particular group to which they belong but because they are enemies.

11. Many of the cases referred to briefly in this discussion of types of genocide are more fully treated in my book *Genocide*. On genocides against indigenous peoples, see also Arens, 1976; Bodley, 1975; Davis, 1977; O'Shaughnessy and Corry, 1977; *Survival International Supplement*, June 1978; *Survival International Review*, Spring 1979 and Autumn/Winter 1980.

12. Lewis, 1976:62–63. See also Arens, ed., 1976.

13. United Nations, H.R. Communication no. 478, 29 Sept. 1969.

GENOCIDE AGAINST HOSTAGE GROUPS

This is the type of mass atrocity most people have in mind when they think of genocide. It is perpetrated against vulnerable minorities who serve as hostages to the fortunes of the dominant groups in the state. The major example of this form of genocide prior to the Genocide Convention was the German genocide against Jews and Gypsies.

The most recent case is the threatened genocide against the Bahá'í religious minority in Iran. Its members are ranked with the American Satan and with the imperialists generally as scapegoats for the woes of the present regime. But the Bahá'ís have always been traditional scapegoats in Iranian society from the earliest origins of the Bahá'í faith in the mid-nineteenth century. They are viewed as heretics, whose blood may be shed with impunity, and they are special anathema to the Islamic fundamentalist theocracy that established its tyrannical and murderous regime in 1979. They were not recognized as a religious minority under the 1906 constitution, and their exclusion continues under the new constitution adopted in 1979. This accords official recognition only to Islam, Christianity, Judaism, and Zoroastrianism, though the Bahá'ís are the largest religious minority, with some 300,000 followers.

The persecutions recall the early stages in the German genocide against the Jews. There are the charges of inernational conspiracy, the incitement of mobs with license for atrocity, the dismissals from government employment, exclusion from schools, desecration and destruction of holy places, expropriation of property, and judicial murder directed against the leaders of the Bahá'í faith. But in contrast to the Jewish victims of the German genocide, the evil decree may be averted by a recantation of faith and conversion to Islam. Most Bahá'ís elect martyrdom.

All the signs indicate a policy directed toward the systematic suppression of the Bahá'í religion in Iran, and a serious threat of genocide against its adherents. And it is carried out (to quote the Iranian ambassador's invocation when defending his country's policy), "In the name of Allah, the Most Merciful, the Most Compassionate."[14]

I have described the Bahá'ís in Iran as a hostage group. But they

14. See the publications and releases of the Bahá'í International Community, 1981–82, and submissions to the Commission on Human Rights and the subcommission: Cooper, 1982; Council of Europe, 1982; E/CN.4/1517; Hakim, 1982; Kazemzadeh, 1982; and Sears 1982. See also Amnesty International, *Report 1982*, 323–29, for discussion of political mass murder in Iran.

are being subjected to a specifically religious persecution designed to eliminate the Bahá'í religion in Iran and comparable therefore to the suppression of the Albigensian and Huguenot "heresies" in thirteenth- and sixteenth-century France.

GENOCIDE FOLLOWING UPON DECOLONIZATION OF A TWO-TIER STRUCTURE OF DOMINATION

The classic cases under this heading are those of Rwanda and Burundi.[15] They were traditional plural societies established by the domination of a small minority of Tutsi pastoralists over Hutu agriculturalists. The Belgian mandate, superimposed on these societies, introduced a further element of pluralism and an additional level of authority.

The two societies were thus closely related in their history and composition and in their subordination to the Belgian authorities, who combined them in a single unit of administration. And yet the patterns of ethnic relations in the movement to independence, and in its aftermath, were almost diametrically opposed.

In Rwanda, the traditional lines of Tusti domination over Hutu remained sharply defined under the Belgian mandate. But democratic reforms later introduced, including a progressive system of electoral representation, began to modify the structure of ethnic relations and served to polarize the society. Political parties consolidated on mainly ethnic lines, with the political parties themselves becoming the agents of ethnic conflict.

There were clear warning signals of impending ethnic massacre. In November 1959, in reaction to Tutsi provocation, Hutu peasants engaged in a jacquerie directed primarily against property. In March 1960 the visit of the United Nations Mission, which was monitoring the movement to independence, provided occasion for further violence, as did the communal elections in June and July 1960. And in March 1962, in reaction to the murder by Tutsi bands of two policemen in one raid and of four Hutu (including one policeman and two civil servants) in another, Hutu engaged in the massacre of between 1,000 and 2,000 Tutsi men, women, and children.

The final large-scale massacres in December 1963 were precipi-

15. For discussion of the background and the genocidal process, see Lemarchand, 1970; Lemarchand and Martin, 1974; Greenland, 1975; Weinstein and Shrire, 1976; and Kuper, 1977:87–107, and 1974:208.

tated by the invasion of a relatively small and poorly armed force of Tutsi refugees from neighboring Burundi. This was about a year and a half after independence, with the Hutus firmly in control and dominant. Their counteraction was immediate and massive. They summarily executed some twenty leading local Tutsi politicians. At the same time, steps were taken to organize civilian "self-defense" groups, and the national radio repeatedly beamed emergency warnings. Inevitably, reprisals took the form of massacre. Between 10,000 and 12,000 Tutsi were murdered in a sequence of events clearly predictable in their general course, if not in their specific detail.

In Burundi, ethnic relations were more fluid. Internal differentiation of the ethnic groups and regional and status differences provided many bases for crosscutting relationships that transcended ethnic exclusiveness, and in the legislative elections preceding independence the party of national unity gained an overwhelming victory. Developments seemed to ensure an ethnic accommodation. And yet the society rapidly polarized, but in contrast to Rwanda, the Tutsi remained in the ascendancy, and it was the Tutsi who engaged in large-scale massacres of Hutu.

Many factors contributed to this genocide. The ethnic divisions were certainly deeply rooted historically, and democratic procedures encouraged ambitious elites to seek political party support on the basis of ethnic affiliation. Then too, the societies of Rwanda and Burundi were so intimately related that Rwanda served as a political paradigm in the process of polarization. The rapid revolutionary assumption of power by Hutu in Rwanda would have raised Hutu aspirations in Burundi, whereas for the Tutsis, it presented the horrifying spectacle of the fate that might await them at the hands of Hutu terrorists. And the presence in Burundi of Tutsi refugees from Rwanda was a further inflammatory element in the relations between the ethnic groups.

In any event, violence and counterviolence set in motion a process of polarization that escalated to massacre and genocide. In 1965, following an attempted coup by Hutu and massacres of Tutsis in the countryside, the Tutsis virtually liquidated Hutu leadership. But this was on a relatively small scale compared with the genocide in 1972, when Tutsis, in reprisal for Hutu massacres, murdered some 100,000 Hutu. Lemarchand described this as a "selective genocide" to emphasize that the educated, the semieducated, the schoolchildren, the employed, that is, the actual and potential leadership, were special targets for revenge. Intermittent killings continued after 1972, with estimates of Hutu deaths ranging from well over 100,000 to 300,000.

With the process of decolonization virtually complete, there are few areas in the world in which this form of genocide can be repeated. It is, however, simply a special case of the genocide described in the next section.

GENOCIDE IN THE PROCESS OF STRUGGLES BY ETHNIC OR RACIAL OR RELIGIOUS GROUPS, FOR POWER OR SECESSION, GREATER AUTONOMY OR MORE EQUALITY

These struggles in plural societies are very widespread. They are often highly destructive of human life, and in extreme cases they threaten world peace. In chapters 4 and 5, I dealt with three ethnic conflicts involving self-determination. In the case of Bangladesh (East Pakistan), the International Commission of Jurists considered that the massacres of Hindus by West Pakistan forces constituted a prima facie case of genocide. I think, too, that in the massive slaughter of Bengali politicians, leaders, and intellectuals and of Bengalis generally there was a prima facie case of genocide within the terms of the Genocide Convention. In Nigeria, the genocidal massacre of Ibos in the north precipitated the movement for secession and the devastation of the Nigerian civil war. In the Sudan, the struggle by African ethnic groups for liberation from Arab domination led to a protracted and highly destructive civil war. Even in cases of political mass murder for the consolidation of despotic rule, the infrastructure of the power struggle will generally be provided, in plural societies, by ethnic rivalry, as notably in Uganda.

Recently, charges have begun to surface that the Guatemalan government has been committing acts of genocide against the indigenous population of Indians, who constitute about 60 percent of the country's 7 million inhabitants.

Various social processes have contributed to the victimization of Guatemalan Indians. For the most part, the situation recalls some of the early processes of colonization. With the development of coffee for the export market, large areas of Indian communal land were expropriated; and the apparatus of the state was applied to securing the necessary Indian labor for the coffee plantations. Meanwhile, non-Indians (Ladinos) began to migrate into Indian areas, assuming positions of authority and undermining the traditional social organization. When cotton was established many years later as a major export crop, thousands of Indians were forced to migrate to the new cotton plantations as a result of growth of population, rural poverty, and landlessness.[16]

At this level, the processes involved are the familiar ones of the colonial exploitation of indigenous labor, with the expropriation of land and the modification of traditional institutions. At a different level, the processes are those of a class war, with the state acting as an agent for the large landowners and brutally suppressing dissent against its regime. The Inter-American Commission on Human Rights, in its report on human rights in Guatemala, concluded that, although the victims of violence were found in all sectors of the society—including the armed forces themselves and the holders of economic and political power—those most affected were the leaders of opposition parties, trade unionists, priests, lawyers, journalists, professors and teachers, and thousands of peasants and Indians. These are the victims of the murders, disappearances, and massacres described in the last chapter and affecting Ladinos as well as Indians.[17]

However, the violations of the right to life have a predominantly ethnic or racial character. Repression falls with maximum destructive effect on Indians as they react against the extreme inequities in economic and political participation by political mobilization and some involvement in the small guerrilla movement. The government and military employ the counterinsurgency strategies rendered familiar in the Algerian and Vietnamese civil wars—assassinations of Indian villagers, torture, display of mutilated bodies, massacres of men, women, and children, aerial bombing, seizure or destruction of crops, sacking and burning of homes, and displacement of population to strategic hamlets. It is particularly these atrocities that form the basis for charges of genocide against the Guatemalan government.[18]

These few examples only touch the fringe of a major world problem, the regulating of internal conflicts within plural societies.

16. I am following the account by Shelton H.Davis, "The Social Roots of Political Violence in Guatemala," *Cultural Survival Quarterly*, 7 (Spring 1983), 5–11.

17. U.N. CHR, E/CN.4/1501, 31 Dec. 1981, p. 4, para. 2.

18. The Spring 1983 issue of *Cultural Survival Quarterly*, vol. 7, no. 1, provides a general analysis and background. On the specific charge of genocide, see the judgment of the Permanent People's Tribunal held in Madrid, 27–31 Jan. 1983, Session Sobre Guatemala, *Separata de Polemica*.

I have drawn a distinction between domestic genocides and those arising in the course of international warfare. The line between the domestic and the international is not always clear. There is often, perhaps almost invariably, an international involvement in the domestic conflicts. This may take the form of training, and the provision of arms and advisers, for one of the combatants, or it may take the form of direct military engagement, as in the intervention by the United States in Vietnam. The destruction inflicted by the U.S. army on the Vietnamese people and their country, and on Laos and Cambodia, was so massive and indiscriminate as to give rise to charges of genocide.[19]

In any event, international warfare, whether between "tribal" groups or city states, or other sovereign states and nations, has been a perennial source of genocide. Indeed there were periods in which total genocide against the vanquished enemy, or the slaughter of the men and the enslavement or other incorporation of women and children, were accepted practice. Protection accorded to noncombatants under the Geneva Conventions should have served as a restraint on genocide in warfare, but this protection was denied in the Second World War by Nazi ideology, or by the invocation of military necessity in the Allies' pattern bombing of civilian populations engaged in war production, or resort to the doctrine of the lesser evil, as in the atomic destruction of Hiroshima and Nagasaki. With the present development of nuclear armament and other technology for mass destruction, and the precedents of the last war, it is difficult to know the current position regarding the rules for the regulation of international warfare. The current nuclear confrontation between the superpowers, with missiles trained on large population centers, is presumably based on a view of military necessity, which includes genocide on a vast scale as acceptable strategy in the struggle for world power.

Two cases of genocide since the founding of the United Nations recall the colonial wars of conquest and annexation. These are the Chinese invasion and occupation of Tibet and the Indonesian invasion and occupation of East Timor.

There is controversy over the precise status of Tibet at the time of the Chinese invasion of the country in 1950. In the view of the Legal Inquiry Committee on Tibet, appointed by the International

19. See, for example, Sartre, 1968:37–42, and Bedau, 1974:5–46.

Commission of Jurists, Tibet was at the very least a de facto independent state.[20] In the view of the People's Republic of China, however,
the Tibetans had a long history as a nationality within the boundaries of China but had been misled by imperialist penetration and de-
ception into adopting an unpatriotic attitude toward the great moth-
erland.[21]

In any event, in 1951, under military duress, Tibet surrendered
its independence by signing the Agreement on Peaceful Measures for
the Liberation of Tibet. By the terms of that agreement, the Central
People's Government of the People's Republic of China recognized
the right of the Tibetan people to exercise national regional autonomy under Chinese leadership. It undertook further that it would not
alter the existing political system or the status, functions, and powers of the Dalai Lama and the Panchan Lama. The religious beliefs,
customs, and habits of the Tibetan people were to be respected and
the lama monasteries protected.[22]

The People's Republic of China violated these undertakings, and
in March 1959 the government of Tibet repudiated the agreement
and resumed its independence. But the independence was only theoretical. The Tibetan rebellion was brutally repressed, and China remained in full control.

The actions of the Chinese during their occupation of Tibet in the
1950s were investigated by a legal inquiry committee of the International Commission of Jurists, which published its preliminary report
in 1959 under the title *The Question of Tibet and the Rule of Law*. It
found that the Chinese had killed tens of thousands of Tibetans and
had deported thousands of Tibetan children; and further, that they
had killed Buddhist monks and lamas on a large scale, destroyed
Buddhist monasteries, desecrated holy places, and publicly humili-
ated religious leaders in a manner calculated to shock the people out
of their age-old religious faith. Moreover, the International Commission of Jurists found that the Chinese had subjected religious leaders
and public officials to forced labor, arbitrary arrest, and torturing
and that they had plundered Tibet on a wide scale, creating wide-

20. International Commission of Jurists, 1960:5. Mullin (1981:7) gives a somewhat different perspective on this issue but agrees that, for 38 years prior to the invasion, Tibet was for all practical purposes independent.
21. Agreement on Measures for the Peaceful Liberation of Tibet (17-Point Agreement of 23 May 1951), International Commission of Jurists, 1960:215.
22. Ibid., 215–18.

spread hunger. The evidence pointed to "a systematic design to eradicate the separate national, cultural and religious life of Tibet." There was at least "a *prima facie* case of Genocide against the People's Republic of China," which merited full investigation by the United Nations.[23] Much use was made of this report in the General Assembly debates on the question of Tibet. In a further report published by the International Commission of Jurists, its legal inquiry committee concluded that acts of genocide had been committed in Tibet in an attempt to destroy Tibetans *as a religious group*, but that there was not "sufficient proof of the destruction of Tibetans as a race, nation or ethnical group as such by methods that can be regarded as genocide in international law."[24]

The account of the Chinese campaign to eradicate Buddhism in Tibet is not complete without reference to the further systematic destruction of monasteries and sacred objects during the Chinese Cultural Revolution. It seems that most of this destruction was carried out by young Tibetans, with the Chinese taking care to stay in the background.[25] An official delegation of the Dalai Lama, which visited Tibet in 1980, reported the desolation wrought on Tibetan Buddhism, the indoctrination of communism, and the suppression of Tibetan language and culture.[26] They were not able to derive much comfort from the new policy of "leniency" toward the Tibetans.

In contrast to the situation in Tibet, Indonesia had no historic claim to East Timor. The territory had never been part of any archipelago-wide administration or political structure,[27] nor had it been part of the Dutch empire that Indonesia succeeded. For 400 years it had been under Portuguese control. But the overthrow of the government in Portugal by the armed forces movement in 1974, the internal struggles for power within East Timor by rival political parties, and the victory of the radical Revolutionary Front, which proclaimed the independence of East Timor in November 1975, provided the opportunity and the motivation for the Indonesian invasion.[28]

Annexation of East Timor, and its "integration" into Indonesia as

23. 1959:17–18, and part 2. I have followed the summary of the findings given by the U.S. delegate during the General Assembly debate in the *Question of Tibet*, p. 490.

24. 1960:3.

25. Mullin, 1981:10.

26. *Tibet News Review*, 1 (Winter 1980/81). A brief account of the new policies will be found in Mullin, 1981:11–12.

27. Weatherbee, 1981:9.

28. See the discussion by Suter, 1979:19–20.

its twenty-seventh province, was effected by a genocidal campaign. In mid-1977, after an initial coastal bombardment and the occupation of the capital, Indonesia, confronted by continued resistance, launched massive aerial bombardments of villages throughout the mountainous interior. This had the effect of destroying the social and economic infrastructure of the society and of driving hundreds of thousands of the inhabitants into the coastal plains, where they were corralled into strategic camps. Here, many died under the harsh conditions of living imposed on them. It was only in the autumn of 1979 that two international agencies were given permission to provide relief services for the "resettlement villages," which by then numbered 150 with a total population of about 300,000.[29] Estimates of the numbers killed in this colonial war and its aftermath range from 60,000 to 200,000 of a preinvasion population of about 650,000—a high cost to pay for the privilege of "integration" into the Republic of Indonesia.[30]

The performance of the United Nations in response to genocide is as negative as its performance on charges of political mass murder. There are the same evasions of responsibility and protection of offending governments and the same overriding concern for state interests and preoccupation with ideological and regional alliances.

However, the record is not totally negative. The United Nations may have contributed in some cases to the prevention of genocidal massacres by its maintenance of peacekeeping forces in troubled areas; and in the case of South Africa, its continuous surveillance has certainly acted as a restraint on the government's use of admonitory or repressive massacres. Some of the confidential intercessions by the secretary-general may also have served as a restraining factor. And the United Nations can generally be relied upon to provide humanitarian relief for the refugees and survivors. Moreover, it has taken up some cases of genocide, and there are now encouraging signs of greater concern for protective action.

The problems of protective action vary with the different situations in which genocides arise. Turning first to the domestic genocides, I would expect that United Nations' action in response to charges of genocide against vulnerable indigenous groups would gen-

29. See Budiardjo, 1982:2–3.
30. Budiardjo, 1982, in an extended analysis of the statistics, defends the upper limit, 177,000 to 217,000.

erally take the form of confidential intercessions by the secretary-general. The intercessions are probably ineffective for the most part, but more information is needed on the extent and the results of this form of action. The physical extinction of these groups, or of their way of life, appears to be an ongoing process in most parts of the world and is widely accepted as an inevitable consequence of the march of history (or progress). In the case of the Aché Indians, four years passed before the United Nations Commission on Human Rights decided to act on the initial complaint. The nature of the action was not disclosed, but it appears to have been a recommendation for intercession by the secretary-general. Earlier, the Inter-American Human Rights Commission had adopted a resolution requesting the government of Paraguay to take measures for the protection of the rights of Aché Indians. The government did respond to these expressions of international concern.[31] I understand that the government proposed a settlement plan that raised a number of issues. Were the Aché consulted? What would be the consequences of the settlement plan for a nomadic people hunting and fishing over a wide area? And since the proposed settlement was on the borders of Brazil, were the Aché to be a buffer against Brazilian expansion?

There is a continuous flow of charges of genocide against indigenous peoples, committed by or with the complicity of governments, and often with multinational corporations as the agents of displacement from traditional areas and means of subsistence. These charges surface briefly in international consciousness through the dedicated campaigns of a few nongovernmental organizations and then recede into oblivion before the seemingly irresistible demand of economic exploitation.

The great majority of deaths in domestic genocides result from struggles for power by ethnic, racial, or religious groups in plural societies or from their struggles for secession, for greater autonomy, or for more equality in human rights and in political participation. I have already referred to the paralysis of the United Nations in the Bangladesh crisis. Performance in relation to the Tutsi genocide against Hutu in Burundi was hardly more encouraging. The massacres were immediately known to the outside world. In May 1972 the Belgian prime minister referred to a veritable genocide in Burundi. The French National Assembly urged action. The United States en-

31. United States Congress, 1979:317.

gaged in humanitarian relief, and it made diplomatic representations, as did other members of the diplomatic corps in Burundi. The secretary-general of the United Nations reported that the U.N. humanitarian mission had confirmed the enormous suffering, with different sources estimating the numbers of the dead as between 80,000 and 200,000. But apart from the active concern of the secretary-general, the various diplomatic approaches, and the provision of humanitarian relief, no serious steps were taken to halt the massacres in either 1972 or 1973.

At its meetings in 1973 the Sub-Commission on Prevention of Discrimination and Protection of Minorities forwarded to the Commission of Human Rights a complaint against Burundi for gross violations of human rights. But when the commission met in 1974, it effectively shelved the matter by appointing a new working party to communicate with the government of Burundi and to report back to the next annual meeting of the commission.

A major preliminary obstacle was presented by the Organization of African Unity, which, according to the policy of the United Nations and of Western diplomats, should be primarily responsible for mediating the conflict and for initiating appropriate action. Whatever representations may have been made privately by members of the organization, its official releases were supportive of the Burundi regime. According to a U.S. report, there was more active concern by a few African heads of state after the ethnic violence in April–May 1973, and this may have restrained in some small measure the fury of genocidal massacre.[32]

Somewhat related to these genocides are the genocidal massacres of ethnic, racial, and religious minorities in the process of establishing and maintaining despotic rule in plural societies. I discussed these in chapter 8. In despotic regimes there is usually a reliance on political formulas. These may be related only marginally to the mass murders and genocidal massacres, as for example, socialism in Equatorial Guinea under Macias or Islam in Uganda under Amin. Or they may be a strongly motivating force, as for example, national chauvinism and Maoism in Democratic Kampuchea. But the differences in legitimating ideologies do not seem to have been particularly significant factors in the final response by the United Nations: performance was equally deplorable in all three cases.

32. United States Congress, 1974:72.

The major hostage and scapegoat genocides I discussed earlier preceded the Genocide Convention, with the German genocide stimulating the resolve to eradicate the crime and the Nuremberg Trials providing a model for its prevention and punishment. The massacres of the Ibo in Northern Nigeria in 1966 have some of the characteristics of the hostage genocide, and these characteristics are also to be found in the expulsions of peoples under hazardous conditions into an outside world unwilling to receive them. The expulsion of Asians from Uganda resulted in the destruction of the way of life of these Asian communities, but not in their physical destruction. In this case, the contribution of the Sub-Commission for Prevention of Discrimination and Protection of Minorities was to transform an immediate concrete issue of survival into an abstract issue of normative regulation. The sub-commission rejected a proposal to send a telegram of concern to the president of Uganda. This was indeed outside their powers, but they evaded the specific issue and recommended instead that the Commission on Human Rights consider the applicability of the present international legal protection of human rights to noncitizens.

The only contemporary case, to which I referred in some detail, is the threatened genocide against the Bahá'ís in Iran; in this case, there was an immediate protective response by the United Nations. The explanation for this radical departure from normal U.N. practice is to be found partly in the somewhat pariah status of Iran, however much protected by its oil wealth and its strategic geopolitical situation. But a more important factor was the role of the Bahá'í International Community in conducting a skillful campaign, in the nature of an international alert, sharply focused on the United Nations.

There are Bahá'í communities in many parts of the world whose members are native born, highly dedicated in their commitment to the unity of mankind, and willing to sacrifice their lives for their religious beliefs. Their dedication and idealism evoked a sympathetic response from the ruling groups they petitioned in their own societies and enabled the Bahá'í International Community to gain the support of European states, both within the European community and in the United Nations. The European Parliament passed unanimous resolutions in 1980 and 1981 condemning the persecutions and calling on the foreign ministers of the member states of the European community to make representations to the Iranian government. There was a similar request in 1980 by the Parliamentary Assembly

of the Council of Europe addressed to the Committee of Ministers of
the member states, and in 1982 this was followed by a resolution
calling on Iran to extend constitutional guarantees to the Bahá'í
Community.

At the United Nations the issue was taken up initially by the sub-
commission in 1980 and again in 1981. In 1982 the commission
passed a resolution requesting the secretary-general to establish direct contact with the government of Iran and to continue his efforts
to ensure that the Bahá'ís were guaranteed full enjoyment of their
human rights. There were also references to the persecution of the
Bahá'ís in the General Assembly, in the Social, Cultural and Humanitarian Affairs Committee, and in the Economic and Social Council.
It is of interest that the issue was not raised as genocide or the threat
of genocide but under the more acceptable categories of violations of
human rights, racial discrimination, and religious persecution.

Notwithstanding these condemnations, the intercessions of the
secretary-general and the diplomatic representations by individual
governments, Iran continues its systematic persecution of the Bahá'í.
But it would seem that international surveillance has restrained the
large-scale massacres which earlier appeared imminent.[33]

United Nations action against genocide in international warfare
is dependent on its success in restraining military aggression, and
here its record is bleak. The new secretary-general, in his report on
his first year of office, gives an account of the many arenas in which
the United Nations was unable to avert war or bring peace. This complaint of U.N. impotence in the discharge of its peacekeeping functions is, of course, an old one. In Vietnam the United Nations proved
powerless to restrain the massive destruction of human life: its role
was both marginal and intermittent. The secretary-general had good
cause to record, in his introduction to the annual report for 1971–72,
his deep concern that the United Nations, created in the aftermath
of a world war to safeguard international peace and security, should
appear to have no relevance to what was happening in Vietnam. And
charges of genocide against the United States were heard by the privately instituted Russell Tribunal.[34]

33. See the publications and releases of the Bahá'í International Community,
1981, and in particular, *The Bahá'ís in Iran*, July 1982;27–31, and appendix III, and
Bahá'í News (June 1982), 3–9.
34. See Sartre, 1968; Bedau, 1974; Coates, Limqueco and Weiss, eds., 1971; Rajan and Israel, 1971; Shawcross, 1979:272–79; and Kiernan, 1982:280–84.

The two cases I cited, under the heading of international war, arose from military invasion and incorporation of territories: a deliberate attempt to eliminate Buddhism in Tibet and genocidal massacres of an ethnic group in East Timor. Both cases were debated in the United Nations.

The question of Tibet was raised first in 1950 by the delegation of El Salvador, which proposed that "the Invasion of Tibet by foreign forces" be included on the agenda of the General Assembly. The view which prevailed, however, was that the United Nations should await the negotiation of a peaceful settlement; and it was only in 1958 that the issue was debated fully in the General Assembly on a draft resolution proposed by the Federation of Malaya and Ireland.

The East European socialist states acted as a solid bloc in defense of China (though with abstention by Yugoslavia). They argued that Tibet was an integral part of the People's Republic of China and that the inclusion of the Question of Tibet on the agenda constituted an intervention in its domestic affairs. Moreover, the Tibetan local government had entered into the 1951 Agreement for the Peaceful Liberation of Tibet, and its leaders had participated in the formulation and adoption of the constitution of the People's Republic of China, which guaranteed regional autonomy to national minorities. The Chinese had introduced much needed reform into the traditional oppressive feudal regime. Nothing could be more absurd, so the argument continued, than a United Nations resolution calling for the restoration of serfdom on behalf of freedom and human rights. Moreover, the atrocities complained of had been committed by Tibetan rebels and reactionaries, and not by the Chinese. The underlying motive in raising the issue was to disrupt the fruitful cooperation between the People's Republic of China and the Asian countries and thus to undermine African-Asian solidarity.

The proposed resolution was a mild affirmation of the principles of the Charter and of the Universal Declaration of Human Rights, and a call to respect the fundamental human rights and the distinctive cultural and religious life of the Tibetan people. Supported significantly by evidence from the first report of the International Commission of Jurists and by statements from the Dalai Lama, the resolution was carried by a majority of 45 votes to 9 (the socialist bloc), with 20 abstentions.

In 1961 the debate was resumed and resulted in a resolution on somewhat similar lines, but specifically including the right of the Tibetan people to self-determination. In the course of the debate, reference was made to the second report of the International Commission of Jurists, and estimates were given of the casualties—80,000 Tibetans killed by March 1959 in a population of about 1,800,000 and more than 42,000 refugees who fled Tibet in 1960. (Mullin, in his study *The Tibetans*, writes that 100,000 are now living in exile.) In 1965 a further resolution was carried by a smaller majority with Yugoslavia and a number of Third World countries joining the opposition. The resolution called for the cooperation of all states in securing the rights of the Tibetan people. Thereafter, the Question of Tibet faded into the international oblivion of the fait accompli.[35]

By contrast with the division within the United Nations on the Question of Tibet, which derived largely from conflicts of interest and ideology between East and West, there was remarkable unanimity regarding the invasion of East Timor. This reflected the strength of Third World rejection of military aggression against smaller nations, and its influence on the United Nations as a whole. Besides, the decolonization of East Timor from Portuguese rule had long been on the agenda of the United Nations.

The U.N. response was immediate and seemed to hold out the promise of resolute action. The General Assembly strongly deplored the military intervention of the armed forces of Indonesia in Portuguese Timor. It called on the government of Indonesia to desist from further violation of the territorial integrity of Portuguese Timor and to withdraw without delay its armed forces in order to enable the people freely to exercise their right to self-determination and independence. Shortly thereafter, the Security Council unanimously adopted a resolution in somewhat similar terms.

The General Assembly renewed its resolutions from year to year, taking up suggestions for steps to initiate a referendum on the form of self-determination and responding to the suffering of the people of East Timor and the need for humanitarian relief.[36] But it would seem that different geopolitical strategies and ideologies have converged to obstruct effective action in the confrontation with Indonesian in-

35. For the United Nations sources, see the General Assembly debates in October 1959 (plenary meetings 826, 831, 832, 833, and 834), December 1961 (plenary meetings 1084 and 1085), and December 1965 (plenary meetings 1336, 1394, 1401, and 1403). The relevant resolutions are 1376 (XIV), 1723 (XVI), and 2079 (XX). For the reference to casualties, see XVI/1084, pp. 1117 and 1126. See also Mullin, 1981: 12, on the present number of Tibetan exiles.

36. See General Assembly Resolutions 3485 (XXX), 31/53, 32/34, 33/39, 34/41, 35/27, 36/50, and Security Council Resolutions 1084 (1975) and 389 (1976).

transigence, and that the resolutions have become somewhat of a ritual performance with little commitment to, or hope for, implementation.

Indonesia is the fifth most populous country in the world and the largest Islamic state. It is an important producer of oil, and it occupies a strategic position across vital sea lanes connecting the Indian and Pacific oceans. According to a recent statement by the American ambassador to Indonesia, support for the country is the cornerstone of U.S. policy in Southeast Asia.[37] Indonesia is also a major arena for U.S. trade and investment, and the United States supplied most of the arms used by the Indonesians against the people of East Timor.[38] Some West European governments also participated in the arms trade and have financial ties with Indonesia.[39] Australia had its own strategic reasons for maintaining cordial relations. In 1976 it abstained on the U.N. General Assembly vote on East Timor, and in 1978 it accorded de facto recognition of "East Timor as part of Indonesia."[40] Major European powers abstained in the voting in the General Assembly, and in 1976 the United Sates actually voted against the General Assembly resolution on East Timor and abstained on the resolution in the Security Council.

The East European socialist states do not appear to have been very actively committed in their support for East Timor. According to a report in the Southeast Asia Chronicle, "in 1979, when the Soviet Union, Vietnam and Cuba were vainly trying to unseat the representative of Democratic Kampuchea in favour of the Vietnam-sponsored Heng Samrin government, an attempt was made to woo Indonesia and her allies with the promise that support for East Timor would be dropped."[41] In the same year, Czechoslovakia and Hungary joined Romania in abstaining on the General Assembly resolution in support of East Timor.

The General Assembly resolutions were carried by the vote of Third World states, but with much division between them, and some ambivalence, because of the prestige of Indonesia for its role in the emergence of the Third World as a force in the international arena.[42]

37. Los Angeles Times, 25 Dec. 1982, p. 8.
38. See the discussion in Chomsky, 1978:5, and Chamberlain, 1982:239–40.
39. Suter, 1979:23.
40. Ibid., 21–22.
41. No. 74 (Aug. 1980), 27.
42. See comment by Suter, 1979:23.

It appears that the same fate that befell Tibet awaits East Timor. The massacres and the large-scale destruction now begin to fade into international oblivion, punctuated by pro forma annual resolutions with diminishing support.[43]

The contrast with the United Nations reaction to the Israeli occupation of Arab territories is startling. For years there have been standing committees engaged in continuous investigation and in the publication of mountains of documentation. There have been routine denunciation and vilification, and regular inclusion of the item on the agenda, with weeks devoted to rituals of repetitive debate. And, finally, there are the campaigns to equate Zionism with racism, with Nazism, and with genocide and to isolate Israel by expulsion from international organizations and by exclusion from the "community" of nations.

These campaigns have been remarkably successful. Waged in the United Nations under Arab leadership and with the support of Third World and socialist states, they have brought increasing unanimity in the rejection of Israel. The equation of Zionism with racism, Nazism, and genocide was already far advanced in United Nations circles prior to the invasion of Lebanon. But this provided the opportunity to carry the charges to a much wider international public, and full-page advertisements appeared in major newspapers denouncing the invasion of Lebanon and the bombing of its cities as an Israeli-perpetrated holocaust.

In the United Nations the Commission on Human Rights, in a convoluted process and by majority vote, found Israel guilty of genocide in connection with the massacres in the Palestinian camps of Sabra and Shatila.[44] These places had fallen under the control of Israel when its forces moved into Beirut in September 1982, after the assassination of the Christian Phalangist leader and Lebanese president. The Israeli military authorities then arranged with Christian militia to disarm the Palestinians in these camps, and it was these Christian militia forces who massacred men, women, and children. The *Encyclopaedia Brittanica Book of the Year 1983* gave an estimate of 328 murdered and 991 missing. Some sources suggest that about 800 Palestinians were massacred.

An Israeli government commission of inquiry concluded that indirect responsibility did attach to Israeli forces. There can be no

43. See Nossiter, *New York Times*, 9 Feb. 1983.
44. See its Resolution, 1983/3, dated 15 Feb. 1983.

doubt of Israeli responsibility. The Israeli army was in military control of the situation. And given the history of communal massacres between Christians and Muslims in Lebanon, on a far larger scale than in the two Palestinian camps, and the immediately preceding assassination of the Christian president, the Israel military authorities should have anticipated that the Christian militia would exact revenge. Moreover, they could have intervened at an earlier stage to stop the massacres.

The General Assembly initiated the first step in a resolution to the effect "that the massacre was an act of genocide." Only the Western democracies and four Third World countries voted against the resolution.[45] To the best of my knowledge, a resolution in these terms is unique in U.N. history and was not applied to any of the genocides in which the victims numbered hundreds of thousands.

The next step was taken by the Commission on Human Rights, which passed the following resolution on 15 February 1983:

The Commission on Human Rights . . .
3. *Condemns in the strongest terms* the large-scale massacre of Palestinian civilians in the Sabra and Shatila refugee camps for which the responsibility of the Israeli Government has been established;
4. *Decides* that the massacre was an act of genocide;
5. *Requests* the General Assembly to declare 17 September a day to commemorate the memory of the victims of Sabra and Shatila.

The resolution carefully omits reference to the role of the Christian militia in carrying out the massacre on its own initiative.

At its meetings in 1983 the sub-commission passed a similar resolution, holding Israel responsible for the massacres, which it characterized as genocide.[46] A suggestion that reference be made to the role of the Phalangist militia was rejected. The vote, 15 to 1, with 5 abstentions, could have been predicted from knowledge of the ideological and regional political alliances, with two exceptions: the expert from Mexico joined the members from the European democracies in abstaining, and the Greek expert cast her vote with the majority from the Arab, East European socialist, and Third World countries.

As for the commission, its condemnation of Israel as guilty of the crime of genocide is in strong contrast to the careful phrasing of its

45. See G.A. Resolution 37/123 D, dated 16 Dec. 1982. The voting was 123 for the resolution and 22 against.
46. See E/CN.4/Sub.2/1983/L.9.

decision on apartheid. During the same session at which it passed the resolution against Israel, the commission decided that "the *Ad Hoc* Working Group of Experts should continue to study the policies and practices which violate human rights in South Africa and Namibia, bearing in mind the effects of *apartheid* on black women and children and the Group's conclusion that the 'criminal effects of *apartheid* amount to a policy bordering on genocide.'"[47]

Against the background of the United Nations' protective stance in many past genocides with tens of thousands, and indeed hundreds of thousands of victims, it is clear that there is a special animosity at work in the resolution on Israel.

If the states organizing the campaigns against Israel really believed in the charges made, there was a simple procedure available to them. In terms of article IX of the Genocide Convention, disputes between contracting parties relating to the responsibility of a state for genocide can be submitted to the International Court of Justice at the request of any of the parties to the dispute. Israel has ratified the convention, and hence many states could apply to the court for an advisory opinion. This at least would have been a judicial process, based on the provisions of the United Nations Convention on the Prevention and Punishment of the Crime of Genocide.

There is little comfort to be drawn from past performance of the United Nations in response to genocide. But there are some encouraging developments for the future in the setting of standards, for example, the proposed declaration on the protection of minorities and the declaration on religious discrimination; in implementation, as in the monitoring potential of the Working Group on Indigenous Populations; and in protection, as exemplified in the resolutions and intercessions on behalf of the Bahá'ís in Iran.

I turn now to consider these developments as they relate to potentialities for effective action against genocide within the United Nations. Clearly, given the many structural and ideological restraints on implementation in the United Nations, outside agencies must continue to perform an activating role. At the same time, they must provide an independent operational base for an international alert. These are the themes I discuss in the concluding section under the headings of the Genocide Convention: punishment and prevention.

47. See Resolution 1983/9.

PART FOUR

PUNISHMENT AND PREVENTION

10

Punishment

The emphasis in the Genocide Convention is on punishment of the crime along the lines of municipal criminal law. This calls for effective procedures and sanctions. But acceptance of the jurisdiction of an international penal tribunal was made optional, and after almost forty years its establishment remains dishearteningly in abeyance. This failure might have been compensated in some measure if the provision for universal jurisdiction had not been eliminated from the original draft. There remains then the jurisdiction of municipal courts, that is, trial and punishment "by a competent tribunal of the State in the territory of which the act was committed." However, since most genocides are committed by or with the complicity of governments, the offending states would be required to prosecute the members of their own governments.

The result is that the Genocide Convention has been almost totally ineffective in securing punishment of the crime. This is evident from a comparison of prosecutions for genocides in the twentieth century, both before and after the adoption of the Genocide Convention. In 1919 and 1920 the Turkish government tried some of those involved in the genocide against Armenians. The accused included leaders of the former government, who were found guilty in absentia. The indictment did not charge genocide (the crime was still nameless), but the evidence supported that charge.[1]

1. See Hovannisian, 1971:419–20; Carzou, 1975:233–46; and Chaliand and Ternon, 1980:121–46.

The term *genocide* was used in the Nuremberg trials of the major war criminals in 1945. The indictment charged the accused with having "conducted deliberate and systematic genocide, viz., the extermination of racial and national groups, against the civilian populations of certain occupied territories in order to destroy particular races and classes of people and national, racial or religious groups, particularly Jews, Poles and Gypsies, and others." This appears to be the first formal recognition of the crime of genocide. But though in its judgment the Nuremberg Tribunal dealt at great length with the substance of the crime of genocide, it did not use this term or make any reference to the concept.[2] In a later trial of one of the Nazi war criminals by the Supreme National Tribunal of Poland, held in August and September 1946, the prosecutor charged the accused with the crime of genocide (claiming it to be a *crimen leasae humanitatis*), and the court found that the wholesale extermination of Jews and also of Poles had all the characteristics of genocide in the biological meaning of the term and embraced in addition the destruction of the cultural life of those nations.[3]

As for punishment of genocide in the postconvention period, there have been only two prosecutions, of Pol Pot and his deputy prime minister in Democratic Kampuchea and of Macías and some of his collaborators in Equatorial Guinea. Curiously enough, both trials were held at about the same time, in August and September 1979. Earlier, in 1973, there had been the projected trial for genocide in Bangladesh.

The performance of national courts in the punishment of genocide is thus hardly impressive. And the reader may recall that one of the two convictions for genocide, that of Macías, was challenged by the legal officer of the International Commission of Jurists. He concluded that (1) Macías was wrongly convicted of genocide, the convention not having been signed or ratified by Equatorial Guinea, nor the crime of genocide incorporated in its laws, and (2) that though mass murder was established, the intentional destruction of national, ethnic, or religious groups in terms of the convention was not proved.[4]

2. *Law Reports of Trials of War Criminals*, vol. 7, 1948:8.

3. Ibid., 1–10. For discussion of early trials for genocide, see United Nations, E/CN.4/Sub.2/416, dated 4 July 1978:6–7.

4. 1979:28–31. Fegley, in a contrary opinion (1978:34–47), expressed the view that the action of the Macias regime against two ethnic groups, the Bubis and Fernandinos, did fall within the U.N. definition of genocide, but he did not address the specific issue of the validity of the charge of genocide under the laws of Equatorial Guinea.

The establishment of an international penal court is, however, not a closed issue. The possibility is raised in relation to other international crimes, most notably for the punishment of apartheid. In this case a number of circumstances combine to encourage resolute action. Member states enjoy relative immunity against the crime, which is rather specific to the South African structure of racial domination, and at the same time, most member states are strongly committed to its suppression. The result is a startling difference between the *Apartheid* and Genocide conventions in respect to the provisions for implementation and punishment and in respect to the actions taken for the suppression of the two crimes.[5]

This is immediately apparent from an examination of the United Nations publication *United Nations Action in the Field of Human Rights*.[6] The index devotes 2 lines to genocide: the initial General Assembly resolution, the convention, and the study of genocide by the sub-commission's rapporteur. No other action is reported, the references being purely expository apart from mention of the punishment of Second World War criminals, humanitarian relief, and publicity. By contrast, the index devotes 32 lines to apartheid. It is the second largest item, being exceeded only by the entries under Women, and it is replete with action. There are the numerous committees—the General Assembly's Commission on the Racial Situation in South Africa and its Special Committee on *Apartheid*, the Expert committee of the Security Council, the Commission's Ad Hoc Working Group of Experts on Human Rights in Southern Africa, the Group of Three, the Centre against *Apartheid*, the United Nations Trust Fund for South Africa, the United Nations Trust Fund for Publicity against *Apartheid*, and an Educational and Training Programme. Then there are the resolutions, reports of the debates, special inquiries and studies, seminars, indeed forests of documentation; and an International Declaration on *Apartheid* in Sport, an International Day for the Elimination of Racial Discrimination, an Annual Day of Solidarity with South African Political Prisoners, an International Anti-*Apartheid* Year, and a variety of measures designed to isolate and to impose sanctions upon South Africa.[7]

We are clearly in the presence of a serious commitment, and this

5. The commission's Ad Hoc Working Group on Implementation of the *Apartheid* Convention relates differences in enforceability to differences in function. See 1980, E/CN.4/1426, para. 20.

6. New York: United Nations, 1980 (Sales No. E.79.XIV 6).

7. Ibid., 76–93, 347–53.

is reflected in the International Convention on the Suppression and Punishment of the Crime of Apartheid. Three paragraphs in the preamble are of special interest. The first links apartheid with genocide by observing that, "in the Convention on the Prevention and Punishment of the Crime of Genocide, certain acts which may also be qualified as acts of *apartheid* constitute a crime under international law." The subtle wording of this preamble derives from a report of the commission's Ad Hoc Group of Experts, who extended a mandate to investigate the torture and ill-treatment of prisoners in South Africa into a sort of preparatory examination of the South African government on charges of genocide. The experts concluded that in the present state of South African legislation, they could not say that the South African government had expressed an intention to commit genocide, but that members of the political groups who had testified did consider that certain elements of genocide existed in the practice of apartheid. In an attempt to resolve the problem of equating apartheid with genocide, the experts recommended in their report the revision of the Genocide Convention to make apartheid policies, as practiced by the South African government, punishable under that convention.[8]

In two other paragraphs in the preamble there is a more positive identification of apartheid with crimes against humanity in the observations that "in the Convention on the Non-Applicability of Statutory Limitations to War Crimes and Crimes Against Humanity, 'inhuman acts resulting from the policy of *apartheid*' are qualified as crimes against humanity" and in the further observation that the General Assembly had adopted a number of resolutions "in which the policies and practices of *apartheid* are condemned as a crime against humanity." There are indeed various U.N. documents in which apartheid is associated with Nazism, genocide, and crimes against humanity,[9] and the experts, in a second report, systematically applied the Nuremberg principles to apartheid. Under the heading of crimes against humanity, they referred to a number of practices as constituting elements of genocide, and they again recommended the revi-

8. See Leo Kuper, *South Africa: Human Rights and Genocide*, 1981:12–13, and the following reports of the commission's Ad Hoc Group of Experts, E/CN.4/950, dated 27 Oct. 1967; E/CN.4/984/Add.18, dated 28 Feb. 1969, paras. 35, 39; and E/CN.4/1075, dated 15 Feb. 1972, paras. 122, 164.

9. See, for example, General Assembly Resolutions 2545, XXIV, dated 11 Dec. 1969, and 2438, XXIII, dated 19 Dec. 1968.

sion of the Genocide Convention to incorporate inhuman acts resulting from apartheid. They also added the recommendation that the Republic of South Africa should be asked to institute penal proceedings against persons who have allegedly committed crimes against humanity, according to the findings of the experts.[10] This is decidedly bizarre—asking members of the South African government to prosecute themselves.

The substantive provisions of the convention open with the declaration that apartheid is a crime against humanity, and that inhuman acts resulting from it are crimes under international law and constitute a serious threat to international peace and security. The crime of apartheid is more fully and systematically defined than the crime of genocide, but with some overlapping. The definition is clearly directed against the practices of the South African government, though with some appearance of more general applicability. Motive, a troublesome aspect of the definition of genocide, is explicitly eliminated in the provision that "international criminal responsibility shall apply, irrespective of the motive involved, to individuals, members of organizations and institutions and representatives of the State" (article III). The jurisdiction of state tribunals is not restricted to the tribunal of the state in the territory of which the act was committed, as stipulated in the Genocide Convention. Instead, states parties undertake to punish, "in accordance with their jurisdiction," persons responsible for, or accused of, the crime of apartheid, "whether or not such persons reside in the territory of the State in which the acts are committed or are nationals of that State or of some other State or are stateless persons" (article IV), and any state party to the convention may try accused persons over whom they acquire jurisdiction.

In both conventions there is provision for the jurisdiction of an international penal tribunal, but it is now only the apartheid tribunal that is being actively promoted. In a report to the commission, *Implementation of the International Convention on the Suppression and Punishment of the Crime of Apartheid*, the Ad Hoc Working Group of Experts concluded that "in the present context, 'implementation' signifies the creation of an international criminal court," and it submitted two drafts, one for the Establishment of an International Penal Tribunal for the Suppression and Punishment of the Crime of

10. E/CN.4/1075, para. 164.

Apartheid and Other International Crimes, and the second, by way of a protocol to the convention, restricted to the penal enforcement of the *Apartheid* Convention. In the first draft, the other international crimes are not specified; article I provides that the states parties may include within the jurisdiction of the tribunal any other international crime by supplemental agreement.[11] In terms of the immediate effect, then, the two drafts provide only for the punishment of the crime of apartheid—or more specifically, for the punishment of "grave breaches" of the *Apartheid* Convention.

States parties have been invited to submit their comments on the proposal for an international penal tribunal. In the meantime, however, the commission has been compiling lists of accused persons and organizations, as authorized by article X of the convention. In a report on the torture and murder of detainees in South Africa, prepared in cooperation with the Special Committee against *Apartheid*, the Ad Hoc Group of Experts investigated 37 cases of murder, torture, and deprivation of liberty and of fundamental rights. The purpose of this inquiry was to establish whether there were sufficient grounds for action against the accused persons. However, the conclusions are expressed as a series of judgments in the following form: "A careful examination of the facts clearly shows the responsibility in the case of _____ , who is guilty of the acts referred to and punishable under the provisions of [Article II ____ , and Article III] of the Convention."[12]

In addition, since 1977, the sub-commission has been compiling lists of "individuals, institutions, including banks, and other organizations or groups, as well as representatives of States, whose activities constituted political, military, economic or other forms of assistance to the colonial and racist regimes in southern Africa." Consideration of these lists is a standing item on the agenda of the sub-commission. In July 1979 there were already 2,605 entries, including not only important military, financial, and industrial trade relations but also stationery, Tampax, chewing gum, pens, tea, books, and so on.[13] *Time*, however, and the *Encyclopaedia Brittanica* were omitted because "a periodical ought to be available throughout the world if it was to perform its mission of providing information effec-

11. E/CN.4/1426, pp. 21–35, 65–86.
12. E/CN.4/1366.
13. E/CN.4/425.

tively, while the *Encyclopaedia Brittanica*, by its very nature, was meant for the whole world."[14] International sports bodies were also listed, including life saving and paraplegic sports.[15]

The lists seem to be more remarkable for zeal than discretion. They are almost entirely restricted to Western firms, and they seem to have been "composed with the underlying thought that the activities of Western—including Netherlands'—enterprises in South Africa are *ipso facto* detrimental to the enjoyment of human rights in South Africa."[16] The original intention in the framing and the publicizing of the lists was to bring the pressure of international public opinion to bear on the firms themselves, and also on the governments of the countries in which the firms are based. However, in 1981 the sub-commission recommended to the commission that the committee set up under the *Apartheid* Convention should be asked to examine whether the actions of transnational corporations that operate in South Africa come under the definition of the crime of apartheid, and whether or not some legal action could be taken under the convention.[17]

Clearly, there is a strong commitment by many member states to an international penal tribunal for the punishment of apartheid. But its establishment would immediately raise the problem of the scale of values. Murder and torture are the first of the two grave crimes of apartheid listed in the draft convention and draft protocol for an international penal tribunal. Then, too, the convention links apartheid to genocide and to crimes against humanity. How then would it be possible to exclude genocide and torture from the jurisdiction of the proposed tribunal?

In a colloquy on war crimes, Tom Farer commented that it seemed to him not inconceivable that an international court would be established in the near future. If it was, he foresaw that it would have jurisdiction only over crimes such as assaults against officials. "Genocide and other crimes against humanity will be ignored. Or, the Convention creating the court might contain a list of crimes and allow each signatory to select those with respect to which it accepts the court's jurisdiction."[18] He seems to have been speaking in jest. But

14. E/CN.4/Sub.2/469, p. 5.
15. E/CN.4/Sub.2/425, p. 136
16. See comment by the Netherlands government, E/CN.4/Sub.2/425/Add.1.
17. Resolution 6 (XXXIV).
18. 1973:44.

the proposal for supplemental agreements could easily result in a checklist of international crimes that would confront many member states with an intolerable dilemma—a readiness to accept penal jurisdiction in respect to (the South African crime of) apartheid while rejecting jurisdiction for genocide and torture.

Even if the United Nations succeeds in overcoming the resistance of many member states to the establishment of an international criminal court for the punishment of genocide, there remain numerous problems relating to the constitution and powers of the court.[19] A particular difficulty is that in most cases the cooperation of the offending state would be required for the surrender of the accused persons.[20] But notwithstanding the difficulties and limitations, a penal tribunal is an essential element in any serious campaign for the punishment of the crime of genocide. Perhaps it may become more feasible with the reopening of the issue for the punishment of apartheid. In the meantime, the United Nations might prepare lists of mass murderers along the lines of the lists of apartheid criminals.

If one extends the concept of punishment beyond the model of municipal criminal courts, there are other possibilities of punitive action open to the United Nations but directed against states and not against individuals. Delegations are highly sensitive to criticism and condemnation, as shown by the steps they take to defend their countries. The brazen and contemptuous self-righteousness in mass murder and atrocity of the Pol Pot regime in Democratic Kampuchea and of the Khomeini regime in Iran is a rarity. This may seem extraordinary in view of the outrageous practices of many of the member states, but presumably the facade of international respectability lends some appearance of legitimacy to oppressive regimes.

Complaints may be raised in many organs of the United Nations and related organizations, as discussed in chapter 6. The resultant adverse international publicity and stigmatization, flowing from the accusations, debates, resolutions, and investigations, offer a modern and genteel equivalent of the pillory and stocks of other days. Moreover, by virtue of article IX of the Genocide Convention, a state party may seek a ruling from the International Court of Justice that another party has failed to fulfill its obligations under the convention.

19. See Stone and Woetzel, eds., 1970, particularly chap. 26 by Stone.
20. E/CN.4/1426, paras. 63 and 64, deals with this problem in relation to apartheid.

And finally, there are the punitive sanctions against offending states by way of the severance or contraction of diplomatic, economic, and other relations—the isolation of which Bolivia complained—and as a last resort, in cases where the mass murders raise a threat to world peace, the sanctions vested in the Security Council. In the meantime, states might exert their influence to secure the preparation of lists of persons against whom there is prima facie evidence of involvement in genocidal and other mass murder, along the lines of the lists of suspected apartheid criminals.

There are many other levels at which it would be possible to take punitive action, if we interpret the term widely.

Under the Genocide Convention the major responsibility for punishment of the crime falls upon states, and they act in both the international and domestic arenas. In addition to action within the United Nations and related international organizations, states may raise issues of genocide in their intergovernmental regional associations. Two of these, the European and the inter-American, offer more scope for effective action on human rights at the present time than the United Nations. This is especially important in the case of the Organization of American States because of a high incidence of political mass murder and genocide on that continent.

The European Commission and Court of Human Rights are well established and have been functioning for many years. The commission has jurisdiction to deal with both interstate applications and individual applications by charging violations of the European Convention for the Protection of Human Rights and Fundamental Freedoms. By ratifying the convention, a state recognizes the commission's competence to hear complaints instituted against it by another contracting state. Some important decisions have been taken pursuant to interstate applications, but states are reluctant to arraign each other, and the right is rarely invoked.

Individuals are the main source of complaints. Article 25 of the convention confers on the commission jurisdiction to receive applications lodged by "any person, non-governmental organization or group of individuals" claiming to be the victims of a violation by a contracting state of a right guaranteed in the convention. This is subject to the proviso that the state has recognized the competence of the commission to receive individual petitions; of the 20 states that have ratified the convention, 16 have accepted the right of individual petition. A further requirement is that the applicant must have exhausted the domestic remedies available.

If the commission fails to obtain a friendly settlement of the dispute, it draws up a report of the facts and its conclusions as to whether there has been a breach of the convention. It may also make proposals relating to the disposition of the dispute. The report is then transmitted to the Committee of Ministers of the Council of Europe and to the states concerned. If the case has not been referred to the Court of Human Rights and if the committee decides that there has been a violation of the convention, it prescribes "a period during which the High Contracting Party concerned must take the measures required by the decision of the Committee of Ministers" (article 32.2). It should be noted that the Committee of Ministers does not prescribe the measures necessary to comply with its decision: that is left to the state party. But under the terms of the convention, state parties undertake to regard the decisions of the committee as binding on them (article 32.4). If the state party fails to take the necessary action, the Committee of Ministers decides what effect is to be given to its original decision, and it publishes the commission's report (article 32.3).

The Court of Human Rights has jurisdiction if the states parties concerned have accepted its jurisdiction as compulsory in all matters concerning the interpretation and application of the convention, or if there is an ad hoc acceptance for the particular case. Eighteen states have made the general declaration accepting the jurisdiction of the court. The right to refer a case to the court is reserved for the commission, the states concerned, or a state party whose national is alleged to have been a victim. The court may decide that a decision or measure taken by a state party is in conflict with its obligations under the convention. When the court finds that a violation has occurred, it may afford "just satisfaction" to the injured party if the internal law of the state affords only partial reparation.[21] The decisions of the court are binding on the states parties concerned in the case. However, it is again left to these parties to draw the necessary conclusions and to decide what remedial action is required. The judgment of the court is submitted to the Committee of Ministers, which has the task of supervising its execution.

The only sanction specifically mentioned in the convention is the

21. See Robertson, 1977:209–10, for a discussion of this issue.

publication of the commission's report by the Committee of Ministers. This is mandatory in cases that have not been referred to the court and in which the state party concerned has failed to take the measures required by the decision of the committee. Publication seems a rather innocuous sanction. But Robertson comments in his study *Human Rights in Europe* that "this is perhaps a more powerful sanction than is generally believed, because no responsible government can view with complacency the prospect of the publication by the Foreign Ministers of eighteen States of a report indicating that it has violated its international obligations regarding respect for human rights." In addition, under the statute of the Council of Europe, the Committee of Ministers may take the more drastic action of suspending or expelling the offending state from membership.[22]

The punitive sanctions thus available are reparation and damages ("just satisfaction"), adverse publicity, and expulsion. Member states may also apply punitive sanctions on their own initiative. Moreover, the Council of Europe may act against nonmember states by denunciation (as, for example, the resolutions of the Parliamentary Assembly on the persecution of the Bahá'ís in Iran) and by diplomatic and other pressures.

The member states of the Council of Europe are for the most part relatively stable and affluent democracies. By contrast, the Organization of American States comprises states at very different levels of economic development, including many military and tyrannical regimes with an appalling record on human rights. There are currently civil wars, armed conflicts between states, numerous claims for territorial revision, and a great vulnerability of indignous groups, the survivors of the initial colonization of the continent who are now threatened with the destruction of their way of life, and indeed with annihilation. Yet the institutional provision for the protection of human rights is quite comparable to that of the Council of Europe, and in some respects potentially more effective.

The Inter-American Commission on Human Rights, like its European counterpart, deals with both individual petitions and interstate complaints. Acceptance of the right of individual petition is mandatory, while the procedures for interstate complaint are optional. Any person or group of persons or any nongovernmental entity legally recognized in one or more member states of the organi-

22. Ibid., 243–44.

zation may lodge petitions containing denunciations or complaints of violation of the convention by a state party. But before one state party may bring such charges against another state party, both states must have made declarations recognizing the competence of the commission to receive and examine interstate complaints. However, only four states have filed that declaration.[23]

If the commission rules that a charge is admissible, it investigates the case and explores the possibility of reaching a friendly settlement on the basis of respect for the human rights recognized in the convention. Failing a friendly settlement, the commission draws a report setting forth the facts and stating its conclusions. The report is submitted to the state concerned, with such proposals and recommendations as the commission sees fit. Thereafter, if within a period of three months from transmittal of the report to the states concerned, the matter has neither been settled nor referred to the Inter-American Court of Human Rights, and if the offending state has failed to take the necessary measures to remedy the situation, the sole sanction available to the commission is the publication of its report.

As for the Court of Human Rights, only the commission and states parties may submit a case. There is the further limitation mentioned above, that the state parties concerned in the case must have accepted the jurisdiction of the court. Of the 32 state members of the organization, 17 have ratified the convention, and 4 have declared their acceptance of the court's adjudicatory functions.

The court, which has only recently begun to function, is required to determine whether there has been a violation of the convention, and the steps that may have to be taken to remedy the violation.[24] It is also empowered to award damages. State parties to the convention are under an obligation to comply with the judgment of the court in any case to which they are parties: and judgments for compensatory damages may be executed in the country concerned, in accordance with the domestic procedures governing the execution of judgments against the state.

In situations of extreme gravity and urgency, when necessary to avoid irreparable damage to persons, the court is empowered to order temporary injunctions (article 63.2). This is an encouraging pro-

23. See Buergenthal in Buergenthal, Norris, and Shelton, 1982:236–37, and his following discussion.
24. See Buergenthal's discussion of article 63.1 (ibid., 240).

vision, seen particularly against the background of the interminable delays in the proceedings of the United Nations Commission on Human Rights, and the profoundly immoral postponement of action against ongoing mass murders from year to year (for example, against the Pol Pot regime in Democratic Kampuchea and against the Amin regime in Uganda).

Thus, the sanctions available to the Organization of American States against genocide and political mass murder are, first of all, denunciation and the directing of international public opinion against the offending state. The reports of the commission provide a valuable source of information and publicity. Then there are the possibilities, still to be explored and developed, of using the court procedures for injunctions, restitution, and damages. But this will be meaningful only when an appreciable number of states, and particularly states with sharp internal divisions, have accepted the jurisdiction of the court. The annual reports by the commission to the General Assembly and notifications by the court of failure to comply with a judgment permit the assembly to adopt whatever political measures it deems appropriate.[25]

In the domestic arena a great variety of diplomatic, trade, and other sanctions can be applied against offending states, without reference to the decisions of intergovernmental organizations, whether international or regional. Under the administration of President Carter, the United Sates emphasized performance on human rights as a criterion for receipt of military, police, and economic aid and as a condition for support in multilateral lending institutions.[26] Though this policy was not consistently pursued, it had some effect in raising the level of international concern for human rights and in restraining gross and systematic violations.[27] Under President Reagan the policy is still professed, but it is corrupted in practice; the administration has found improved performance in human rights not visible to other observers, notably in the case of El Salvador. But, in fact, the administration was misleading the country in basing its case for further military aid to El Salvador on improved performance in human rights. The correct tests, in terms of United States legislation relating to El Salvador, are, inter alia, that the government is making a con-

25. Ibid., 241. For further general discussion of the European and American conventions, see ibid. generally; Frowein, 1980; Krüger, 1980; and Waldock, 1980.
26. Fisher, 1982:27–28.
27. Refer to Alston, 1982:162.

certed and significant effort to comply with internationally recognized human rights, and that it is achieving substantial control over all elements of its own armed forces so as to bring to an end the indiscriminate torture and murder of Salvadoran citizens by these forces.[28] It is only recently that there begins to be some evidence of an attempt to comply with these requirements.

The above actions in the domestic arena are directed against states. They do not address the problem of the punishment of individual criminals. The record in this respect is almost totally negative. As discussed earlier, the explanation is partly that the mass murderers are likely to be protected by their own governments. One of the most notorious examples of this nurturing of genocidal criminals is provided by Austria in the years following the Second World War. In his memoirs Simon Wiesenthal, the Nazi hunter, gives many accounts of the protective stance of the government, administrators, and courts toward Austrian war criminals, the often derisory sentences for mass murder, and the public celebration of travesties of trial and acquittal.[29] This is by no means surprising in view of Austrian enthusiasm for Nazism and the massive participation of Austrians in the genocide against Jews.[30] The many prosecutions by the German government of German mass murderers, though touching only the fringe of the problem, and the large scale of the reparations paid to the survivors of the genocide are exceptional.[31] If the mass murderers flee their own countries, they are likely to find sanctuary in other countries, as Wiesenthal has recorded in his memoirs. And recently there have been exposures of collaboration after World War II by government agencies of the United States with well-known genocidal murderers, who were smuggled into the country, given protec-

28. There are checks on administrative malpractice in this regard, both by Congress and by vigilant nongovernmental organizations, who recently initiated action to set aside the certification of El Salvador. The conditions for certification are set out in the International Security and Development Cooperation Law of 1981. I am indebted to Paul Hoffman for these comments.

29. See 1967.

30. In "A profile of Simon Wiesenthal" (ibid., 189), we read that "although the Austrians accounted for only eight per cent of the population of the Third Reich, *about one third of all people working for the SS extermination machinery were Austrians. Almost half of the six million Jewish victims of the Hitler regime were killed by Austrians*" (italics mine).

31. Sentences were, however, "fantastically lenient. . . . Thus, Dr. Otto Bradfisch, of the *Einsatzgruppen*, the mobile killing units of the SS in the East, was sentenced to ten years of hard labour for the killing of fifteen thousand Jews" (Arendt, 1969:15). See also her general discussion in chap. 1.

tion, and accorded American citizenship against the express prohibition of Congress and in violation of several criminal laws.[32]

But quite apart from these protective barriers, there are the negligible jurisdiction conferred on states by the Genocide Convention and the exclusion of political groups in the definition of the crime. I commented in chapter 6 that this exclusion might be remedied in some measure by the framing of a protocol extending the "protection" of the convention to political groups. The same objections would be raised as in the past, and there would be difficulties in securing the adoption of a protocol and its ratification by state parties, but as a U.N. official commented in making this suggestion, it was important to initiate a process that would keep the issue alive.

As for the limited jurisdiction conferred on states, I assume that the principle of territorial competence, which replaced the original proposal for universal jurisdiction, does not exclude the right of any state to bring to trial before its own tribunals any of its nationals for genocide acts committed outside its territory.[33] But even with this extension, the effect of the convention is to render genocide virtually a crime without punishment. A strong case can be made for universal jurisdiction in crimes against humanity.[34] However, the states themselves would be the final arbiters of the recognition to be accorded international crimes in their courts.

The issues are very complex.[35] In some states there may be sufficient uncertainty to allow pressure to be exerted for the extension of domestic jurisdiction to include jurisdiction over such major international crimes as genocide and other crimes against humanity, regardless of the place where the crimes were committed or the nationality of the accused. Initiatives for this type of extension might come from nongovernmental organizations (particularly lawyers' groups concerned with human rights) and from individuals. At the different level of torts, there may also be opportunities, in favorable circumstances, for individuals to institute actions for punitive damages suf-

32. See the general account by Loftus, 1982:89ff., and Holtzman, 1983. In 1978 the United States passed legislation to authorize deportation of Nazi war criminals. It should be added that French and British intelligence units also entered into protective collaboration with well-known war criminals.

33. This may be controversial. See the discussion in E/CN.4/Sub.2/416, paras. 212–14.

34. For example, Beres, 1982:22–23.

35. For discussion of the many factors likely to be taken into account, see Bassiouni, 1979:260ff.; Lillich, 1981; and Sohn and Buergenthal, 1973:913ff., 981–82.

fered by reason of genocidal acts and mass murder committed in the territories of other states.

Given the poor record of intergovernmental organizations and of states in the punishment of genocide and mass murder and the paucity of formal interstate complaints, the major initiative rests with individuals and nongovernmental organizations. And they have been taking this initiative with increasing impact on international public opinion and on intergovernmental organizations, as notably in the campaigns against disappearances and torture. They act in both the international and domestic spheres. In the international organizations they are the main source of charges of gross violations of human rights. Nongovernmental organizations, in particular, carry out the important task of investigating and publishing the facts, and the reports of such bodies as Amnesty International have high credibility in international circles. Domestically, these organizations, and individuals, may be able to exert pressure on their own governments to take some action against offending states by diplomacy and by the more positive restraints of trade sanctions and the denial of aid. They themselves may organize boycotts and protests. But there is in fact very little that they can do about the punishment of mass murderers.

The survivors of genocide have sometimes taken the law into their own hands. One of the most celebrated of these cases was the execution in 1926 of Simon Petlura by Samuel Schwartzbard. Petlura was the Ukrainian leader responsible for the pogroms in 1919 in which, according to an estimate of the Red Cross, about 50,000 Jews were murdered.[36] The massacres were carried out with great atrocity, and their scale and organization were such that we would now describe them as genocide.

Schwartzbard, a Ukrainian Jew, had survived many pogroms, in which 15 members of his own family had perished. He moved to Paris, served in the French army during the First World War, and was awarded the Military Cross. Wounded, and discharged after convalescence, he returned to Russia in 1917, where he remained until 1920 caring for the survivors of the pogroms who had taken refuge in Odessa. Back in Paris and having learned that Petlura was also there, he finally traced him and shot him down.[37]

The case was remarkable in two respects. First there were the

36. Torrès, 1928:v.
37. Ibid., i–ix.

circumstances of the assassination. Petlura was usually accompanied by a woman and a young girl, and Schwartzbard was not prepared to shoot him in their presence, waiting for an occasion when he was unaccompanied. One notices the sharp contrast with contemporary terrorism, in which victims are murdered in the presence of their families and in which the cause is deemed to justify the indiscriminate taking of lives totally unrelated to the original crime. The trial was remarkable also for the support extended to the accused, with many distinguished Frenchmen willing to testify on his behalf, and for his acquittal, to the acclamation of those present with cries of "Vive la France."[38]

In the course of his plea, the defense counsel, Henry Torrès, referred to an earlier, similar trial in 1921. This was the trial in Berlin, "devant les célèbres bourgeois de la cité berlinoise," of Soghomon Teilirian for the murder of Talaat Bey, one of the leaders responsible for the genocide against the Armenians. Notwithstanding the evidence of General Liman van Sanders, "casqué de fer et éperonné,"[39] that Talaat Bey was a great friend of the Germans, their protégé, their ally, Teilirian was acquitted. About the same time, there were further assassinations by Armenians of Turkish leaders for their participation in the massacres.[40]

In his memoirs Wiesenthal describes a planned assassination, which he averted. This was at the trial of an Austrian mass murderer, Murer. With difficulty, Wiesenthal had prevailed on a survivor, Jacob Brodi, to give evidence. Murer had killed Brodi's son in his presence. During the trial, Murer's two sons and his wife, sitting in the front row, laughed, grimaced, and sneered at the witnesses, with the indulgence of the court. Brodi then told Wiesenthal that they would stop sneering when he was called to the witness stand. He had not come to testify, but to act, and he pulled out a long knife. Wiesenthal was finally able to persuade him to give up his plan, and he writes that a few days after Murer was acquitted to the cheers of those present and showered with flowers, he met Brodi in the lobby of a Vienna hotel. "He looked through me as if I hadn't been there. I understood. I may have saved Murer's life. It is not a very pleasant thought, but there was nothing else I could have done."[41]

38. Ibid.
39. Ibid., 36. See also Carzou, 1975:201–08.
40. Chaliand and Ternon, 1980:135ff.
41. Wiesenthal, 1967:77.

I am not advocating the extralegal execution of genocidal or other mass murderers. Although I have some ambivalence about the matter, I understand all too well the threat to innocent people of license to self-appointed executioners. An alternative procedure, proposed by Peter Benenson, founder of Amnesty International, seems somewhat innocuous by comparison. This is the documentation of the crimes committed by mass murderers, comparable to the compiling of data by the United Nations War Crimes Commission established in 1942. This was also the approach adopted by Wiesenthal. But Wiesenthal was working in relation to procedures for the prosecution of war criminals, which, however inadequate, enabled him to make an outstanding contribution, whereas the present contemplated documentation would have to await more adequate provision for the punishment of mass murderers. Nevertheless, it would be available for future trials, and its existence might perhaps serve in some cases as a mild deterrent. In the ordinary course of events, the United Nations would be the appropriate body to prepare this documentation and the lists of mass murderers, but it does not have the necessary moral stature. One can readily envisage the atmosphere of vendetta and *protetzione* in which it would carry out the framing of lists. It seems best that the documentation should be undertaken by an independent body based on nongovernmental organizations, many of which would have relevant information from their own research units.

In favorable circumstances it may be possible to institute action for damages. The case of Filartiga against Pena-Irala, decided in the United States in 1980, may have set a valuable precedent in that country.

In a complaint filed jointly with his daughter, Dolly, Dr. Joel Filartiga, a well-known Paraguayan physician and artist and an opponent of President Alfredo Stroessner's repressive regime, alleged that members of that regime's police force had tortured and murdered his son, Joelito. On June 30, 1980 the Court of Appeals for the Second Circuit found that since an international consensus condemning torture has crystallized, torture violates the "law of nations" for purposes of the Alien Tort Statute. United States Courts, it was held, therefore have jurisdiction under the statute to hear civil suits by the victims of foreign torture, if the alleged international outlaws are found in the United States.[42]

42. I am following the account of Beres, 1982:32. The case is reported in *Filartiga* v. *Pena* 630 F.2d 876 (1980). A general discussion was published by Human Rights Advocates in 1982.

The court has now awarded the plaintiffs compensation and punitive damages of $10,385,364 (United States District Court, Eastern District of New York, 10 January 1984).

A similar suit (*Siderman* v. *Argentina*) was filed in a U.S. district court in Los Angeles for the return of property wrongfully seized and for $100 million in punitive damages from those who tortured the plaintiff or from the government of Argentina. However, the cause of action differed from the Filartiga case in two respects: the torturers were not present in the United States, and the plaintiff sought to extend liability to a government. In October 1984, the District Court granted José Siderman and his wife, Lea, a default judgment of $2.7 million.

Possibilities of legal action would certainly be available in U.S. courts against genocidal and political mass murderers. One such suit, *Handel et al.* v. *Artukovic*, was recently filed, again in the U.S. district court in Los Angeles. Five survivors of the Nazi Holocaust were seeking compensatory and punitive damages against a former Nazi official residing in the United States for the personal losses sustained by the plaintiffs and other victims and by the immediate relatives of those killed or injured (*Los Angeles Daily Journal*, 8 March 1984).

At a different level of action, directed against states, there are the nongovernmental international tribunals. Their existence is a measure of the failure of domestic and international jurisdiction over major international crimes. They correspond to the documentation processes, but they are public events conducted on the lines of court proceedings, and they conclude with a formal judgment.

The First Russell Tribunal, held in 1966–67, investigated charges of genocide against the United States for its role in the Vietnam War. It concluded that the United States had committed acts of aggression against Vietnam, that it was guilty of the deliberate, systematic, and large-scale bombardment of civilian targets and populations, and that it was also guilty of repeated violations of the sovereignty, neutrality, and territorial integrity of Cambodia. The governments of Australia, New Zealand, and South Korea were found to be accomplices in the aggression against Vietnam. In a second session the United States was found guilty of genocide in Vietnam.[43]

The Second Russell Tribunal, in 1973–75, dealt with violations

43. Coates, Limqueco, and Weiss, 1971:185, 365–66.

of human rights in Latin America. It found that Brazil, Chile, Uruguay, and Bolivia were guilty of serious, repeated, and systematic violations of human rights of such a nature as to constitute crimes against humanity. There were similar findings against Guatemala, Haiti, Paraguay, and the Dominican Republic, while the government of Brazil was also found guilty of the crime of genocide.[44]

The Third Russell Tribunal in 1978–79, dealing with violations of human rights in West Germany, seems somewhat offbeat or out of the general pattern of the tribunals.[45] The Fourth Russell Tribunal in 1980, published as *The Rights of the Indians of the Americas*, investigated 14 complaints of violations of human rights, received mostly from Indian national groups. The accused were judged guilty, 7 for crimes that included genocide.[46] The following year, the jury of the Permanent Tribunal of the Peoples, which was the successor to the Russell Tribunal, found El Salvador guilty of genocide, seemingly using the term for political mass murder in a sense that departs from the convention.[47] In 1981 and 1982 the Peoples' Tribunal held sessions on the situation in Afghanistan and found the Soviet government guilty of aggression and both the Soviet and Afghanistan governments responsible for violation of humanitarian law applicable to warfare.

Three recent sessions of the Peoples' Tribunal have been concerned with the crime of genocide. In June 1981 the Indonesian government was found guilty of genocide in East Timor, and in January 1983 the Guatemalan government, as mentioned in the last chapter, was held to have committed the crime of genocide against its Indian population.

In April 1984 the tribunal decided that the Young Turk government had committed genocide by the extermination of the Armenian population in 1915–17. This last hearing was a response to the Turkish government's consistent denial of responsibility for the genocide and to its recent efforts to block inquiry into, or even acknowledgment of, the genocide in international forums and academic meetings. I have included a copy of the judgment (appendix 2). It complements my account of the original handling of the historical record in

44. See Spokesman Pamphlet no. 51, *Found Guilty*, 1975.
45. See Spokesman Pamphlet no. 61, *Berufsverbote Condemned*, 1978, and no. 69, *Censorship, Legal Defence and the Domestic Intelligence Service in West Germany*, 1979.
46. *Report of the Fourth Russell Tribunal*, 1980.
47. Navarro, 1981:1–16.

the United Nations Sub-Commission on Prevention of Discrimination and Protection of Minorities (appendix 3 of my book *Genocide*).

The First Russell Tribunal made a very strong impact on international public opinion, and its proceedings reinforced the peace movement in the United States. Later trials have been far less resonant. Still, they do serve to direct attention to major international crimes and are a means for documenting genocidal and political mass murders. But there are many disquieting elements in this procedure.

Bertrand Russell opened the second session of the First Russell Tribunal with the following statement: "We are not judges. We are witnesses. Our task is to make mankind bear witness to these terrible crimes and to unite humanity on the side of justice in Vietnam."[48] But in fact the tribunals do judge, and they do pronounce judgments of guilt on the accused, who are not represented, being naturally reluctant to submit to the proceedings of the court, however generously invited to attend. The investigations sometimes seem perfunctory, and the verdict seems preordained. And yet, notwithstanding their shortcomings, these tribunals do make some contribution to the pathetically limited possibilities of action for the punishment of genocide.

A further possibility is the establishment of a World Genocide Tribunal, as proposed by Luis Kutner in a paper presented to the International Conference on the Holocaust and Genocide.[49] It could be along the lines of the Russell tribunals, or, at a more ambitious level, one might seek to bring about the establishment of the World Genocide Tribunal by multilateral treaty with an initial approach to the Council of Europe or its member states. This might have the further function of stimulating the United Nations to implement the Genocide Convention.

The punishment of genocide addresses the crime after the annihilation of a people, whereas the crucially significant problem is that of prevention. And the United Nations is more likely to extend its cooperation for prevention of the crime, since punishment is threatening to the governments of many member states.

Nevertheless, it remains important to establish adequate institutions and procedures for punishment, although no punishment

48. Coates, Limqueco, and Weiss, 1971:9.
49. Kutner, 1982.

could possibly fit the crime, outside some of the torments reserved for unrepentant sinners in Christian theology. The probability of prosecution immediately after the crime or as a lifelong threat to the criminal would certainly serve as something of a deterrent. Thus, the Argentinian military junta, finding it increasingly difficult to resist the return to civilian rule, sought to protect itself (unsuccessfully, as it later transpired) against Nuremberg-style prosecutions. Accordingly, it passed a law that granted the military and the police immunity from prosecution for crimes committed during the war against leftist terrorists. The law also extended immunity to persons suspected of terrorist activity, but not to those already convicted or in exile.[50] Earlier, the military regimes in Greece and Spain had negotiated amnesties before surrendering their power to civilian rule.

Moreover, the prosecutions for genocide may be expected to reactivate revulsion for the crime. Wiesenthal comments that the trial of Eichmann in Jerusalem was the greatest setback to the growth of the neo-Nazi movement in Germany and in Austria.[51] So, too, the contemporary trial of Klaus Barbie, "the Butcher of Lyons," brings back shameful memories of French participation in the Holocaust and reawakens sentiment against the crime. The Russell-type tribunals, notwithstanding their many limitations, give expression to an international conscience that is outraged by world indifference to punishment of the crime, and they sensitize and mobilize a wider international public.[52] And finally, there is the aspect Wiesenthal stresses— the bearing of witness, the duty owed to the victims and the survivors and to the potential victims of future genocides.

50. See Freed, 1982; Cohen, 1982:234; and Schumacher, 1983:1.
51. Wiesenthal, 1967:8. See also Wiesenthal, 1977:83–87.
52. See the discussion by Cassese, ed., 1979:254–56.

11

Prevention
A General Comment

There are different levels of approach to the prevention of genocide, and these, in turn, are linked to different theories of genocide. From the many theories, I select three for brief comment.[1]

A wide range of psychological and sociobiological theories emphasize the innate destructiveness in man. Lorenz derives human destructiveness, expressed in the killing of members of his own species, from instinctual aggression, which has taken an exaggerated form in the course of evolution. Unexpected explosions of devastatingly destructive violence may result from its frustration. It is all the more likely, Lorenz argues, since the invention of weapons has the effect of destroying the functional equilibrium between the aggressive instinct and the mechanisms that inhibit the killing of members of one's own species; particularly in modern warfare, impersonal methods of killing at ever increasing distances remove these inhibitions.[2]

Koestler, in a discussion of man's persistent pursuit of intraspecific warfare, describes him as alone (apart from some controversial phenomena among rats and cats) in killing members of his own species on an individual and a collective scale for motives ranging from sexual jealousy to quibbles about metaphysical doctrines. Homo sapiens, he argues, may be an aberrant biological species, an evolutionary misfit, afflicted by an endemic disorder, the source of which lies

1. For a more general discussion of theories of genocide, see chapter 3 of my book *Genocide*.
2. See Lorenz, 1977:265, 228–90, and 1970:3–5, 51–56.

in the conflict between the new and the old structures of the brain. The neocortex, seat of our intellect, has failed to establish proper control over our ancient brain, seat of archaic emotion-based beliefs—the horse and the crocodile that we carry inside our skulls.[3]

Charny, in a more recent and less pessimistic prognosis, finds the source of human destructiveness in the fear of death and the fear of nonaliveness.[4] It is the projection of these fears that leads "to 'nearly every one of us' being available to participate in genocide or to support genocidal acts. . . . Driven by nameless, overwhelming fears, men turn to the primitive tools of self-protection, including the belief that they may spare themselves the terrible fate of death by sacrificing another instead of themselves." The intervening mechanism in this process is the dehumanization of the victim as not deserving the protection due to members of our species.[5]

When we review these theories from the perspective of possibilities of action for the prevention of genocide, it is clear that we cannot hope to restructure the human psyche in the foreseeable future. So, of necessity, we are obliged to move away from this level of analysis. There is also a further relevant, but less pragmatic, consideration. These sociopsychological and sociobiological theories postulate universals in human nature. But not all societies experience genocide. Hence, the theoretical problem is transposed to a different level of analysis, that of the conditions under which the destructive impulses in man find expression in genocidal massacre. This Charny fully recognizes, and much of his work is devoted to the analysis of these predisposing conditions.

Nevertheless, these theories are important as offering a partial explanation for the wide prevalance of genocide. They suggest that genocide is not an aberrant pathological phenomenon but close to the nature of man. Mass murderers always seem to be available to carry out the genocidal massacres and other mass murders, and there are many reports of the joyous abandon with which they perpetrate the most horrifying atrocities. The theories also oblige us to reexamine the liberal assumption that the inhibitions against killing members of our own species are of such strength as to require the ideological dehumanization of the victims as a precondition for massacre.

3. Koestler, 1978, prologue.
4. *How Can We Think the Unthinkable? Genocide: The Human Cancer*, 1982.
5. Ibid., 207.

The search for the economic determinants of almost all social phenomena is now firmly established in the social sciences. But, strangely enough, the East European socialist states did not advance a Marxist theory of genocide during the debates on the convention. Presumably, this would have taken the form of equating ethnic and racial conflicts with the class struggle. But the application of a class model of analysis to the conflicts within *plural societies* has often been quite misleading and raises many problems.[6]

The racial or ethnic boundaries are usually not coterminous with the class divisions. A particularly disturbing feature, in terms of a Marxist class perspective, is the failure of solidarity between members of the same class but of different ethnic or racial background. Where there is inequality in the incorporation of different groups in the structure of the society, a decisive factor in the life chances of the worker will be the relationship to the means of power, and not the relationship to the means of production; and workers in the dominant group are likely to be the most hostile to the aspirations of subordinate groups for equality of participation. Moreover, in situations of extreme conflict, polarization tends to follow the lines of ethnic or racial cleavage rather than those of class structure.

Generally speaking, however, the material interests are an important factor in genocide. Their role is most marked in the genocides of colonization, in the sacrifice of indigenous groups to economic development, in many of the struggles for power between ethnic, racial, and religious groups, and in the genocides of international war. But they may have little or no significance in the genocides against hostage groups. They were quite irrelevant to the German genocide against Gypsies, which seems to have been motivated by pure malevolence, ideologically rationalized. Or to take the example of pogroms against Jews in Europe, there was a quite varied significance of economic motivations. One recalls Cohn's study of the exterminatory anti-Semitism that leads to attempts at genocide, and his conclusion that it can exist almost regardless of the real situation of Jews in society. "It can prosper where Jews form a large, cohesive and clearly recognizable minority, but also where the only Jews are a few scattered individuals who hardly regard themselves as Jews at all. And if it thrives on the spectacle of rich and influential Jews, it does not necessarily wilt where all Jews are poor. Most striking of all,

6. See Kuper, "Political Change in Plural Societies: Problems in Racial Pluralism," in 1974, chap. 9.

it can be found among people who have never set eyes on a Jew and in countries where there have been no Jews for centuries."[7] This deadliest kind of anti-Semitism, he argues, has little to do with real conflicts of interest between living people.

While recognizing the significant role of material interests in genocide, it is difficult to see what contribution even the most effective networks of nongovernmental organizations could possibly make to the economic restructuring of societies. Quite apart from the problem of obtaining access to the centers of power, there are difficulties in knowing what strategy to pursue. Capitalist societies have in the past tended to emphasize economic growth as contributing to the promotion of human rights, and the proposed new international economic order would seem to hold out promise. But the benefits of economic growth in plural societies are likely to be appropriated by the power elites and may contribute little to the advancement of subordinate groups. Thus, in Guatemala, with its traditional repression of Indian peasants, the gross national product grew more than 5 percent annually from 1960 to 1980; yet, according to studies by the Agency for International Development and the World Bank, the living standards of the peasants declined.[8] And we have seen how inimical Third World ideologies of development can be to the promotion of civil and political rights.

Socialist policies seem to favor equalization among racial, ethnic, and religious groups in a society. In an earlier chapter, I mentioned the view of the sub-commission's Rapporteur Cristescu, in his report *The Right to Self-Determination*, that "public ownership of the means of production . . . remains the decisive factor in achieving equitable distribution of the national income, economic and social democratisation and social justice."[9] But the issue is not ownership of the means of production. It is the control of access to the means of production, and the vesting of this control in the Communist party leadership and in the centralized state bureaucracies, that lays down the infrastructure for an immense concentration of power inimical to civil and political rights. Nor has the record of socialist states with respect to minorities been such as to encourage optimism.

In an important paper, Richard Falk analyzes the comparative protection of human rights in capitalist and socialist Third World

7. *Warrant for Genocide*, 1967:252, 16.
8. See Nairn, 1983.
9. Chap. 5, p. 55.

countries at the different levels of deep structure and ideology, theory, and practice.[10] He writes that socialism would seem to be better adapted *structurally* than capitalism to the realization of fundamental human rights, especially in the setting of the Third World.

In a world of resource and environmental constraint, of population pressures, and mass poverty amid rising material expectations and dissolving traditional bonds, the adoption of a socialist model of development appears to be a necessary precondition for the realisation of human rights, although it is of course not sufficient. . . . Capitalist models of development necessarily produce a privileged elite that appropriates a large proportion of the capital surplus not allocated for further development, and a substantial fraction of that elite may not even be resident in the country.[11]

This is at the level of theory. In practice, Falk arrives at

the uncomfortable conclusion that the human rights records of both socialism and capitalism are so poor in the Third World at this point that it is quite unconvincing to insist that one approach is generically preferable to the other. . . . The transition costs of moving to socialism have turned out to be so heavy, the absence of any tradition of checks and balances or pluralist politics and culture have made the administration of power in socialist states so totalitarian, and the effectiveness of control has been so great as to make popular control over a socialist state so difficult to exert that we cannot conclude, with confidence, that a given Third World society is better off "socialist." In effect, my position is that socialism *as applied* to date in the Third World deprives it of the moral advantage associated with socialism, *as theory* or as an ideological perspective.[12]

In Falk's comparison of capitalist and socialist societies, which focuses on the special conditions of the Third World, he mentions particularly the diversity of antagonistic ethnic elements contained within many Third World state boundaries as strengthening the disposition toward repression.[13] This element of ethnic diversity and antagonism is understated in applications of Marxist theory but is given full weight in plural society theory. It is for this reason, among others, that I prefer the more comprehensive perspectives of the latter theory, particularly for the analysis of domestic genocides, in which the victims are national, ethnic, racial, or religious groups within a society and the murderers are members of other groups in the same society. Because the domestic genocides are a phenomenon

10. 1979:3–29.
11. Ibid., 12.
12. Ibid., 5.
13. Ibid., 6.

of the plural society, their analysis calls for a theory of the plural society.

There is a close relationship between plural societies and domestic genocide, since plural societies contain the same types of groups as are victims of genocide.[14] Recapitulating some of the earlier argument on plural societies, I do not mean simply the presence of racial, ethnic, or religious groups in a society, but I refer to special conditions of accentuated cleavage. The extreme form is represented by South African apartheid, in which race differences are elaborated in a comprehensive system of discrimination affecting all aspects of life.[15]

Plural societies have the following characteristics to a greater or lesser extent.

1. There is a superimposition of differences, cultural differences and occupational differentiation, for example, being superimposed on race, ethnicity, and other factors. In most domestic genocides, the murderers and their victims are of different religion.
2. There is generally either de jure or de facto differential incorporation in the political structure, with inequality of participation by the different groups.[16] This inequality is the basis for further differentiation, which is ramified throughout the society.
3. Some degree of dissociation characterizes the relationship between the different groups. They tend to participate in different religious, communal, and other institutions. There is usually some physical separation. In extreme form, indigenous populations surviving the decimation of colonization are forced into the remote periphery of the society. In many cases, however, groups have lived together in some proximity for long periods of time and participate in the same economy, thus establishing a great variety of relationships that cut across the basic cleavages.
4. There is often a history of conflict, which is expressed in the crystallization of historic memories and in hostile and dehumanizing perceptions of other groups. Issues of conflict tend to coincide with the plural divisions.

14. Kuper, 1977:281f.
15. The basic theory of the plural society was introduced by Furnivall (1939, 1945, 1948). It was greatly refined and elaborated by M. G. Smith (1960, 1965, 1969).
16. See Smith, 1969:91f., 431–36.

5. The effect is to create a general status, a total identity, based on race, nationality, ethnicity, or religion.

Social processes in plural societies have many distinctive qualities that affect the various types of genocide in different ways. However, these processes share in common a tendency to destructive violence.[17]

Small surviving indigenous groups in peripheral areas are quite marginal to the society. They live in relative isolation, maintaining few relationships with the outside world, and they are readily treated as expendable in the interests of economic development. Their destruction has little resonance in the wider society.

Hostage groups engage in wider social relationships with members of the environing society. These relationships may be very extensive or limited mainly to economic transactions, but in neither case are the groups integrated into the society. They are often foreigners, though they may have been domiciled in the society for many generations, and they maintain, or are obliged to maintain, or are perceived as maintaining, a separate and distinctive identity based on cultural differences, particularly religious, and on participation by some members of the group in lucrative and coveted occupations. In some cases, they are indigenous populations incorporated by conquest. Whatever their background, they share a common vulnerability. Their destruction, whether by mass expulsion or by physical annihilation, is usually, perhaps invariably, preceded by campaigns of vilification, with many similar elements of imagery and stereotype. There is not the same indifference, or indeed ignorance, that attends the destruction of peripheral indigenous settlements. Because of the functions these hostage groups perform and because their removal provides joyful occasion for the appropriation of property, and for physical atrocity, their destruction is more widely felt in the environing society. I regard these hostage groups as permanently at risk, especially in times of social change or of threat to the ruling groups.

Colonization continues, as by the Indonesians in East Timor, but in general neocolonialism is the contemporary form of colonization; and it makes its own contribution to destructive group violence in plural societies. The superpowers, in particular, manipulate the plural divisions of other societies for the advancement of their own in-

17. Kuper and Smith eds., 1969:10–16.

terests in world and nuclear supremacy. Not only do they often provide the arms and the training, which encourage violent conflicts
between the plural sections of the society or which raise the conflicts
to higher levels of destructive violence, but they also place, or maintain in power, regimes that engage in political mass murder and genocidal massacre. At a different level, there are the activities of multinational corporations, which become at times the agents for the
destruction of the way of life, and indeed the survival, of indigenous
groups in peripheral areas.

The most destructive of the domestic genocides arise out of
struggles for power between ethnic or racial groups, or for self-
determination taking the form of change in the conditions of incorporation. In the present state of international relations, external
intervention is almost inevitable. But these struggles have a highly
destructive potential in their own right, regardless of such intervention.

A number of characteristics of the plural society contribute to
the tendency to polarization of group relations and to destructive
violence in situations of challenge to the dominant group. The central process in polarization is the increasing aggregation of a population into exclusive groups. This is facilitated by the general status
accorded race or ethnicity. At the subjective level, aggregation is associated with a heightened salience of sectional identity and with an
increasing perception in terms of antagonistic racial or ethnic interests. At the objective level, it is expressed in the growth of exclusive
organizations, in the further superimposition of lines of cleavage, and
in the rapid escalation of local and specific disturbances to the level
of general, nationwide intersectional conflict.

Extreme polarization may result from nonviolent conflicts, but
the process is likely to accelerate to much higher levels under the
stimulus of violence, particularly when acts of violence so intermesh
in reciprocal action as to generate cycles of polarization. It is as if
the whole process moves into high gear. In the course of this process,
the contending parties destroy the middle ground of interethnic or
interracial relations that might restrain the final violent confrontation.

The cycles of polarization are, of course, quite varied, related in
their detailed manifestations to such factors as the relative numbers
in the contending groups, their geographical concentration or disper-
sion, the scale of societal development, the extent of economic inter-

dependence, and other conditions of pluralism referred to above. For example, groups that are geographically concentrated in appreciable numbers may seek change in the conditions of incorporation by initially demanding equal participation in the society or a measure of regional autonomy. The state will almost certainly respond by outright rejection of the demands, or by evasion, or by the offer of quite derisory concessions, thereby encouraging leaders of the group to seek the more radical solution of secession. With the hardening of the conflict, the state engages in systematic repression. Relations increasingly polarize as violence and counterviolence escalate, and the state suspends civil rights in the offending area and imposes collective punishment. In the extreme case, the state resorts to admonitory massacres of noncombatants and to vast relocations of population.

The study of these cycles of polarization is important in devising strategies for the prevention of genocide. They yield the necessary indicators of impending violence and of escalating violence against racial, ethnic, or religious groups. My book *The Pity of It All* is devoted to the analysis of the polarization of race and ethnic relations in a number of plural societies.[18] *Pluralism in Africa*[19] and *Race, Class and Power*[20] also include relevant chapters. Helen Fein, in the paper she presented to the International Conference on the Holocaust and Genocide in Israel, provides a number of models of genocide, which analyze a range of cycles of polarization,[21] and there is valuable comparative material and analysis available in the work of Pierre van den Berghe,[22] Crawford Young,[23] and Jack Porter.[24] M. G. Smith, in addition to his major contributions to the theory of plural societies, is now working on a comprehensive study of the relationship between violence and different conditions of pluralism.

Many of the plural sections are, of course, minorities, and the effective protection of minorities would be a major contribution to the prevention of genocide. But this has proved to be a somewhat intractable problem in both the international and domestic arenas.

In an organization such as the United Nations, in which primary

18. 1977.
19. Kuper and Smith, 1969, chaps. 5, 9, 13, 14.
20. Kuper, 1974, part 2.
21. Fein, 1982.
22. See van den Berghe, in Kuper and Smith, 1969, chap. 3.
23. 1976.
24. 1982.

values in the relations between states are respect for state sovereignty, territorial integrity and unity, and domestic inviolability, there are serious obstacles to the protection of minorities. Self-determination, in the form of a movement for secession, directly challenges the territorial integrity and unity of the state. Even movements for greater autonomy, falling far short of secession, are seen as a threat to the unity of the state; and protection against discrimination involves a restructuring of power relations and a diminution in the prerogatives of ruling elites. Then, too, minority movements provide occasion for intervention. They may be used by other states to overthrow an unfriendly government, to further territorial claims, or to advance their competitive interests in other ways that pose a threat to world peace.

Since a great many member states are plural societies, recently independent and still seeking to integrate the diversity of their peoples, protection of minorities is charged with apprehension. But even well-established polities are not immune to the fear of disturbance by minority movements. Indeed, the evasion of the issue and the ambivalence about protection of minorities go back to the very earliest days of the United Nations, when it was under the domination of Western powers.[25] Bruegel comments that "after the Second World War the slogan was no longer 'protection of minorities' but 'protection from minorities.'"[26]

The Charter makes no specific provision for the protection of minorities, but it does proclaim the principles of equal rights and self-determination of peoples, and respect for human rights and fundamental freedoms for all without distinction as to race, sex, language, or religion. The principle of nondiscrimination is, of course, an essential element in the protection of minorities.

The Universal Declaration of Human Rights also fails to deal with the protection of minorities. A Russian proposal to include a provision relating to the rights of national minorities was rejected by the General Assembly. However, on the same day that the General Assembly adopted the Universal Declaration (10 December 1948), it passed a resolution on the "Fate of Minorities." This stated that the United Nations could not remain indifferent to their fate but that it was difficult to adopt a uniform solution to this complex and delicate question, which had special aspects in each state in which it arose.[27]

25. See Bruegel, 1971:413–42, and Humphrey, 1970:164–65.
26. Bruegel, 1971:413.
27. E/CN.4/Sub.2/384/Rev. 1, pp. 26–27.

Almost twenty years later, in December 1966, the International Covenant on Civil and Political Rights dealt with the question in the following terms: "Article 27. In those States in which ethnic, religious or linguistic minorities exist, persons belonging to such minorities shall not be denied the right, in community with the other members of their group, to enjoy their own culture, to profess and practice their own religion, or to use their own language." The principles embodied in this article became the basis of a major work, the *Study on the Rights of Persons Belonging to Ethnic, Religious and Linguistic Minorities*, carried out by Francesco Capotorti, as special rapporteur of the sub-commission, and published in 1979. In his introduction to the study, the rapporteur comments that article 27 was "the first internationally accepted rule for the protection of minorities."[28] It will be noted, however, that the rule applies to persons belonging to minorities, and not to the minorities themselves, and the rapporteur's own mandate was for the study of the rights of *persons belonging* to ethnic, religious and linguistic minorities, and not the rights of minorities. But in article 27 there is an implicit incorporation of the collective aspect in the reference to the enjoyment of the rights "in community with the other members of their group." Moreover, the rapporteur does deal, quite unavoidably, with many of the collective aspects of minority rights.

There have been other activities of the United Nations relevant to the protection of minorities. The mandate of the Commission on Human Rights includes the protection of minorities, and this is, of course, a major function of the sub-commission (which was established on the initiative of the Soviet Union).[29] Then, too, the United Nations has provided special protective measures in specific situations, and it has, at times, acted against gross violations of human rights affecting particular minorities. In addition, various conventions are relevant for the protection of minorities: the Genocide Convention of 1948, the ILO Convention of 1957 concerning indigenous and tribal populations, the UNESCO Convention of 1960 against Discrimination in Education, the U.N. Convention of 1965 on the Elimination of All Forms of Racial Discrimination, and the International Convention of 1973 on the Suppression and Punishment of the Crime of Apartheid.[30] It is only at the present time, however, after 35 years,

28. Ibid.
29. See Humphrey, 1970: 165, on the role of the cold war in the establishment of the sub-commission.
30. See the discussion of relevant U.N. action in the report by Capotorti,

that the United Nations is finally settling down to the task of framing a comprehensive declaration for the protection of minorities. Yugoslavia had submitted a draft declaration to the Commission on Human Rights, which dealt directly with the rights of minorities as collectivities, as well as with the individual rights of its members. And this is now being redrafted by a working group of the commission.[31] The redrafting proceeds quite tortuously, but one can reasonably hope that the General Assembly will approve a declaration on minority rights before the year 1990 and then proceed to the adoption of a convention. The Minority Rights Group, a nongovernmental organization with consultative status, has already submitted an excellent draft for a "Convention on the Protection of National or Ethnic Groups or Minorities."[32]

There are, of course, very real difficulties in the framing of a convention and in the establishment of procedures for implementation. The United Nations has not yet agreed upon a definition of minorities, and the process of defining minorities is laden with controversy. In his *Study on the Rights of Persons Belonging to Ethnic, Religious and Linguistic Minorities*, the special rapporteur proposed the following definition:

A group numerically inferior to the rest of the population of a State, in a nondominant position, whose members—being nationals of the State—possess ethnic, religious or linguistic characteristics differing from those of the rest of the population and show, if only implicitly, a sense of solidarity, directed towards preserving their culture, traditions, religion or language.[33]

This definition was drawn up solely with reference to the application of article 27 of the Covenant on Civil and Political Rights. From the point of view of protection against genocide, however, I favor a definition of minorities that would include numerical *majorities* (as, for example, Hutu in Burundi or Africans in South Africa). That is to say, I would place the emphasis on the nondominant (subordinate) position in the society. I would also include racial groups, national groups (an item of controversy in the framing of the declaration on the protection of minorities), and settled populations of aliens. Agreement on a definition should not raise any insuperable problems.

1979:26–41, and in the United Nations publication, *Protection of Minorities*, 1967.

    31. See E/CN.4/L. 1367/Rev. 1, E/CN.4/L. 1579, and E/CN.4/1982/WG. 5/1.

    32. E/CN.4/NGO/231. The draft convention will also be found in Fawcett, 1979, appendix C.

    33. Para. 568.

Much more difficult questions are presented by the great diversity of societal contexts and of ruling political philosophies. A distinction is sometimes drawn between societies of immigration and societies of colonization, with societies of immigration tending to favor policies of assimilation. The distinction is not all that valid, since the societies of immigration were often established by colonization and the annihilation of indigenous groups. In addition to differences in their origins, minority groups vary in type, in number and demography, in the past history of their relations with dominant groups, in the extent of their regional concentration or dispersal, and in the mode of their incorporation into the political, economic, and other social structures of the society. As for the societies themselves, they differ in scale, forms of economy, level of development, political structure and ideology, social structure and culture, and international relations.[34] Indeed, the variety is almost infinite in its detailed manifestations.

Political philosophies relevant to minorities range from the refusal to acknowledge the existence, or the salience, of minority divisions (as in some of the Latin American countries) to an extreme emphasis on these divisions as the basis of political and social organization (notably, for example, in South Africa). In the former case, that of assimilationist policies, the recognition of minorities may be viewed as endowing them with legal status and as, in fact, creating minority problems. On the contrary, however, it is forced assimilation—by the suppression of minority languages, for example—that may be expected to exacerbate group relations and ignite violent confrontation.

Where recognition is accorded minority groups, a great variety of constitutional approaches are available. Official recognition may be used to erect a structure of political domination, with systematic discrimination too in other institutions of the society (the South African apartheid policy). Or it may be the basis for the sharing of political power in consociational arrangements (with success in Switzerland and catastrophic consequences in Lebanon, appreciably influenced by the intrusion of many extraneous factors). Or minority members may have the same rights as other nationals in the public domain but are free to pursue their community interests in the private domain, with or without state support.

It is clear that in the context of this great diversity of societal

34. See my discussion in *Pluralism in Africa*, edited with M. G. Smith, 1969, chap. 14. See also the comments in Capotorti, 1979:45–50.

conditions and political philosophies, the United Nations will experience difficulty in devising effective measures for the protection of minorities. Member states will certainly seek formulations that promote the interests of their ruling elites. But the protection of minorities is an important element in the prevention of domestic genocide.

The successful framing of a convention for the protection of minorities and its ratification by many member states lie well in the future. The declarations, and the assumptions of treaty obligations, however, are at best only a preliminary step toward implementation. Meanwhile, minorities will continue to remain in their present state of vulnerability to destructive violence.

12

Prevention
A Program of Action

At the deeper levels of the structure of states and of their international relations, many of the conditions that might encourage domestic genocide could be eliminated, as for example by the abolition of inequality between groups and their full incorporation into the political and other institutions of the society. Or again, if socialism is indeed a more effective guarantee of human rights than other social systems, and if socialist states are less likely to engage in imperialist expansion—both highly doubtful propositions—then the goal should be a global conversion to socialism. Since totalitarian societies are probably more inclined to domestic genocide and political mass murder than democratic societies, they should be dismantled and replaced by democratic socialist states—not simply in nomenclature, as for example Democratic Kampuchea, but in substantive reality. The destructive intervention of outside powers in the domestic affairs of other societies could be eliminated by the establishment of a cooperative global system of international relations. And the genocides of international warfare and the threat of humanicide or omnicide by nuclear "deterrence" might be removed quite simply by the effective abolition of warfare.

These and other ideal prescriptions that appear in the literature are important in helping to shape international public opinion and its goals for long-term collective endeavor. But the deeper levels of the structure of states and of their international relations are not remotely accessible to nongovernmental organizations with modest means. Moreover, it would be extremely difficult to secure wide agreement at the level of what Jacques Maritain described as "speculative ideology," and to which I referred in my discussion of conflicts of norms and values.

In place of these ideal prescriptions, I am therefore setting out more immediate and realizable strategies and objectives, accessible to organizations with limited resources working both within, and outside of, the United Nations. They are strategies and goals at the level of "practical ideology and principles of action," designed to make or facilitate a contribution to the prevention of genocide; and they are closely related to current trends in the promotion and protection of human rights.

Some of the recent trends in standard setting and institution building within the United Nations have encouraging implications for the protection of minorities and for preventive action against genocide. Of course, the United Nations already has a plethora of standard-setting declarations, resolutions, and covenants for the regulation of human rights; and the continuous mounting of new resolutions, new declarations, new covenants is eloquent testimony to the failure of the international community to honor its commitments. Indeed, the ceaseless manufacture of normative documents without implementation may be a disservice. It deflects action away from implementation, encouraging abstract formulation as a substitute for practice; and formal adherence to ideal norms may engender a self-righteousness that serves as license for gross violation of human rights. Thus it is common practice for governments to respond to charges of massacre and other gross violations of human rights by reference to the provisions of their constitutions and laws; and representatives of governments in the United Nations seem to experience no qualms (indeed, to the contrary, they seem to experience a moral exaltation) in castigating the very sins in other countries that their governments freely practice in their own. But the movement in recent years from standard setting to concern for implementation, however halting and inconsistent, and the more active response of the commission and sub-commission to gross violations of human rights do offer some basis for the hope that the new declarations and undertakings will enable U.N. delegates and nongovernmental organizations to intervene on behalf of threatened groups with more effect than in the past. In the early stages of the genocidal process, there are likely to be many infringements of human rights (increasing repression, incitement, detention without trial, torture, murder, massacre) and various humanitarian issues, which would provide different opportunities for bringing pressure to bear on offending governments.

In chapter 8, I mentioned encouraging developments in the approach to political mass murder by the interweaving of normative regulation and protective action. As governments responded to international concern with many ingenious devices, the U.N. Commission on Human Rights and its sub-commission were able to relate the setting of standards and of procedures for implementation in a more effective and comprehensive strategy for action against mass murder. The combination of normative regulation and of working groups (or of other surveillance institutions) seems a particularly promising development.

The two groups that I view as continually at risk are indigenous groups inhabiting areas with exploitable resources, and hostage groups. Pressure on the survival of vulnerable indigenous groups in the interests of economic development will certainly continue. Under conditions of extreme poverty, with high death rates from starvation, malnutrition, and readily preventable disease, it is inevitable that primacy should be given to economic development. But these groups are also threatened in such rapidly developing and potentially rich countries as Brazil and for that matter, too, in economically developed societies. In this process many lives are lost, and many distinctive cultures destroyed, with consequent impoverishment of human society. The indigenous groups have little or no voice in the national affairs of the societies in which they live and are mostly dependent on the active concern of the United Nations and of nongovernmental organizations for their survival. However, they are now beginning to organize and to represent their own interests in international gatherings. They find a ready forum in the U.N. Working Group on Indigenous Populations, and the sub-commission, at its meetings in 1982, asked that a fund be established to enable their representatives to participate in the activities of the working group.[1]

At the same meetings, the sub-commission reviewed the U.N. *Study of the Problem of Discrimination Against Indigenous Popula-*

1. See Resolution 1982/31, dated 10 Sept. 1982.

tions, an extremely detailed report, which has dragged its weary length over many years.[2] It emphasized the need for special and urgent attention to "cases of physical destruction of indigenous communities (genocide) or destruction of indigenous cultures (ethnocide)"; and it defined as one of its primary tasks, the identification and development of standards concerning the rights of indigenous populations,[3] which would lay the basis for a declaration and convention. It continued its review and discussions in 1983. From these proceedings and annual reviews, there should emerge standards of accountability for governments and multinational corporations whose development projects threaten the rights and indeed the survival of indigenous populations; and these standards will certainly have wider applicability to other situations of gross violations of their human rights, as in the actions of the governments of Guatemala against the Mayan Indians and of Nicaragua against the Miskito Indians.

There are many other encouraging developments. The International Labour Organisation maintains contact with problems relating to the rights, protection, and development of indigenous populations, pursuant to a convention ratified by 27 countries. In 1979 the Nordic countries established an informal intergovernmental working group to promote the rights of the indigenous populations. In 1981 nongovernmental organizations held the important Conference on Indigenous Peoples and the Land, and in the same year there was a Conference of Specialists on Ethnocide and Ethnodevelopment in Latin America. These developments by no means ensure effective action for the protection of indigenous populations, but they do indicate an increasing international awareness and concern, and they lay down an infrastructure for implementation of international obligations. The survival of many indigenous groups, however, continues to be under serious threat.

Developments for the protection of hostage groups are far less encouraging, more particularly since there is an increasing threat of mass expulsion as a result of rapid population growth in the host countries and the contemporary vigorous assertion of nationalism. If the recent recommendations in Prince Sadruddin Aga Khan's report *Human Rights and Massive Exoduses* are implemented, they would

2. See E/CN.4/Sub.2/476 and addenda, and E/CN.4/Sub.2/1982/2 and addenda. The final report was submitted in 1983 (E/CN.4/Sub.2/1983 and addenda).

3. Resolution 1982/31, cited above.

provide some protection mainly at the level of pragmatic action, against these mass expulsions.[4] The following key recommendations combine an early warning system with the establishment of a supranational agency.

(7) The introduction of an early-warning system based on impartial information gathering and data collection concerning potential mass exodus situations, leading to expeditious reporting to the Secretary-General of the United Nations and competent intergovernmental organs for the purpose of timely action, if required;

and

(8) The appointment of a Special Representative for Humanitarian Questions whose task, defined briefly in the preceding section, would basically be (a) to forewarn; (b) to monitor; (c) to depoliticize humanitarian situations; (d) to carry out those functions which humanitarian agencies cannot assume because of institutional/mandatory constraints; (e) to serve as an intermediary of goodwill between the concerned parties.

The special representative would be assisted by a corps of humanitarian observers.

I mention these recommendations in detail because they have a relevance extending beyond situations of genocidal threat arising from mass expulsion. Persecution of hostage groups by means other than expulsion is also likely to give rise to a refugee problem at an early stage, and the proposed monitoring system could thus provide timely warning of an imminent threat to survival. But, in addition, the recommendations offer a model for some forms of preventive action against genocide.

The proposed declaration on minorities and the adoption of a convention would set standards for protection against genocide of hostage groups, and of minority groups in general, but this is already provided in the Genocide Convention; and the experience of the United Nations and of the Anti-Slavery Society and other organizations is that the setting of standards, without effective measures for implementation, makes little or no contribution to the prevention of international crimes, though it may *ultimately* shape an international moral consciousness.

One of the consistent features in the campaigns in the United Nations for more effective implementation of human rights obligations has been the search for supranational institutions, or for depo-

4. 1981:i, ii (following p. 61).

liticized surveillance mechanisms, that would transcend the primacy of, and frustration by, state interests. The most promising proposal, theoretically, has been for the appointment of a high commissioner for human rights. In 1982, in a further episode in the tormented history of this proposal, the sub-commission succeeded in passing by a narrow majority a resolution formulating possible terms of reference for the mandate of a high commissioner. His proposed tenure of office would be five years. His duties would be to promote and protect the observance of human rights and fundamental freedoms; to initiate direct contacts with governments of a "prompt, confidential, and exclusively humanitarian" nature; and to pay "particular attention to urgent situations appearing to involve threats to life, . . ." When reports of mass and flagrant violations of human rights called for urgent action, he would be empowered, within the United Nations system, to sound what virtually amounts to an international alert.

At its session in 1983, the sub-commission pursued the matter further by framing, at the request of the commission, detailed recommendations for the functions and responsibilities of the high commissioner. These recommendations are decidedly modest, carefully preserving the "correct" relations with U.N. organs and member governments.[5] They are far from attaining the supranational watchdog role necessary for the most effective action against gross violations of human rights, but they are realistic, and the appointment of a high commissioner, even in these guarded terms, could make some contribution to the prevention of domestic genocides in general—not only the genocides against indigenous and hostage groups but also those arising in the course of colonization and neocolonialist intervention or in the struggles against discrimination and for self-determination.

At present, neocolonial interventions have become almost routine in international relations, and they resist restraining action by the United Nations. The main problem is that the principal offenders in this aggression are the superpowers. They might be more responsive to U.N. resolutions if the middle-range powers could agree on a coordinated strategy. In the case of Afghanistan, there has been a general condemnation of the neocolonialist intervention by the Rus-

5. The full terms of the resolutions will be found in Resolution 1982/27, dated 10 Sept. 1982, and Resolution 1983/14, dated 6 Sept. 1983. An encouraging feature of the 1983 resolution was the strong vote in its support. The secretary-general's review of the history of the proposal for the appointment of a high commissioner will be found in E/CN.4/Sub.2/1982/26.

sians, but there is no indication that the USSR intends to withdraw its army of occupation. In democratic societies, there is the possibility of control by democratic process (as in the Vietnam War, but only after an immense internal struggle within the United States and massive destruction in Vietnam, Cambodia, and Laos). But even a vigilant Congress, supported by nongovernmental human rights organizations, may not be able to control the interventions of the American government, under a president with a Khomeini-like vision of international relations, in which the USSR is cast in the role of Satan playing dominoes with the Central American states.

The old-style colonial conquests are now rare, and since they constitute a breach of the peace, the most effective sanctions within the United Nations would be available. Moreover, there is a sufficient consensus in the United Nations against wars of aggression and against colonialism to ensure the passing of resolutions for withdrawal of the invading forces and respect for the right to self-determination of the conquered people. But given the structure of the United Nations and of international relations in the context of the cold war, sanctions are rarely applied, and the colonized become a restive population falling under the domestic jurisdiction of the aggressor state. This seems the likely fate of the people of East Timor. It is also one that now threatens Palestinians in the delayed aftermath of the Israeli occupation of the West Bank and Gaza following the 1967 Six Day War.

As for the highly destructive conflicts between racial, ethnic, and religious groups in plural societies, I argued earlier that some of them might be regulated by recognition of the right to self-determination, and that it was entirely consistent with the many declarations in the Charter and in United Nations resolutions and conventions that this right should be generally available and not restricted to societies under colonial or other foreign domination.

Maximum resistance is to be expected from governments when the demand takes the form of secessionist self-determination. I recall a discussion at Geneva with the ambassador for Sri Lanka, who commented, with I think a note of horror in his voice, that the Tamil opposition party was seeking to secede. "No government," he added, "would agree to that." And I suppose this is generally true, but it is no reason for excluding the possibility of secession. However, criteria for legitimacy need to be established. Buchheit, in a major study of secession, makes some valuable suggestions for establishing legitimacy on the basis of a calculus between the internal merits of the case and its potentially disruptive consequences for the parent state, for other states, and for the general international order.[6]

Claims for self-determination in the form of a measure of autonomy or for more equality in rights and opportunities are certain to be more tractable. But in practice they tend to be resisted, with resultant polarization. A more flexible and responsive approach could be of considerable benefit to the society as a whole, without necessarily threatening the elites of the dominant group. In many cases, it would reduce divisive and potentially destructive conflicts, release energy for cooperative enterprise in developing the resources of the country, and eliminate some of the opportunities for outside intervention offered by internal discord.

There is a large body of research on possible forms of self-determination. Claire Palley has examined the range of policies available in different institutions of the society. Her discussion is particularly valuable for its detailed specification of legal constitutional arrangements designed to promote assimilation or to balance the sharing of common institutions with a measure of institutional "separateness."[7] The U.N. Cristescu report devotes some sections to a general discussion of forms of self-determination.[8] Then there are the broad political approaches of the "consociational school," associated with the names of Lijphart, Daalder, Nordlinger, and others, which also provide a basis for social engineering.[9]

My concrete suggestion, therefore, is to seek to establish a more tolerant and flexible approach to self-determination in its great variety of forms and to publicize the many contributions it could make to the reduction of destructive internal conflicts. This should be linked to a technical advisory service to assist the governments of member states to respond constructively to claims for self-determination or to other contentious issues arising out of the relations of racial, ethnic, and religious groups in plural societies.

The establishment of the standards and institutions outlined above constitutes policy for many delegations in the Western liberal camp. Indeed, these standards and institutions enjoy broader support within the United Nations and among the nongovernmental or-

6. 1978, Chap. 4.
7. 1978.
8. Paras. 304–28.
9. See, for example, Lijphart, 1977; Daalder, 1968; and Nordlinger, 1972.

ganizations with consultative status. They would greatly strengthen existing procedures for action against genocide.

As I commented earlier, the United Nations, notwithstanding the many obstacles to its functioning for the protection of human rights, still represents potentially the major channel for preventive action against genocide. And there have been marked improvements in its response to gross violations of human rights. But, even so, given the conflicts of ideologies and interests, which are deeply embedded in its structure and take precedence over the concern for human rights, including the right to life, there is a crucial role to be performed by outside agencies, both in activating the United Nations and in providing an independent base for action. This role has been performed in the past largely by the international nongovernmental organizations, and their involvement continues to be an essential requirement for any effective program of preventive action.

In recent years, there has been a great proliferation of human rights organizations, responding partly to the success of the United Nations in promoting standards and reacting also against its failure to implement those standards. Human Rights Internet recently identified almost 2,000 nongovernmental organizations actively concerned with some aspect of the promotion and protection of internationally recognized human rights.[10] Cassese comments that the entry of these bodies into international society has shattered its traditional structure, which rested on sovereign and independent states and which tended to legitimize the state's monopoly over its subject peoples. As a result, new protagonists had emerged from their earlier "confinement" to express new interests and new needs on the international plane.[11]

The proliferation of organizations has been associated with considerable diversification. Some organizations, such as the scientific and professional ones, are highly specialized in terms of their objectives or of their constituencies. Others have broad objectives and a grass-roots constituency. Many are transnational, maintaining contact with other bodies in the local areas of their branches, as well as internationally. And recently we have seen the establishment of national networks of associations. These provide a structural base for coordinated national campaigns and for effective liaison with orga-

10. Wiseberg and Scoble, 1982.
11. "Progressive Transnational Promotion of Human Rights," 1979:252.

nizations and networks in other countries. There are all the indications of the growth of a vigorous international human rights association parallel to that of the United Nations.[12]

In the past, there were no human rights organizations specifically concerned with genocide, and the contribution of special interest groups, as for example the Working Group on Disappearances, is strong argument for the need to establish such an organization. Of course, the objectives of an organization may of necessity assign a central role to protection against genocide. Thus, the Minority Rights Group, having as its principal aims justice for minority or majority groups suffering discrimination and prevention of dangerous and destructive conflicts, is inevitably concerned with genocide, and many of its research reports have dealt with genocidal situations. Other organizations have a major interest in the prevention of genocide by reason of their constituents. This applies to organizations of indigenous groups or organizations representing the interests of these groups, since their major problems relate to genocide, ethnocide, and the expropriation of land and other necessary resources for survival. Religious groups have so often been the target, as hostage groups, of genocidal or other mass murder that they cannot but be interested in the prevention of genocide, though unfortunately this interest is often narrowly focused on threats to their own members. But the common concern of these and other groups needs to be coordinated by an activating secretariat or through an organization specifically devoted to international action against genocide. And in 1983 and 1984, a beginning was made in the establishment of human rights groups specifically concerned with the prevention of genocide.

Short of restructuring the member states of the United Nations, the most desirable preventive action against genocide is at the early stages, when there are indications of mounting repression against racial, ethnic, or religious groups, or of increasing polarization, or when there are other indications of a possible threat to the survival of these groups. This calls for the introduction of an early warning system based on the impartial gathering of information about potential genocidal situations along the lines proposed in the study of massive exoduses. It would need to be linked with procedures to forewarn, to monitor, and to initiate preliminary preventive action.

12. See Wiseberg and Scoble, "Recent Trends in the Expanding Universe of NGOs Dedicated to the Protection of Human Rights," 1981:229–60, and 1982. See also Forsythe and Wiseberg, 1979.

The secretary-general of the United Nations could readily make a major contribution to such an early warning system by arranging with U.N. agencies in different countries that they keep him informed of threatening developments affecting racial, ethnic, and religious groups. This reporting could provide a basis for initiating necessary action in the United Nations. A similar contribution could also be made through the embassies of member states.

Recently, Israel Charny and Shamai Davidson of Tel Aviv University opened an institute for the setting up of an early warning system. It will be based on comprehensive data collection concerning genocidal situations but extending also to other violations of human rights that fall short of genocide, and there are plans to develop and test a series of social indicators of genocidal threat. Apart from providing an important research facility, the organizers propose to alert international public opinion to gross violations of human rights by means of an information service.[13]

Realization of this project lies well in the future, but the setting up of an early warning system with related monitoring is immediately practicable. It would rest on the cooperation of nongovernmental organizations, those concerned with human rights and others with interests related to action against genocide. These nongovernmental organizations, and nongovernmental organizations in general, would provide a rich source of information from which early warning signals can be derived. In the past, the destruction of the way of life of indigenous groups was usually well advanced before information surfaced in the outside world. But this is now less likely, with the contemporary mobilization of indigenous groups and of organizations devoted to their interests. Where hostage groups are members of a religious denomination or sect with an international membership, there is almost certain to be advance knowledge of persecution and of increasing threat.

The genocides or mass murders in plural societies arising out of struggles for power between racial, ethnic, or religious groups, or out of movements against discrimination or for a measure of autonomy, are generally indicated by early warning signals, such as campaigns of vilification, assassinations, the imposition of states of siege or other states of exception, imprisonment without trial, torture, and the flight of refugees to surrounding territories. In the case studies I

13. See Charny and Rapaport, 1982, chap. 13.

have reported, there has generally been an awareness in the outside world of the imminent threat of massacre, or at the very least of the first massacres, and, with few exceptions, these genocides and mass murders have lasted long enough to provide opportunity for international intervention. And humanitarian relief has often been extended to the refugees.

Information from these nongovernmental sources would certainly be uneven in quality and coverage, and continents would be quite varied in the level of information available. Some organizations, such as Amnesty International, have excellent and extensive research facilities, and their reports are particularly relevant to many of the social indicators of destructive violence referred to above. The special investigations of the International Commission of Jurists, as a further example, have high reliability. Information from these sources could be supplemented by an academic support system. There are large numbers of scholars, especially social scientists, who have worked in different parts of the world and maintain a high level of knowledge of conditions in the areas of their specialization. I am sure that academic cooperation would be readily available for the purposes of preventive action against genocide.

These purposes would not call for comprehensive coverage or for an attempt to develop worldwide surveillance. Instead, the objective would be to select a few cases for concentrated and coordinated action. Some cases would be automatically excluded because they are already under intense surveillance.

Criteria for selection might be governed by the following considerations. In the first place, since it is important to gain experience in the planning of effective strategies against the different forms of genocide, a variety of cases of genocide should be chosen with this in mind. Second, cases might be selected also on the basis of the urgency of the threat, the most promising situation from the point of view of preventive action being one of long-known risk rather than of immediate threat.

When in February 1982 I expressed alarm to the Sri Lanka ambassador in Geneva at the threatening nature of the ethnic conflict between the majority Buddhist Sinhalese and the minority Tamils, largely Hindu, the situation seemed to be one of long-term risk. The background to the conflict was the British decision, in 1833, to bring together the two separate, ancient, and disparate communities of Sinhalese and Tamils into a single colonial unit, thereby establishing the plural society of Ceylon (Sri Lanka), in the administration of which it tended to favor the Tamils. On independence in 1948, the majority Sinhalese proceeded to rectify this past imbalance and to engage in reverse discrimination. Ethnic relations then began to polarize in a familiar pattern, with political affiliation tending to coincide with ethnic division. The government, again in a familiar pattern, responded inadequately to Tamil demands, thereby stimulating claims for self-determination in the form of greater regional autonomy, and indeed separation (secession).

The operations of a small "terrorist" ("liberation") movement among the Tamils added an inflammatory element to an already tense situation, which was punctuated by episodes of communal violence against the Tamils; and the conflict finally escalated in the latter part of July 1983 into a highly destructive conflagration after the murder of 13 soldiers by Tamil terrorists. In what appeared to be an organized massacre, Sinhalese groups murdered Tamils with great atrocity and burned and looted their businesses and homes.

The government acknowledged 380 deaths in the nine days following the murder of the soldiers, while the leader of the Tamil opposition party gave an estimate of about 2,000 murdered in the two months of ethnic unrest that culminated in the latter part of July. The estimated damage to property may be well over $100 million. And in addition, perhaps as many as 100,000 Tamils were displaced, creating a vast refugee problem and a movement of Tamils to areas of traditional Tamil settlement reminiscent of the relocation of religious groups in Northern Ireland after an extreme outburst of sectarian violence.

By the time the sub-commission met in August, the government had already restored "law and order." But some of the legal and administrative steps taken polarize relations still further. The government was reluctant to acknowledge the communal roots of the violence, initially alleging a foreign conspiracy of subversion by a series of communal riots and later tending to blame the victims for the atrocities inflicted upon them. Two measures were particularly disturbing. The first was an amendment to the constitution that bans any political party advocating secession of any part of the country. This was clearly directed against the main Tamil opposition party at a time when communal atrocities lent additional justification to demands for separation, as was the case in Nigeria after the massacres of Ibos in the North. The second was an extraordinary announcement that the state would take over all damaged property, including housing and industrial premises, as a temporary measure in the interests of rapid reconstruction.

The sub-commission was immediately "seized" of the issue, a great change from the old days of evasion and subterfuge. But there were many complex issues in the debate. The Sri Lanka government is held in high esteem by many members of the sub-commission, and it argued against U.N. involvement on the ground that it might disturb present delicate negotiations; it also circulated its own version of the events. Then, too, the Indian government had interceded, and discussions were proceeding. But there were also political currents observable in the alignment of members, though I could not altogether fathom the geopolitical considerations involved. In the end, a very mild resolution was passed calling for information from the Sri Lanka government and recommending that the commission examine the situation at the next meeting in the light of the information available.[14] There was, however, only a bare majority for the resolution (10 for, 8 against, and 4 abstaining). It is unfortunate that the United Nations did not take a firm stand at this stage. The Sinhalese army is now engaging in large-scale massacres of Tamils, and the conflict has escalated, seemingly beyond control.

Other current cases of immediate urgency are the Iranian persecution of the Bahá'ís and the Guatemalan massacres of Indians. In the case of the Bahá'ís, there has been the appreciable international concern shown by the European Council and the United Nations, with some modest pressure by the U.N. Human Rights Committee, which frustrated the expectations of Iran that its report would be received in a spirit of brotherhood with unqualified admiration for its Islamic justice.[15] But given the murderous self-righteousness of the Iranian government and its continuing need for scapegoats, the situation calls for a most urgent international alert.

The selection of cases would be approved by the participating organizations. These might be networks, or organizations with related interests. Or participation might be on an ad hoc basis for each

14. See resolution of the sub-commission, no. 1983/19, the statement submitted by the International Commission of Jurists, (1983), and its earlier report (1981).

15. See the report on the session of the committee (1982:393–403). On the role of the secretary-general in relation to Iran and general surveillance of its gross violations of human rights, see Resolution 1982/25 of the sub-commission, dated 8 Sept. 1982.

particular case, though I hope it would be possible to rely on a stable core of actively involved organizations.

The next stage would be the planning of the strategies to be followed in the campaigns. This planning of action within and outside the United Nations would be related to the type of genocidal threat, the qualities of the offending government (or other agent) and of the victims, and the general international context relevant to preventive action in the particular situation. I participated recently in some of the discussions of a lawyers' group planning legal action in cases of gross violations of human rights, and I was very impressed by the contribution that an imaginative and creative approach could make to effective planning.

If there is to be effective pressure within the United Nations it is essential to enlist the support of friendly governments who are carefully briefed in advance. This was a major factor in the successful campaign of the Bahá'ís. Without this support, submissions often fall into a curious void, or worse still, the decibels mount in the conference hall, reflecting the indifference of many delegations or their contemptuous hostility.

In earlier chapters of this book, especially in the section on implementation, I discussed different channels and procedures for action within the United Nations and in the regional and other related intergovernmental organizations. For convenience, and to present a different perspective, I quote the following summary from an excellent paper presented by Laurie Wiseberg and Harry Scoble to the Amnesty Conference on Extra-Legal Executions, in which they outline *An International Strategy for NGO's (Non-Governmental Organizations) Pertaining to Extra-Legal Executions*.

One may wish to target inter-governmental organizations directly, through the use of diverse petition procedures or written or oral interventions. This might involve filing a confidential 1503 with the Sub-Commission; a 1235 public intervention with the Sub-Commission or Human Rights Commission; providing information to the Working Group on Disappearances, the Working Group on Indigenous Peoples (just created in 1982), the Working Group on Slavery, the Special Rapporteur on Summary or Arbitrary Executions, the Human Rights Committee, or other U.N. bodies; filing petitions with, or sending information to, the Specialized Agencies of the United Nations including not only the International Labor Organization, the United Nations Educational, Scientific and Cultural Organization, but also the

World Bank and the International Monetary Fund; presenting information to regional bodies including the Inter-American Commission on Human Rights and the European Commission on Human Rights (and, when established, the African Commission) and also regional specialized bodies such as the Inter-American Development Bank.

With respect to inter-governmental organizations (IGO's), it is important to carefully select the arena in which, and the procedure through which, one may have the greatest impact. Thus, fifty letters to the World Bank—which is not used to being targeted by human rights NGO's—may provide more mileage than the same 50 letters to the U.N. Commission on Human Rights. A public debate under resolution 1235 may be more immediately productive than a 1503 confidential complaint. Feeding information to members of the Human Rights Committee, when a country report is up for consideration, may be of vital importance; but less important after the country review is completed. That is, human rights NGO's must begin to become sophisticated in their lobbying of—in their dissemination of information to—inter-governmental organizations. They must be sensitive to timing, to sympathetic and hostile committee members, to contacting sympathetic government representatives, to support that can be gained by committed international civil servants.

Mention should also be made of the possibility of enlisting the good offices of the U.N. secretary-general.[16]

Besides action within the intergovernmental organizations, there are two major tasks to be performed at this early warning stage. The first is to alert international public opinion. This calls for the processing of information and its dissemination by all available means. At the same time, steps would be taken to enlist wider support in preparation for an emergency campaign.

The second task is that of exerting some pressure on the offending government in the hope that it can be prevailed upon to exercise restraint while the genocidal process is still under control. Representations might be made directly to the responsible minister in the government, petitions presented to consulates, and campaigns initiated along the lines of the Amnesty International campaigns on behalf of prisoners of conscience. One hopes that friendly governments would be willing to intercede. At the very least, there should be sufficient international impact to make known to the offending government that it is under surveillance. If the threat against survival arises in part from the activities of multinational corporations, other means of persuasion and pressure can also be found.

If these representations in the early warning stage should fail

16. See discussions by Ramcharan (1982, 1983).

and the situation deteriorate, and if there are increasing episodes of murderous violence, then the time has clearly arrived to launch a full-scale international alert with all urgency. Violent conflict in plural societies can escalate with startling rapidity, as was evident in the case of Sri Lanka. Some seemingly minor event may set off disturbances in many different sectors and quickly engulf the entire society in violence. The first massacres, which appear to outside observers as a final settlement, may be only the prelude for genocide after a period of quiescence, as in Burundi. And once the massacres are under way, there is less inducement for the government to cry halt because the leaders are already criminally involved. Moreover, the genocidal process may have gained its own momentum and be quite resistant to governmental restraint.

All possible means would then be used in an attempt to halt the mass murders. They would include activating different organs of the United Nations and related organizations through national delegations, and where possible by direct representations, making use of the different channels for urgent action.[17] One would hope for active concern by the Security Council, which is so organized as to be able to function continuously and which commands powerful sanctions when it determines that there exists a threat to the peace or a breach of the peace. Under present conditions, however, as we have seen, the Security Council is almost certain to be paralyzed by the veto. When the Security Council has failed to discharge its primary responsibility for maintenance of the peace, the General Assembly may pass a "uniting for peace" resolution, but this too is limited to special circumstances and would also be quite an exceptional measure. Still, there are possibilities for securing resolutions in some of the organs of the United Nations, by means of which international pressure can be mounted against offending governments.

At the same time, approaches would be made to regional intergovernmental organizations and to national governments for their assistance. It may be possible, through supportive governments, to bring pressure to bear by the suspension or threatened suspension of aid agreements or by other limitations on relations with offending governments. As a last resort, there is the possibility of forceful humanitarian intervention.

In three of the cases discussed in this book, murderous regimes

17. See Ramcharan, 1981.

were overthrown by outside intervention—in Pakistan by India, in Uganda by Tanzania, and in Kampuchea by Vietnam. All three cases *could* have been defended as humanitarian intervention. The Indian government's policy fluctuated over the crisis period from March to December 1971, but at the May meetings of the Economic and Social Council, the Indian ambassador urged the United Nations to couple relief and rescue measures with a call to the government of Pakistan to restore human rights to its people and to abide by the declarations, resolutions, and conventions on human rights;[18] and the Indian government consistently emphasized, in its memoranda to the secretary-general and in the debates, the humanitarian aspects of the situation. In the Security Council debate on the Vietnamese occupation of Kampuchea, the representative of the Soviet Union raised, in defense of the action of its Vietnamese ally, the charge of genocide by the Khmer Rouge. Tanzania's intervention followed the invasion of its own territory by the Ugandan army, but it could have been defended as a humanitarian intervention.

I am in no position to comment on the current status of this controversial doctrine in international law.[19] I have discussed the matter with a number of experts, whose immediate reactions were of rejection on the ground of the historical experience that these interventions are invariably, or almost invariably, contaminated or driven by other motives. But given the many failures of the United Nations to act against regimes engaging in continuous massacres of their subjects, it seems to me that there is a great need for individual nations, or preferably groups of nations, to reassert under carefully defined conditions the right of humanitarian intervention against genocide and other gross, consistent, and murderous violations of human rights.

I would hope, then, that governments individually, but preferably in cooperation, would assert a right of humanitarian intervention when:

1. the United Nations fails to take action under its peacekeeping machinery (where the genocide raises a threat to peace), or by the exercise of other powers in cases of the more purely domestic genocides;

18. Franck and Rodley, 1972:145.
19. See, for example, International Commission of Jurists, *The Events in East Pakistan, 1971*, 1972, part III; Lillich, ed., 1973; and Moore, ed., 1974.

2. a regional intergovernmental organization, with interests in the area, similarly fails to act; and
3. the offending regime is deaf to appeals.

Representations could be made to governments for such intervention.

There remain the pressures that can be exerted directly by the participating nongovernmental organizations, which can draw on extensive experience in a great variety of campaigns, such as the anti-apartheid movement, or the campaign against the Vietnam War, or the present peace and antinuclear movements. These pressures would include an intensification of the publicity campaign, demonstrations, and the sanctions that can be applied through public support by means of economic boycotts, the refusal to handle goods to or from offending states, and selective exclusion from participation in international activities and events. Representations would also be made to governments or campaigns would be mounted to enlist their support in the application of these sanctions.

All these measures should make some contribution to the prevention of genocide or the restraint of genocidal massacres in the particular cases selected for action, and this is the main and immediate objective. But the further objective would be to establish, by experiment, planned and coordinated procedures for effective early preventive action, to demonstrate what could be achieved and to contribute by these means to the growth of an international movement against genocide. The campaign against "disappearances" in Argentina attracted international attention, contributing greatly to the present revulsion against the crime. It is an example of what one might hope to achieve by successful campaigns against genocide in carefully selected cases.

Thus far, the analysis and the suggestions for preventive action have been concerned very largely with the domestic genocides. There are only passing references to the genocides of international warfare. This is, in part, because I do not feel that I have any special contribution to make toward a program of action against international warfare. But it is also because the scale of the action called for greatly exceeds the potentialities of the modest organization outlined in these pages as an immediately practical contribution. The proliferation of contemporary international warfare, and the power of the entrenched interests of governmental, industrial, and military establishments in this warfare, are such that only a massive grass-roots international peace movement, with the participation of influential political leaders, can hold out any hope of imposing a measure of restraint. But I cannot conclude without brief comment on some of the implications of nuclear armaments, which now present an overwhelming threat of genocide, and indeed of omnicide, the extinction of our species.

Epilogue
The Nuclear Arms Race and Genocide

The nuclear age began, not with atoms for peace and the promise of infinite nuclear energy, but with the dropping of atomic bombs by the United States on the defenseless inhabitants of Hiroshima and Nagasaki. And this intimate relationship with genocide remains inherent in the very nature of nuclear armaments.

The annihilation of the civilian populations of these two Japanese cities is generally justified in U.S. circles by the argument that it was a necessary measure to bring the war to an early close, thereby saving lives, especially American lives. There are, however, suggestions in the literature that the Japanese were about to surrender, and there is a Russian view that the American destruction of Hiroshima and Nagasaki in August 1945, with the surrender of Japan already imminent, was primarily a demonstration of force designed to intimidate the USSR.[1] But whatever the motivations (and they were doubtless mixed), the wide acceptance by Americans of the justifica-

1. See Medvedev and Medvedev, 1982:159, and Hertsgaard, 1983:14. See also the discussion by Falk, 1982:191–96, especially his comment (p. 195) that "the military occasion was routine, certainly lacking in any compelling necessity. National survival was in no way at stake. Even the outcome of the war was patently clear, and possibly the atomic bomb achieved no more by way of war goals than saving a few weeks' time. Whatever the appraisal of the Hiroshima decision, there is common ground that it didn't take much for the United States back in 1945 to leap across the nuclear threshold." The issue is taken up also in an exchange of correspondence between Alsop, Joravsky, and Ward (1980, 1981).

tion of this horrendous war crime raises serious questions regarding their scale of values in international relations.

American world domination in the period after the Second World War was reinforced by its possession of the atomic bomb and its preeminence in the development of nuclear technology and armaments; and on a number of occasions, the United States threatened the use of these weapons.[2] The threat was rendered all the more credible by the precipitate employment of the atomic bomb against the totally vulnerable inhabitants of Hiroshima and Nagasaki, an event described by Pope Paul VI as a "butchery of untold magnitude."[3] The United States has the unhappy distinction of being the only country to have deployed the annihilating weapons of the nuclear age.

As the USSR came to challenge American nuclear supremacy by the amassing of a formidable nuclear arsenal and as the superpowers engaged in a frenetic nuclear arms race, they acquired the capacity to destroy each other, and indeed the whole world, many times over. At this stage, American strategic analysis emphasized deterrence, not superiority, the deterrent sanction being that of mutual assured destruction (MAD).[4] For both parties, nuclear warfare seemed unthinkable.

However, this may have been largely for popular consumption, that is, to provide some measure of reassurance that the annihilating power of nuclear weapons would not be unleashed. But probably, at more discrete levels, there has always been some aggressive planning for nuclear warfare. The continued piling up of armaments beyond the level of mutual assured destruction and the technological innovations in which the United States has taken the lead seem to be intelligible only in the context of a struggle for nuclear superiority, with an increasingly credible threat of the deployment of nuclear weapons.

In any event, in the last decade there has been a radical change in American strategic thinking. Desmond Ball, a strategic analyst, describes this as a movement from the earlier concerns over the conditions of viable mutual deterrence, the prevention of accidental nuclear war, and the promotion of nuclear nonproliferation to concerns relating to the period *following* the initiation of a strategic nuclear

2. Ellsberg, 1981:v, vi; Falk, 1982:179; Schell, 1982:210–13.
3. United States Catholic Bishops, 1983:13.
4. Falk, 1982:178.

exchange, with *controlled escalation* as "the central operational concept in current US strategic doctrine."[5] The American public has begun to hear of the *clean surgical strike, nuclear exchange,* and *limited nuclear warfare* and is told that the Department of Defense under President Reagan has put high priority on attaining the capacity, if necessary, to fight a *protracted nuclear war* and to *prevail.* There are widely publicized policy directives in which the U.S. secretary of defense has instructed the military services to prepare for fighting "limited" and "protracted" nuclear wars.[6] I have an impression that there is a slow infiltration of the idea of nuclear warfare and a conditioning of the American public to its acceptance.

At this time, the U.S. administration is advocating a huge expansion of its nuclear forces quite consistent with strategic interest in the waging of nuclear warfare, and in May 1983 it took a dramatic step toward the enhancement of its nuclear arsenal. This was congressional approval, however reluctant, of the president's plan to base 100 MX missiles in existing shelters under the plains of Wyoming and Nebraska, and the allocation of $625 million for engineering and testing.

The new weapon is a formidable intercontinental ballistic missile with a promise of high accuracy. Each missile would mount ten warheads and have sufficient weight to crush the deep-hardened silos in which the Russians house their own intercontinental ballistic missiles. But at the same time, the MX missiles themselves would be vulnerable to Soviet attack. Moreover, in times of crisis, the concentration of 1,000 warheads would offer a most tempting target and invite a preemptive first strike.

This highly threatening combination of menace and vulnerability seems almost certain to escalate the nuclear arms race, as the Russians further extend the development of new weapons and thereby render the threat of nuclear war more imminent. Yet, incredibly, the MX missile project was rationalized as necessary to achieve arms control in the president's declaration that, in the congressional debate on the MX missile, the future of arms reduction was at stake—"*balanced, verifiable arms reductions that can make the world a safer place for all the earth's people*"[7] (italics mine). And in a flight of Orwellian fantasy, the president described the new weapon as the

5. Ball, 1981:1.
6. See Union of Concerned Scientists, 1983; Draper, 1983; and Rothschild, 1983.
7. *New York Times*, 28 May 1983.

"Peacekeeper" missile. And now it seems that the Russians may have responded by hardening their silos to a level which would frustrate, or render less effective, the present MX strategy.

But this is only a further absurdity in the general intellectual and moral absurdity of the nuclear arms race. There are so many absurdities at so many different levels that it is difficult even to find the rational criteria for selecting the most salient among them. And indeed, as Richard Falk observes, "to adopt a tone of rationality is to gloss over the quintessentially absurd reality of contemplating the use of apocalyptic weaponry for the sake of the secular state based upon a rushed decision by poorly qualified politicians and generals."[8] I mention here only a few of the absurdities.

There is the absurdity of overkill in a continuing arms race, with the accumulation and perfection of more and more genocidal weapons, when the superpowers already have enough genocidal weapons to destroy each other, and indeed the whole world, many times over. Then there is the absurdity of seeking national security in the possession of annihilating weapons that are accessible to other powers, and the holding of the peoples of the United States, the USSR, and Europe as hostages in the struggle between the two superpowers for world hegemony.

At a different level, there is the absurdity of the vast waste of resources and ingenuity and creativity in the accumulation of annihilating weaponry when there is an overwhelming need for a new international economic order that would bring sustenance and economic development to the starving peoples of the world. To be sure, the public was reassured in the past that these weapons were designed only for deterrence because their use was unthinkable. But this reassurance merely serves to emphasize the intellectual absurdity and moral repugnance of the whole enterprise.

In thinking about this earlier reassurance of a purely deterrent function, I recalled the potlatch ceremonies of the Kwakiutl Indians, during which costly copper sheets were destroyed in a competitive struggle for prestige.[9] And I reflected that if the American and Russian leaders could engage in similar contests to determine world supremacy by the dismantling of the greatest number of warheads, many of the vested interests of ruling elites, government bureaucra-

8. Lifton and Falk, 1982:128.
9. See Codere, 1972:75ff.

cies, and military and industrial establishments in a "defense" (war) economy would be served without threatening the extinction of our species. This outrageously wasteful consumption of resources would still be overwhelmingly absurd, but at least it would be somewhat less morally repugnant.

Then there are the psychological absurdities analyzed by Robert Jay Lifton.[10] We purchase psychological security at the expense of escalating the danger of extermination. "We feel the pain of loss of security, credibility and stability; we embark on the literally impossible quest to regain these by stockpiling the very nuclear devices (along with accompanying secrets) responsible for their loss; and we are left with a still greater sense of vulnerability and insecurity, along with further decline in credibility and integrity." Faced with our inability to think about the unthinkable reality of a nuclear holocaust, we retreat into the absurdity of irrelevant images derived from past experience and find security in nuclear illusion. "Bomb-induced futurelessness becomes a psychological breeding ground for further nuclear illusion, which in turn perpetuates and expands current arrangements including bomb-induced futurelessness and so on."[11]

And now in the United States, we seem to be plunging into the extreme absurdity of preparations for nuclear warfare. We are introduced to advertising slogans and campaigns reminiscent of the marketing techniques for deodorants and washing machines. But the new slogans, interminably repeated, such as "the window of vulnerability" and "the missile gap," are designed to soften resistance against the allocation of more and more funds for the escalation of nuclear armaments. Benign phraseology camouflages the genocidal reality, quite reminiscent of Nazi circumlocutions to disguise the reality of the planning and execution of genocide. We hear of the "clean surgical strike" drawing on the prestige of medical surgery and suggesting that only military targets are threatened, with quite minor and acceptable levels for the collateral annihilation of civilians. We read of "nuclear exchanges," suggesting rules of the game, in which the contestants take turns to obliterate each other's weapons, as in the Atari video games. And we are encouraged to believe in the illusion of "nuclear defense," expressed at its most absurd in the following quotation from a deputy under secretary of state:

10. Lifton and Falk, 1982.
11. Ibid., particularly pp. 5, 25, and 80.

Dig a hole, cover it with a couple of doors and then throw three feet of dirt
on top. . . . It's the dirt that does it . . . If there are enough shovels to go
around, everybody's going to make it.[12]

And, finally, there is the ultimate illusion of a protracted nuclear war,
from which the contestants would emerge with regrettable but seemingly acceptable casualties of 20 million or 50 million or 100
million[13] and with ability to reconstruct their societies. This is the
illusion that nuclear warfare can be controlled, when there are enormous arsenals readily available on land and sea and air, when the
tempo of nuclear warfare would move at lightning speed, demanding
almost instantaneous decisions by leaders exposed to all the uncer-
tainties of revolutionary military strategies and working through
command structures, which are themselves vulnerable to enemy attack.[14]

Given the catastrophic threat of nuclear arsenals and the absurdities of nuclear warfare, the only rational level of discourse is how to
disengage from the nuclear arms race and how to move toward disarmament and the outlawing of nuclear weaponry. Of course, the
problem is more basic: the elimination of warfare as a means of re-
solving international disputes and a return to the fundamental prin-

12. Extracts from interview in Scheer, 1982, chap. 2, quoted on the dust cover of
the book.
13. Estimates vary widely. I quote here recent estimates by the Union of Concerned Scientists of the destruction which would be caused by the detonation of a
single one-megaton nuclear device.

Within a mile and a half, all living beings would be instantly destroyed by the
blast and the incredible heat. Within the next mile, about half the people would be
killed immediately, almost all the rest severely injured, and all the homes destroyed.
Within the next two miles, "only" five percent of the people would be killed but
nearly half would be injured. Over half of the buildings would be destroyed by the
resulting fire. Three miles further, few would be killed, but one-quarter would be injured.
All this would happen in the *first few minutes*. Then, the prolonged suffering
would begin. In any city, nearly one-third of the population would be injured, most
suffering from severe burns and exposure to massive doses of radiation. But all of the
downtown hospitals would have been destroyed and most of the doctors killed, so no
help would be available.
Those who continue to live would face a world turned upside down. Fallout
would produce radiation sickness and agonizing death for hundreds of miles down-
wind. People would be hideously affected by the massive doses of radiation.
And this describes only the effects of the detonation of a single, moderate-sized
bomb over one city.
14. See the discussion by Ball, 1981.

ciples of the U.N. Charter. However, until there is progress in this direction, we will have to live with nuclear arms, while resisting, by all means, any conditioning to the acceptance of their deployment. I fear that this conditioning has already gone far in American society, and presumably a similar process unfolds in the USSR. But I write now only of the American scene, since I am a witness to it.

Many sources of conditioning to nuclear warfare derive from quite ordinary routines in industry, government bureaucracies, and the armed forces. Some of the implications of their conditioning appear more clearly in the context of Nazi experience.

It would have been comforting to believe that the Nazi planning and execution of genocide were the deranged atrocities of psychopathic personalities. But this belief cannot readily be defended. Quite apart from the large-scale involvement of the German people in different aspects of the genocidal process, which lends little credibility to the view that only psychopaths planned and executed the genocides, there is the accumulated evidence in postwar psychological studies of normal personality development in some of the major genocidal murderers. This has encouraged two different types of explanation. One emphasizes the inherently destructive nature of man as, for example, in the theory of the "genocider" within each of us developed by Israel Charny; the other seeks an explanation or contributory factor in the ordinary everyday routine—"the banality of evil."

The following epigraph to one of the chapters in Charny's book *How Can We Commit the Unthinkable?* captures this banality while conveying a deep sense of shock at the routine efficiency of involvement in genocide.

The Nazis ran closed bids for the construction of the gas chambers:
1. A. Tops and Sons, Erfurt, manufacturers of heating equipment: "We acknowledge receipt of your order for five triple furnaces, including two electric elevators for raising the corpses and one emergency elevator. . . ."
2. Vidier Works, Berlin: "For putting the bodies into the furnace, we suggest simply a metal fork moving on cylinders. . . ."
3. C. H. Kori: "We guarantee the effectiveness of the cremation ovens, as well as their durability, the use of the best material and our faultless workmanship."[15]

15. 1978:185.

But what is the difference, from a purely business point of view, between tenders for the construction of a furnace to fire clay pots and
tenders for the cremation of the victims of genocide?

In these examples, the involvement, though facilitating the genocidal process, is not a direct involvement in mass murder, in contrast
to those cases in which German industrialists participated directly
in genocide—as in the extreme exploitation of the slave labor of the
genocidal victims, who were regarded as totally expendable. So too,
in the present context, a distinction can be drawn between involvement in a variety of subsidiary operations supportive of the missile
industry and involvement in the actual production of the nuclear
missiles.

Bureaucracies have their own insulating mechanisms against
human awareness. Henry Nash describes these in an article entitled
"The Bureaucratization of Genocide," in which he reviews his experience as an intelligence analyst in the Air Targets Division of the U.S.
Air Force during the 1950s and 1960s, "the hot years of the Cold
War."[16] His task was to identify Communist party headquarters in
various Soviet cities as targets for inclusion in the official catalogue
of strategic targets, the *Bombing Encyclopedia*. Fellow analysts in
other offices were engaged in identifying other types of strategic targets—petroleum depots, airfields, and industrial centers.

As he looks back on this experience about twenty years later,
Nash is haunted by a disturbing question. What was it about work
with Air Targets that made him insensitive to its homicidal implications? He and his colleagues never experienced guilt or self-criticism.
Their office behavior was no different from that of men and women
who might work for a bank or an insurance company. What enabled
them calmly to plan to incinerate vast numbers of unknown human
beings without any sense of moral revulsion?[17] And he finds the explanation, in part, in the crisis conditions of the cold war but also in
the bureaucratic organization of the tasks: the division of labor, the
fragmentation of knowledge, the strong technological and quantita-
tive orientation, the absorption in the hierarchical relationships of
the bureaucracy and one's own position within it, and the benign
terminology—"*Should we deliver ten or fifteen baby nukes on the Ir-
kutsk Party Headquarters?*"—the image of the lovable "baby bomb"
lending innocence to the inquiry. And then, too, there was the ob-

16. In Thompson and Smith, eds., 1981.
17. Ibid., 150.

scuring of the relationship between cause and effect, since decisions as to the deployment of the weapons would be taken at a different level.

For personnel whose task it is to fire the missiles or to drop the bombs, the relationship between cause and effect is surely inescapable. Of course, the operational techniques are such as to provide a substantial measure of insulation against a sensitive awareness of the impending annihilation. I assume that the men who are to launch the intercontinental ballistic missiles would be working in a highly sanitized, neon-lighted environment closed to the outside world—a totally dehumanized laboratory-type setting. And the bombers would be raining down desolation from Olympian heights. It is these impersonal methods of killing in modern warfare at ever-increasing distance that Lorenz emphasizes as removing the inhibitions against killing members of one's own species. Still, the moral dimension in man must introduce an incalculable and disturbing element in the planning of nuclear campaigns.

This appears very clearly in a startling comment by Richard Falk. He describes his participation in a tour of the Strategic Air Command headquarters of the Air Force, which was designed to impress the visitors "with the ingenious quality of the electronics then available to monitor events everywhere in the world enabling devastating American military responses, as necessary, in a matter of minutes to security challenges." He mentions the extreme preoccupation of most of the high-ranking officers he met "with the malicious designs and great capabilities of the Russian bear," and he records his impressions of the junior personnel.

They seemed to be virtual extensions of the computer terminals they were seated at, as close to robots as I have ever seen. Some years later I read some classified studies of "human reliability" that helped explain this impression. The personnel chosen to operate sensitive equipment associated with nuclear weapons were supposed to be selected, in part, on the basis of their *absence* of moral scruple. The express idea was that individuals with an active conscience might hesitate in a crisis to follow orders leading to nuclear war, that such soldiers would, in this decisive military sense, be unreliable.[18]

Still, there seems to be no effective way of totally neutralizing this moral dimension, save by fully mechanizing the operations and installing robots programmed to exclude all moral considerations. But since these remain a factor, they introduce sharp conflicts of duty

18. Lifton and Falk, 1982:130.

between patriotism and obedience to superior orders on the one hand, and the duty to refrain from crimes against humanity on the other.

At the level of affairs of state, the moral dimension becomes an issue in the scale of values. And here there are many discouraging elements in the past American record and in its present policies.

The United States is the only country to have used the new nuclear inventions for mass murder. When the president announced that the United States had dropped an atomic bomb on Hiroshima, he took pride in an achievement by which his country had harnessed, for war, "the basic power of the universe," and he added that "the force from which the sun draws its power had been loosed against those who brought war to the Far East."[19] But the bomb was loosed on defenseless men, women, and children, killing some 200,000, many of whom were incinerated instantly, while others were condemned to mutilation and a long and painful dying. Whatever the motives—experimentation, demonstration of power, termination of the war, revenge—it was a sorry distortion of values, which accorded primacy to American national interests over the right of other peoples to survival. As Richard Falk observes, "Hiroshima provides the touchstone of legitimacy for the entire subsequent edifice of nuclearism."[20]

Then, in the 1960s, there was the American intervention in Vietnam, with the deployment of highly destructive long-range weapons, massive bombardment, search and destroy missions, free fire zones, defoliation, indiscriminate reprisals against villagers, and the large-scale relocation of population. In the course of this intervention and in the pursuit of their enemies, American forces dropped half-a-million tons of bombs on neutral Cambodia. Adding to the loss of human lives, they destroyed Cambodia's economic infrastructure and agricultural productivity, thereby contributing to the horrors of the Pol Pot regime. And the intervention was justified as undertaken at the instance of the South Vietnamese government and for the defense of Vietnam and the free world against communist aggression. Again, concern for the state interests of the United States took precedence over the right to life of other peoples.

The same distortion of values has been a marked characteristic of the foreign policies of the United States in its competitive struggle

19. Schell, 1982:11.
20. Lifton and Falk, 1982:189.

with the USSR. America intervenes freely in the domestic conflicts of other states as it seeks to secure the ascendancy of parties favorable to its own interests—a policy, of course, also pursued vigorously by the Soviet Union. Procommunist regimes are threatened with destabilization and indeed with active American support for their enemies, while anticommunist regimes are almost automatically perceived as allies against the USSR and eligible for military and economic aid. Unfortunately, many of the anticommunist regimes are the world's most "repressive"—to use a euphemism for the practices of torture, disappearances, extralegal executions, and mass murder. During the Carter administration, the United States sought, however inconsistently, to reverse these policies by linking American aid to acceptable human rights practices; but the Reagan government has now aggressively reinstated the old policies in a most extreme form.

The justification again is the protection of freedom and democracy in America, and in the free world, against communist totalitarianism. There is certainly much to admire in the increasing respect for human rights within the United States and in its democratic institutions. But it is a narrow concept of freedom and democracy that confines itself to the domestic scene, with little concern for the record of the United States in international relations, and it is a strange scale of values that associates the defense of democracy and freedom at home with support for tyrannical and murderous governments abroad. And now there is the playing around with the idea of nuclear war in which civilian populations, including those of the United States, are held as hostages in the struggle for world supremacy.

The saving grace is that the fear of nuclear war has brought forth strong domestic reactions to the extremism of the Reagan administration. There is the recent Roman Catholic bishops' pastoral letter speaking out against any use of nuclear weapons and enlisting support from other religious groups. Scientists, physicians, and concerned members of the public in general campaign against the nuclear threat with increasing grass-roots support and organization. And there are strong movements within the U.S. Congress to introduce a "nuclear freeze" and to bring pressure to bear on the president to negotiate *in good faith* for the reduction of nuclear armaments. Perhaps these movements, the present opposition to President Reagan's "Star Wars" initiative, and measures in Congress to restrain military commitment in support of tyrannical governments abroad may introduce some measure of balance and morality in the U.S. scale of values in international relations, as was briefly achieved by the citizens' campaign for disengagement in Vietnam.

Since the United States is probably the major nuclear power, these internal reactions against the nuclear arms race and against nuclear aggression are particularly significant. But they are only a pale reflection of the peace and antinuclear movements in Europe, whose inhabitants have good reason to fear that nuclear exchanges or war between the superpowers will be waged on their territories. So, too, Third World states have good reason to fear the nuclear arms race, which not only threatens survival but immediately frustrates, in lavish and useless expenditure, their hopes for a new international economic order. This explains the substantial majorities in the United Nations General Assembly, in 1981 and 1982, for a wide range of resolutions that seek the reduction of military budgets, the establishment of a disarmament fund for development, the cessation of all test explosions of nuclear weapons, the creation of nuclear-weapon-free zones, the prohibition of new types of weapons of mass destruction, and, generally, nuclear disarmament and the prevention of nuclear catastrophe.[21]

The cold war between the United States and the Soviet Union, and the primacy they accord to their competitive relations, have been a major obstacle to United Nations action against genocide and mass murder. If, however, the movements for nuclear disarmament succeed in restraining their obsessive preoccupation with national self-interest and introduce a measure of cooperation in promoting the broad interests of the United Nations, it should become possible to take more effective action for the prevention of genocide and related atrocities. Conversely, the international campaigns against torture, disappearances, extralegal executions, mass murder, and genocide may contribute to restraint on nuclear aggression by promoting a consciousness of interdependence and a community of interest between nations.

21. See General Assembly Resolutions 36/92–100, 37/70–85, and 37/95–100J.

Convention on the Prevention and Punishment of the Crime of Genocide

The Contracting Parties

Having considered the declaration made by the General Assembly of the United Nations in its resolution 96 (1) dated 11 December 1946 that genocide is a crime under international law, contrary to the spirit and aims of the United Nations and condemned by the civilized world;

Recognizing that at all periods of history genocide has inflicted great losses on humanity; and

Being convinced that, in order to liberate mankind from such an odious scourge, international co-operation is required;

Hereby agree as hereinafter provided

ARTICLE I

The Contracting Parties confirm that genocide whether committed in time of peace or in time of war, is a crime under international law which they undertake to prevent and to punish.

ARTICLE II

In the present Convention, genocide means any of the following acts committed with intent to destroy, in whole or in part, a national, ethnical, racial or religious group, as such:

    (a) Killing members of the group;
    (b) Causing serious bodily or mental harm to members of the group;
    (c) Deliberately inflicting on the group conditions of life calculated to bring about its physical destruction in whole or in part;
    (d) Imposing measures intended to prevent births within the group;
    (e) Forcibly transferring children of the group to another group.

ARTICLE III

The following acts shall be punishable:

    (a) Genocide;
    (b) Conspiracy to commit genocide;
    (c) Direct and public incitement to commit genocide;
    (d) Attempt to commit genocide;
    (e) Complicity in genocide.

ARTICLE IV

Persons committing genocide or any of the other acts enumerated in article III shall be punished, whether they are constitutionally responsible rulers, public officials or private individuals.

ARTICLE V

The Contracting Parties undertake to enact, in accordance with their respective Constitutions, the necessary legislation to give effect to the provisions of the present Convention and, in particular, to provide effective penalties for persons guilty of genocide or any of the other acts enumerated in article III.

ARTICLE VI

Persons charged with genocide or any of the other acts enumerated in article III shall be tried by a competent tribunal of the State in the territory of which the act was committed, or by such international penal tribunal as may have jurisdiction with respect to those Contracting Parties which shall have accepted its jurisdiction.

ARTICLE VII

Genocide and other acts enumerated in article III shall not be considered as political crimes for the purpose of extradition.

The Contracting Parties pledge themselves in such cases to grant extradition in accordance with their laws and treaties in force.

ARTICLE VIII

Any Contracting Party may call upon the competent organs of the United Nations to take such action under the Charter of the United Nations as they consider appropriate for the prevention and suppression of acts of genocide or any of the other acts enumerated in article III.

ARTICLE IX

Disputes between the Contracting Parties relating to the interpretation, application or fulfilment of the present Convention, including those relating to the responsibility of a State for genocide or any of the other acts enumerated in article III, shall be submitted to the International Court of Justice at the request of any of the parties to the dispute.

ARTICLE X

The present Convention, of which the Chinese, English, French, Russian and Spanish texts are equally authentic, shall bear the date of 9 December 1948.

ARTICLE XI

The present Convention shall be open until 31 December 1949 for signature on behalf of any Member of the United Nations and of any non-member State to which an invitation to sign has been addressed by the General Assembly.

The present Convention shall be ratified, and the instruments of ratification shall be deposited with the Secretary-General of the United Nations.

After January 1950, the present Convention may be acceded to on behalf of any Member of the United Nations and of any non-member State which has received an invitation as aforesaid.

Instruments of accession shall be deposited with the Secretary-General of the United Nations.

ARTICLE XII

Any Contracting Party may at any time, by notification addressed to the Secretary-General of the United Nations, extend the application of the present Convention to all or any of the territory for the conduct of whose foreign relations that Contracting Party is responsible.

ARTICLE XIII

On the day when the first twenty instruments of ratification or accession have been deposited, the Secretary-General shall draw up a *procès-verbal* and transmit a copy of it to each Member of the United Nations and to each of the non-member States contemplated in article XI.

The present Convention shall come into force on the ninetieth day following the date of deposit of the twentieth instrument of ratification or accession.

Any ratification or accession effected subsequent to the latter date shall become effective on the ninetieth day following the deposit of the instrument of ratification or accession.

ARTICLE XIV

The present Convention shall remain in effect for a period of ten years as from the date of its coming into force.

It shall thereafter remain in force for successive periods of five years for such Contracting Parties as have not denounced it at least six months before the expiration of the current period.

Denunciation shall be effected by a written notification addressed to the Secretary-General of the United Nations.

ARTICLE XV

If, as a result of denunciations, the number of Parties to the present Convention should become less than sixteen, the Convention shall cease to be in force as from the date on which the last of these denunciations shall become effective.

ARTICLE XVI

A request for the revision of the present Convention may be made at any time by any Contracting Party by means of a notification in writing addressed to the Secretary-General.

The General Assembly shall decide upon the steps, if any, to be taken in respect of such request.

ARTICLE XVII

The Secretary-General of the United Nations shall notify all Members of the United Nations and the non-member States contemplated in article XI of the following:

(a) Signatures, ratifications and accessions received in accordance with article XI;
(b) Notifications received in accordance with article XII;
(c) The date upon which the present Convention comes into force in accordance with article XIII;
(d) Denunciations received in accordance with article XIV;
(e) The abrogation of the Convention in accordance with article XV;
(f) Notification received in accordance with article XVI.

ARTICLE XVIII

The original of the present Convention shall be deposited in the archives of the United Nations.

A certified copy of the Convention shall be transmitted to all Members of the United Nations and to the non-member States contemplated in article XI.

ARTICLE XIX

The present Convention shall be registered by the Secretary-General of the United Nations on the date of its coming into force.

APPENDIX 2
Judgment of the Permanent Peoples' Tribunal on the Genocide of the Armenians
Paris, 13–16 April 1984

Madjid BENCHIKH (Algeria), Professor of International Law at the University of Algiers

Georges CASALIS (France), Theologian, Professor emeritus at the Institut Protestant de Théologie, Paris

Harald EDELSTAM (Sweden), Former ambassador to Chile and Algeria

Richard FALK (United States), Professor of International Law at Princeton University

Ken FRY (Australia), Member of Parliament

Andrea GIARDINA (Italy), Professor of International Law at the University of Rome

Sean MAC BRIDE (Ireland), Jurist, President of the International Peace Bureau, Nobel and Lenin Laureate, and [recipient of] American Medal for Justice

Leo MATARASSO (France), Lawyer, Paris

Adolfo PEREZ ESQUIVEL (Argentina), Nobel Peace Laureate, General Coordinator of the "Servicio Paz y Justicia en America Latina"

James PETRAS (United States), Professor of Sociology at the State University of New York

François RIGAUX (Belgium), Professor at the Faculté de Droit Université Catholique, Louvain

Ajit ROY (India), Economist and Journalist

George WALD (United States), Professor emeritus of Biology, Harvard University, Nobel Laureate in Physiology or Medicine, 1967.

THE PERMANENT PEOPLES' TRIBUNAL

was called upon by the following organizations to devote a session to the case of the genocide of the Armenians:

—Groupement pour les Droits des Minorités (Paris, France)
—Cultural Survival (Cambridge, Mass., U.S.A.)
—Gesellschaft für Bedrohte Volker (Göttingen, West Germany)

which ask that the following questions be answered:

1. Is it established that the Armenian people was the victim of deportations, massacres, etc. in the Ottoman Empire during World War I?
2. Do these facts constitute a "genocide" in the sense of the International Convention on the Prevention and Punishment of the Crime of Genocide (1948) and, consequently, do they fall under the 1968 Convention on the Non-Applicability of Statutory Limitations to War Crimes and Crimes against Humanity?
3. Which are the consequences of this both for the international community and for the concerned parties?

The President of the Tribunal declared this request to be admissible in accordance with Article 11 of the statutes, and drew it to the attention of the Turkish government in application of the provisions of Articles 14 and 15. The Turkish government was invited to send representatives or written documents to make its position known.

Since the Turkish government did not reply to this invitation, the Tribunal decided to insert into the record the two documents cited below, which contain the arguments of the Turkish party in support of its denial of the genocide of the Armenians.

The Tribunal held public hearings on 13 and 14 April 1984, at the Sorbonne in Paris, and the jury considered the matter on 15 April 1984.

At the conclusion of this discussion, the Tribunal handed down the following sentence:

Considering the Universal Declaration of Human Rights of 10 December 1948,

Considering the Convention on the Prevention and Punishment of the Crime of Genocide, of 9 December 1948,

Considering the Nuremberg principles formulated by the International Law Commission and adopted by the United Nations General Assembly, in 1951,

Considering the Convention on the Non-Applicability of Statutory Limitations to War Crimes and Crimes against Humanity, of 26 November 1968,

Considering the Universal Declaration of the Rights of Peoples (Algiers, 4 July 1976),

Considering the Statutes of the Permanent Peoples' Tribunal (Bologna, 24 June 1979),

Having heard reports from:

—Richard G. HOVANNISIAN, Professor at the University of California at Los Angeles (U.S.A.), on the Armenian question from 1878 to 1923;

—Gerard J. LIBARIDIAN, historian, Director of the Institute for contemporary Armenian Research and Documentation (Cambridge, Mass., U.S.A.), on the intent to commit genocide and the ideology of the "Young Turk" movement;

—Christopher WALKER, historian and author, on British sources concerning the Armenian genocide;

—Tessa HOFFMANN, Freie Universität, West Berlin, on the Austrian and German sources concerning the Armenian genocide;

—Yves TERNON, historian and author, on the Armenian genocide in the Ottoman Empire in 1915–1916;

—Joe VERHOEVEN, Professor at the Catholic University in Louvain, on the Armenian people and international law;

—Dickran KOUYMJIAN, Professor at California State University (Fresno), on the destruction of Armenian historical monuments;

Having heard testimony from:

—Mr. INDJIRABIAN (France)
—Mrs. Haigoui BOYAJIAN (United States)
—Mr. GUZELIAN (France)
—Mr. NAHABEDIAN (United States)

survivors to the massacres;

Having heard:

—a report sent in by and read for Professor Leo KUPER of the University of California at Los Angeles, on the concept of genocide as it applies to the massacre of the Armenians;

—a memorandum written by and read for Professor Theo Van BOVEN, former Director of the U.N. Human Rights Division, on the deletion of the reference to the massacre of the Armenians when the issue was under study by the United Nations Human Rights Commission:

Having taken note of:

—the many documents presented by the rapporteurs in support of their reports, including the documents coming from British and, in particular, from German sources;
—the important and abundant body of documentation from American sources;
—the documentation on the Unionists' trial in 1919 and the trial of Soghomon TEHLIRIAN held in Charlottenburg, Berlin, in 1921;
—the document entitled "The Armenian Problem: Nine Questions, Nine Answers" (Foreign Policy Institute, Ankara), stating the viewpoint of the current Turkish government;
—the testimony given by Professor ATAOU of the University of Ankara to the Criminal Court in Paris in January 1984, which repeats the arguments of the Turkish government.

PREAMBLE

The most fundamental of all assaults on the right of peoples is the crime of genocide. Nothing is graver in a criminal sense than a deliberate state policy of systematic extermination of a people based on their particular ethnic identity. This centrality of genocide to the works of the Permanent Peoples' Tribunal is embodied in its basic framework of law set forth in the Universal Declaration of the Rights of Peoples (Algiers, 4 July 1976).

Article 1 of the Algiers Declaration asserts: "Every people has the right to existence." Article 2: "Every people has the right to respect of its national and cultural identity." Article 3: "Every people has the right to retain peaceful possession of its territory and to return to it if it is expelled."

And finally, Article 4 confronts directly the reality of genocide: "None shall be subjected, because of his national or cultural identity, to massacre, torture, persecution, deportation, expulsion or living conditions such as may compromise the identity or integrity of the people to which he belongs."

Yet, it may still be asked, why so many years after the alleged genocide, should the Tribunal devote its energies to an inquiry into the allegations of the Armenian people. After all, the basic grievance of massacre and extermination is fixed in time sixty-nine years ago in 1915. The Tribunal is convinced that its duties include the validation of historic grievances if these have never been properly brought before the bar of justice and acknowledged in an appropriate form by the government involved.

In this instance, the basis for an examination and evaluation of the Armenian allegations is especially compelling. Every government of the Turkish state since 1915 has refused to come to grips with the accusation of responsibility for the genocidal events.

In recent international forums and academic meetings, the Turkish Government has made a concerted effort to block inquiry or acknowledgement of Armenian genocide.

Furthermore, the current Turkish Government has not taken cognizance of these most serious charges of responsibility for exterminating the Armenian people. On the contrary, additional charges implicate the present Turkish Government in continuing these exterminist policies.

Particularly relevant in this regard are the charges of deliberate destruction, desecration and neglect of Armenian cultural monuments and religious buildings. The Tribunal adopts the view that charge of the crime of genocide remains a present reality to be examined and if established, to be appropriately and openly acknowledged by leaders of the responsible state. The victims of a crime of genocide are entitled to legal relief even after this great lapse of time although this relief must necessarily reflect present circumstances.

Here, also, the attitudes of the Armenian survivors and their descendants are also relevant. Any people rightfully insist and seek a formal recognition by legal authorities of crimes and injustices found to have been committed at their expense. The more extreme the injustice and the longer it is covered up, the more profound is this longing for recognition. The Tribunal notes with regret that the frustration arising from this denial of acknowledgement has seemingly contributed to the recourse to terroristic acts against Turkish diplomats and others. The hope of the Tribunal is to facilitate a constructive process of coming to terms with the Armenian reality which may lead to a resolution or moderation of the conflict that may arise from it.

Genocide is the worst conceivable crime of state. Often, the state responsible is protected from accountability by other states and by the international framework of organizations, including the United Nations, composed exclusively of states. One striking feature of the Armenian experience is the responsibility of other states who, for reasons of geopolitics, join with the Turkish government in efforts to prevent even at this late date a thorough inquiry and award of legal relief.

The Permanent Peoples' Tribunal was brought into existence partly to overcome the moral and political failures of states as instruments of justice. The Tribunal has inquired into the Armenian grievances precisely because of the long silence of the organized international society and, especially, of the complicity of leading Western states (with the recent exception of France) who have various economic, political and military ties with the Turkish state.

The Tribunal also acts because it is deeply concerned with the prevalence of genocide and genocidal attitudes in our world. As members of the Tribunal we believe that the uncovering and objective documentation of allegations of genocide contributes to the process of acknowledgement. To uncover and expose the genocidal reality makes it somewhat harder for those with motives of cover up to maintain their position. By validating the grievances of the victims, the Tribunal contributes to the dignity of their suffering and lends support to their continuing struggle. Indeed, acknowledging genocide is itself a fundamental means of struggling against genocide. The acknowledgement is itself an affirmation of the right of a people under international law to a safeguarded existence.

FOR THESE REASONS
in answer to the questions which were posed, the Tribunal hereby states that:

  —the Armenian populations did and do constitute a people whose fundamental rights, both individual and collective, should have been and should be respected in accordance with international law;
  —the extermination of the Armenian populations through deportation and massacre constitutes a crime of genocide, not subject to statutory limitations within the Convention of 9 December 1948 on the Prevention and Punishment of the Crime of Genocide. With respect to the condemnation of this crime, the aforesaid Convention is declaratory of existing law in that

it takes note of rules which were already in force at the time of the incriminated acts;

—the Young Turk government is guilty of this genocide, with regard to the acts perpetrated between 1915 and 1917;

—the Armenian genocide is also an "international crime" for which the Turkish state must assume responsibility, without using the pretext of any discontinuity in the existence of the state to shun that responsibility;

—this responsibility mainly implies the obligation to recognize officially the reality of this genocide and the consequent damages suffered by the Armenian people;

—the United Nations Organization and each of its members have the right to demand this recognition and to assist the Armenian people to that end.

Bibliography

Alexander, Yonah, and Robert A. Friedlander, eds. *Self-Determination: National, Regional, and Global Dimensions*. Boulder, Colo.: Westview Press, 1980.

Alsop, Joseph, David Joravsky, and Geoffrey Ward. "Was the Hiroshima Bomb Necessary? An Exchange." *New York Review of Books*, 23 Oct. 1980, pp. 37–42, and 19 Feb. 1981, pp. 44–45.

Alston, Philip. "International Trade as an Instrument of Positive Human Rights Policy." *Human Rights Quarterly*, 4 (Spring 1982), 155–183.

Amnesty International. *The Human Rights Situation in Uganda*. London: Amnesty International, 1977.

———. "What Happened in Indonesia? An Exchange." *New York Review of Books*, 9 Feb. 1978, p. 44.

———. *Guatemala: A Government Program of Political Murder*. London: Amnesty International, 1981.

———. *Extra-Legal Executions in Uganda*. Amnesty International Conference on Extra-Legal Executions, 30 Apr.–2 May 1982. Repr. in *Political Killings by Governments*. London: Amnesty International, 1983, pp. 44–49.

———. *Mass Political Killings in Indonesia (1965–1966) and Kampuchea (1975–1979)*. Amnesty International Conference on Extra-Legal Executions, 30 Apr.–2 May 1982. Repr. in *Political Killings by Governments*. London: Amnesty International, 1983, pp. 34–43.

———. *A Study of Extra-Legal Executions in Argentina, 1976–1981*.

Amnesty International Conference on Extra-Legal Executions, 30 Apr.–2 May 1982. Repr. in *Political Killings by Governments*. London: Amnesty International, 1983, pp. 50–60.

———. *Report 1982*. London: Amnesty International, 1982.

———. *Political Killings by Governments*. London: Amnesty International, 1983.

Anderson, Benedict R., and Ruth T. McVey. *A Preliminary Analysis of the October 1, 1965 Coup in Indonesia*. Ithaca: Southeast Asia Program, Cornell University, 1971.

Anthropological Resource Center. *ARC Newsletter*. Temple Place, Boston.

Anti-Slavery Society for the Protection of Human Rights. *Annual Reports*. 1947–79.

———. *The Anti-Slavery Reporter and Aborigines' Friend*. London: Anti-Slavery Society, 1947–76.

Arendt, Hannah. *Eichmann in Jerusalem*. New York: Viking Press, 1969.

Arens, Richard. "Death Camps in Paraguay." *American Indian Journal*, 4 (July 1978). In Porter, *Genocide and Human Rights*, 1982, pp. 218–237.

Arens, Richard, ed. *Genocide in Paraguay*. Philadelphia: Temple University Press, 1976.

Arlen, Michael J. *Passage to Ararat*. New York: Farrar, Straus, & Giroux, 1976.

Artucio, Alejandro. *The Trial of Macias in Equatorial Guinea: The Story of a Dictatorship*. London: International Commission of Jurists and International University Exchange Fund, 1979.

Bahá'í International Community. *Submissions to the United Nations Sub-Commission on Prevention of Discrimination and Protection of Minorities*, under agenda item 6, 28 Aug. 1981, and under item 7, Aug. 1982.

———. *Submissions to the 38th Session of the United Nations Commission on Human Rights*, under agenda 20, and under agenda item 12, 9 Mar. 1982.

———. *The Bahá'í's in Iran*. New York: Bahá'í International Community, June 1982.

———. *Bahá'í News* (July 1982), pp. 2–10.

Ball, Desmond. *Can Nuclear War Be Controlled?* Adelphi Paper 169. London: International Institute for Strategic Studies, 1981.

Barron, John, and Anthony Paul. *Peace with Honour*. London: Hodder & Stoughton, 1977.

Bassiouni, Cherif M. "International Law and the Holocaust." *California Western International Law Journal*, 9 (Spring 1979), 202–305.

Bauer, Jehuda. *A History of the Holocaust*. New York: Franklin Watts, 1982.

Beamish, Tufton, and Guy Hadley. *The Kremlin's Dilemma: The Struggle for Human Rights in Eastern Europe*. London: Collins & Harvill Press, 1979.

Bedau, Hugo Adam. "Genocide in Vietnam?" In Held, Morgenbesser, and Nagel, *Philosophy, Morality and International Affairs*, 1974, pp. 5–46.

Bedjaoui, Mohammed. *Towards a New International Economic Order*. UNESCO, New York and London: Holmes & Meier, 1979.

Bell, Wendell, and Walter E. Freeman, eds. *Ethnicity and Nation-Building*. London: Sage Publications, 1974.

Beres, Louis René. "Reason and Realpolitik: International Law and the Prevention of Genocide." Paper delivered at the International Conference on the Holocaust and Genocide, Tel Aviv, June 1982.

Bergesen, Helge Ole. "Human Rights: The Property of the Nation State or a Concern for the International Community? A Study of the Soviet Positions Concerning UN Protection of Civil and Political Rights since 1975." *Cooperation and Conflict*, 14, no. 4. (1979), 239–254.

Berlin, Isaiah. *Russian Thinkers*. London: Hogarth Press, 1978.

Berman, Maureen R. "Grappling with Unsolvable Problems: For over Two Decades Louis Henkin Has Been Seeking the Elusive Route to Worldwide Recognition of Human Rights." *Columbia* (Winter 1979), 53–55.

Bibo, Istvan. *The Paralysis of International Institutions and the Remedies: A Study of Self-Determination, Concord among the Major Powers, and Political Arbitration*. Harwich, Brighton: Harvester Press, 1976.

Birnbaum, K. E. "Human Rights and East-West Relations." *Foreign Affairs*, 55 (1977), 783–799.

Boasson, Charles. "Self-Determination and Violence." In Marion Mushkat, ed., *Violence and Peace-Building in the Middle East*. Munich: K. G. Saur, 1981, pp. 63–71.

Bodley, John H. *Victims of Progress*. Menlo Park, Calif.: Cummings, 1975.

Bokor, Hanna. "Human Rights and International Law." In Halász, *Socialist Concept of Human Rights*, 1966, pp. 267–309.

Bos, Maarten, ed. *The Present State of International Law*. Deventer, The Netherlands: Kluwer, 1973.

Boulier, Jean Abbé. *The Law above the Rule of Law: A Criticism of an Enterprise of the Cold War*. Brussels: International Association of Democratic Lawyers, 1958.

Brandt, Willy, et al. *North-South: A Programme for Survival*. Report of the Independent Commission on International Development Issues. London: Pan Books, 1980.

Bruegel, J. W. "A Neglected Field: Protection of Minorities." *Revue des droits de l'homme*, 4, nos. 2–3 (1971), 413–442.

Bryce, Viscount J., and Arnold Toynbee. *The Treatment of Armenians in the Ottoman Empire*. London: His Majesty's Stationery Office, 1916.

Buchheit, Lee C. *Secession: The Legitimacy of Self-Determination*. New Haven and London: Yale University Press, 1978.

Budiardjo, Carmel. "The Abuse of Human Rights in Indonesia." In Foundation for the Study of Plural Societies, *Case Studies on Human Rights and Fundamental Freedoms: A World Survey*, vol. 3, 1975–76, pp. 209–241.

———. "Genocide: The Case of East Timor." Paper presented at a conference on genocide in London, Mar. 1982.

Buergenthal, Thomas, Robert Norris, and Dinah Shelton. *Protecting Human Rights in the Americas*. Arlington, Va.: Engel, 1982.

Bukovsky, Vladimir. *To Build a Castle: My Life as a Dissenter*. London: André Deutsch, 1978.

Bundy, McGeorge. "The Bishops and the Bomb." *New York Review of Books*, 16 June 1983, pp. 3–8.

Capotorti, Francesco. *Study of the Rights of Persons Belonging to Ethnic, Religious and Linguistic Minorities*. Report Submitted to the United Nations Sub-Commission on Prevention of Discrimination and Protection of Minorities. E/CN.4/Sub. 2/384 and Add. 1–7, 20–30 June 1977. (Sales No. E.78. XIV.I) New York: United Nations, 1979.

Carr, Edward Hallett. *The Bolshevik Revolution, 1917–1923*. Vol. 1. London: Macmillan 1950.

Carrynnyk, Marco. "The Famine the 'Times' Couldn't Find." *Commentary*, 76 (November 1983), 32–40.

Carzou, Jean-Marie. *Un Génocide exemplaire: Arménie 1915*. Paris: Flammarion, 1975.

Cassese, Antonio. "Foreign Economic Assistance and Human Rights: Two Different Approaches." *Human Rights Review*, 4, no. 1 (1979), 41–44.

———. "Progressive Transnational Promotion of Human Rights." In Ramcharan, *Human Rights: Thirty Years after the Universal Declaration*, 1979, pp. 249–262.

Cassese, Antonio, ed. *U.N. Law/Fundamental Rights: Two Topics in International Law*. Alphen aan den Ryn: Sijthoff and Noordhoff, 1979.

Chaliand, Gerard, and Yves Ternon. *Génocide des Arméniens*. Brussels: Complex, 1980.

Chalidze, Valery. *To Defend These Rights: Human Rights and the Soviet Union*. London: Collins & Harvill, 1975.

Chamberlain, Mike. "The People of East Timor." In Porter, ed., *Genocide and Human Rights: A Global Anthology*, 1982, pp. 238–243.

Charny, Israel. *How Can We Commit the Unthinkable? Genocide: The Human Cancer*. In collaboration with Chanan Rapaport. Boulder, Colo.: Westview Press, 1982.

Charny, Israel W., ed. *Strategies against Violence: Design for Nonviolent Change*. Boulder, Colo.: Westview Press, 1978.

Chaudhuri, Kalyan. *Genocide in Bangladesh*. Bombay: Orient Longman, 1972.

Chomsky, Noam. Statement re East Timor Delivered to the Fourth Committee of the United Nations General Assembly. A/C.4/33/7/ Add. 3. Nov. 1978.

Chomsky, Noam, and Edward S. Herman. *After the Cataclysm: Postwar Indochina and the Reconstruction of Imperial Ideology*. Nottingham: Spokesman, 1979.

———. *The Political Economy of Human Rights*. Boston: South End Press, 1979.

Clark, Roger S. "Does the Genocide Convention Go Far Enough? Some Thoughts on the Nature of Criminal Genocide in the Context of Indonesia's Invasion of East Timor." *Ohio Northern University Law Review*, 8 (Apr. 1981), 321–328.

Claude, Richard Pierre. "The Case of Joelito Filártiga and the Clinic of Hope." *Human Rights Quarterly*, 5 (Aug. 1983), pp. 275–301.

Claydon, J. "The Transnational Protection of Ethnic Minorities: A Tentative Framework for Inquiry." *Canadian Yearbook of International Law*, 13 (1975), 25–60.

———. "Internationally Uprooted People and the Transnational Protection of Minority Culture." *New York Law School Law Review*, 24 (1978), 125–151.

Coates, Ken, Peter Limqueco, and Peter Weiss, eds. *Prevent the Crime of Silence*. London: Allen Lane, Penguin Press, 1971.

Codere, Helen. *Fighting with Property: A Study of Kwakiutl Potlatching and Warfare, 1792–1930*. Seattle: University of Washington Press, 1972.

Cohen, Roberta. "Human Rights Diplomacy: The Carter Administration and the Southern Cone." *Human Rights Quarterly*, 4 (Spring 1982), 212–242.

Cohn, Norman. *Warrant for Genocide*. New York: Harper & Row, 1967.

Committee for the Compilation of Materials on Damage Caused by the Atomic Bombs in Hiroshima and Nagasaki. *Hiroshima and Nagasaki: The Physical, Medical, and Social Effects of the Atomic Bombings*. Trans. Eisei Ishikawa and David L. Swain. New York: Basic Books, 1981.

Connor, Walker. "Self-Determination: The New Phase." *World Politics*, 20 (Oct. 1967), 30–53.

———. "Nation-Building or Nation-Destroying?" *World Politics*, 24 (Apr. 1972), 319–355.

———. "The Politics of Ethnonationalism." *Journal of International Affairs*, 22, no. 1 (1973), 1–21.

Cooper, Roger. *The Bahá'ís of Iran*. London: Minority Rights Group, 1982.

Council of Europe. Parliamentary Assembly, *Report on Persecution in Iran*. Strasbourg: Doc. 4835, 18 Jan. 1982.

Cristescu, Aureliu. *The Right to Self-Determination: Historical and Current Development on the Basis of United Nations Instruments*. UN E/CN.4/Sub.2/404/Rev.1. New York: United Nations, 1981 (Sales No. E. 80.XIV.3).

Daalder, Hans. "The Consociational Democracy Theme." *World Politics*, 26 (July 1968), 721–747.

Davis, Shelton H. *Victims of the Miracle: Development and the Indians of Brazil*. Cambridge: Cambridge University Press, 1977.

———. "The Social Roots of Political Violence in Guatemala." *Cultural Survival Quarterly*, 7 (Spring 1983), 5–11.

Dawidowicz, Lucy S. *The War Against the Jews, 1933–1945*. New York: Holt, Rinehart & Winston, 1975.

———. *The Holocaust and the Historians*. Cambridge: Harvard University Press, 1981.

Debré, François. *Cambodge: La révolution de la forêt*. Paris: Flammarion, 1976.

Dominguez, Jorge, Nigel S. Rodley, Bryce Wood, and Richard A. Falk, eds. *Enhancing Global Human Rights*. New York: McGraw-Hill, 1979.

Draper, Theodore. "On Nuclear War: An Exchange with the Secretary of Defense." *New York Review of Books* (14 Apr. 1983), pp. 27–32.

———. "Nuclear Temptations," *New York Review of Books* (19 Jan. 1984), pp. 42–50.

Duff, Ernest, and John McCamant. *Violence and Repression in Latin America*. New York: Free Press, 1976.

Dugard, C. J. R. "The Organisation of African Unity and Colonisation: An Inquiry into the Plea of Self-Defence and Justification for the Use of Force in the Eradication of Colonialism." *International and Comparative Law Quarterly*, 16 (Jan. 1967), 157–190.

Eide, A., and A. Schou, eds. *International Protection of Human Rights.* Nobel Symposium 7. New York: Interscience Publishers, 1968.

Elias, T. O. *Human Rights and the Developing Countries.* Strasbourg: International Institute of Human Rights, 1977.

Emerson, Rupert. *Self-Determination Revisited in the Era of Decolonization.* Occasional Paper 9. Center for International Affairs, Harvard University, Dec. 1964.

Ellsberg, Daniel. "Introduction." in Thompson and Smith, eds., *Protest and Survive,* 1981, pp. 1–xxviii.

———. "Self-Determination." *American Journal of International Law,* 65 (June 1971), 459–471.

———. "The Fate of Human Rights in the Third World." *World Politics,* 27 (Jan. 1975), 201–226.

Espiell, H. Gros. "The Evolving Concept of Human Rights: Western, Socialist and Third World Approaches." In Ramcharan, *Human Rights: Thirty Years after the Universal Declaration,* 1979, pp. 41–65.

———. *The Right to Self-Determination: Implementation of United Nations Resolutions.* E/CN.4/Sub.2/405/Rev.1. New York: United Nations, 1980 (Sales No. E. 79. XIV.5).

Falk, Richard. "The American Attack on the United Nations: An Interpretation." *Harvard International Law Journal,* 16 (Summer 1975), 566–575.

———. "Comparative Protection of Human Rights in Capitalist and Socialist Third World Countries." *Universal Human Rights,* 1 (Apr.–June 1979), 3–29.

———. *Human Rights and State Sovereignty.* New York: Holmes & Meier, 1981.

———. "Political Anatomy of Nuclearism." In Lifton and Falk, *Indefensible Weapons,* 1982, pp. 128–265.

Falk, Richard, ed. *The International Law of Civil War.* Baltimore: Johns Hopkins Press, 1971.

Farer, Tom. Contributions in "Vietnam and the Nuremberg Principles: A Colloquy on War Crimes." *Rutgers Camden Law Journal,* 5 (Fall 1973), 1–58.

Fawcett, James. *The International Protection of Minorities.* London: Minority Rights Group, 1979.

Fegley, Randall. "The U.N. Human Rights Commission: The Equatorial Guinea Case." *Human Rights Quarterly,* 3 (Feb. 1981), 34–47.

Fein, Helen. "A Formula for Genocide: A Comparison of the Turkish Genocide (1915) and the German Holocaust (1939–1945)." In Tomasson, *Studies in Sociology,* vol. 1, 1978, pp. 271–294.

———. *Accounting for Genocide.* New York: Free Press, 1979.

————. "Crimes without Punishment: Genocide after the Holocaust." In Nelson and Green, *International Human Rights*, 1980, pp. 251–264.

————. "Anticipating Deadly Endings: Models of Genocide and Critical Responses." Paper presented to the International Conference on the Holocaust and Genocide, Tel Aviv, June 1982.

Fisher, Stewart W. "Human Rights in El Salvador and U.S. Foreign Policy." *Human Rights Quarterly*, 4 (Spring 1982), 1–38.

Ford Foundation. "Confronting Man's Inhumanity." *Foundation News*, Nov.–Dec. 1978.

Forsythe, David P., and Laurie S. Wiseberg. "Human Rights Protection: A Research Agenda." *Universal Human Rights*, 1 (Oct.–Dec. 1979), 1–24.

Foundation for the Study of Plural Societies. *Case Studies on Human Rights and Fundamental Freedoms: A World Survey*. 5 vols. The Hague: Martinus Nijhoff, 1975–76.

Franck, Thomas M., and Nigel S. Rodley. "The Law, the United Nations, and Bangla Desh." *Israel Yearbook on Human Rights*, 2 (1972), 142–175.

————. "After Bangladesh: The Law of Humanitarian Intervention by Military Force." *American Journal of International Law*, 67, no. 1 (1973), 275–305.

Freed, Kenneth. "Fate of Argentina's 'Disappeared' Haunts Government." *Los Angeles Times*, 5 Dec. 1982, part 1-B.

Friedlander, Robert A. "Self-Determination: A Legal Political Inquiry." In Alexander and Friedlander, *Self-Determination: National, Regional and Global Dimensions*, 1980, pp. 307–331.

Frowein, Jochen A. "The European and the American Conventions on Human Rights—A Comparison." *Human Rights Law Journal*, 1, nos. 1–4 (1980), 44–65.

Furnivall, J. S. *Netherlands India: A Study of Plural Economy*. London: Cambridge Press, 1939.

————. "Some Problems of Tropical Economy." In Rita Hinden, ed., *Fabian Colonial Essays*, London: Allen & Unwin, 1945. Pp. 161–184.

————. *Colonial Policy and Practice: A Comparative Study of Burma and Netherlands India*. London: Cambridge University Press, 1948.

Galey, M. E. "Indigenous People, International Consciousness Raising and the Development of International Law on Human Rights." *Revue des droits de l'homme*, 8 (1975), 21–39.

George, Susan. *How the Other Half Dies: The Real Reasons for World Hunger*. London: Penguin, 1976.

Glaser, Kurt, and Stefan T. Possony. *Victims of Politics: The State of Human Rights*. New York: Columbia University Press, 1979.

Gonzales, Theresa D. "The Political Sources of Procedural Debates in the United Nations: Structural Impediments to Implementation of Human Rights." *Journal of International Law and Politics*, 13, no. 3 (1981), 427–472.

Goodin, Robert E. "The Development Rights Trade-Off: Some Unwarranted Economic and Political Assumptions." *Universal Human Rights*, 1 (Apr.–June 1979), 31–42.

Gotlieb, Allan, ed. *Human Rights, Federalism and Minorities*. Toronto: Canadian Institute of International Affairs, 1970.

Graefrath, B. "Cooperation between States to Promote and Safeguard Human Rights." German Democratic Republic Communication, *Human Rights Bulletin*, 1, no. 5 (1977).

Greenidge, C. W. W. *Slavery*. London: Allen & Unwin, 1958.

Greenland, Jeremy. "Ethnic Discrimination in Rwanda and Burundi." In Foundation for the Study of Plural Societies, *Case Studies on Human Rights and Fundamental Freedoms: A World Survey*, vol. 4, 1975, pp. 97–133.

Hakim, Christine. *Les Bahá'ís ou victoire sur la violence*. Lausanne: Pierre-Marcel Favre, 1982.

Halász, J., ed. *Socialist Concept of Human Rights*. Budapest: Akadémiai Kiadó, 1966.

Harris, John. *A Century of Emancipation*. London: John Dent & Sons, 1933.

Harvard Nuclear Study Group. *Living with Nuclear Weapons*. Cambridge: Harvard University Press, 1983.

Hawk, David. "The Killing of Cambodia." *New Republic*, 15 Nov. 1982, pp. 17–21.

Held, Virginia, Sidney Morgenbesser, and Thomas Nagel, eds. *Philosophy, Morality and International Affairs*. London: Oxford University Press, 1974.

Henderson, Conway W. "Multinational Corporations and Human Rights in Developing States." *World Affairs*, 33 (Summer 1979), 17–32.

Henkin, Louis. *How Nations Behave*. New York: Praeger, 1968.

——. "The United States and the Crisis in Human Rights." *Virginia Journal of International Law*, 14 (Summer 1974), 653–671.

——. *The Rights of Man*. London: Stevens & Sons, 1975.

——. "The Covenant on Civil and Political Rights." In Lillich, *U.S. Ratification of the Human Rights Treaties*, 1981, pp. 20–26.

Henkin, Louis, ed. *World Politics and the Jewish Condition*. New York: Quadrangle Books, 1972.

Hermassi, Elbaki. *The Third World Reassessed*. Berkeley and Los Angeles: University of California Press, 1980.

Hertsgaard, Mark. *Nuclear Inc.: The Men and Money Behind Nuclear Energy*. New York: Pantheon Books, 1983.

Hilberg, Raul. *The Destruction of the European Jews*. Chicago: Quadrangle Books, 1961.

Hildebrand, George, and Gareth Porter. *Cambodia—Starvation and Revolution*. New York: Monthly Review Press, 1976.

Hoffman, Stanley. *Duties Beyond Borders*. Syracuse: Syracuse University Press, 1981.

Holtzman, Elizabeth. "Examine U.S. Aid to Nazi Criminals." *New York Times*, 23 Apr. 1983, p. Y17.

Horowitz, Irving Louis. *Taking Lives: Genocide and State Power*. New Brunswick: Transaction Books, 1980.

Hovannisian, Richard G. *Armenia on the Road to Independence*. Berkeley and Los Angeles: University of California Press, 1967.

———. *The Republic of Armenia*. Vol. 1, Berkeley and Los Angeles: University of California Press, 1971.

———. "The Critics' View: Beyond Revisionism." *International Journal of Middle East Studies*, 9 (Aug. 1978), 379–388.

Human Rights Advocates. *International Human Rights Law: What It Is and How It Can Be Used in State and Federal Courts*. Berkeley: Human Rights Advocates, 1982.

Humphrey, John P. "The Sub-Commission on Prevention of Discrimination and Protection of Minorities." *American Journal of International Law*, 62 (1968), 869–888.

———. "The World Revolution and Human Rights." In Gotlieb, *Human Rights, Federalism and Minorities*, 1970, pp. 147–179.

———. "The Right of Petition in the U.N." *Human Rights Journal*, 4 (1971), 463–475.

———. "The International Law of Human Rights in the Middle Twentieth Century." In Bos, *The Present State of International Law*, 1973, pp. 75–105.

Hussein, M. "Les droits de l'homme dans le Tiers Monde." *Le Nouvel Observateur*, 16 May 1977.

Ijalaye, David A. "Notes and Comments: Was Biafra at Any Time a State in International Law?" *American Journal of International Law*, 65 (July 1971), 551–559.

Indian Ministry of External Affairs. *Bangla Desh Documents*. Madras: B. N. K. Press, 1971.

International Commission of Jurists. *Under False Colours*. The Hague: International Commission of Jurists, 1955.

———. *The Question of Tibet and the Rule of Law*. Geneva, 1959.

————. *Tibet and the Chinese People's Republic.* Report by the Legal Inquiry Committee on Tibet. Geneva, 1960.

————. "Right of Self-Determination in International Law." East Pakistan Staff Study, *International Commission of Jurists Review,* 8 (June 1972), 43–52.

————. *The Events in East Pakistan, 1971.* Study by the secretariat. Geneva, 1972.

————. "Equatorial Guinea." *The Review,* 13 (Dec. 1974), 10–13.

————. *Violations of Human Rights and the Rule of Law in Uganda.* Geneva, 1974.

————. *Uganda and Human Rights: Reports to the United Nations.* Geneva, 1977.

————. "Equatorial Guinea." *The Review,* 21 (Dec. 1978), 1–5.

————. *The Trial of Macias in Equatorial Guinea.* Report by Alejandro Artucio. Geneva, 1979.

————. Report by the Secretary-General. "Self-Determination and the 'Independent' Bantustans." *I.C.J. Newsletter,* Jan.–Mar. 1981, pp. 25–38.

————. "Eritrea." *The Review,* 26 (June 1981), 8–14.

————. American Association. *Human Rights and U.S. Foreign Policy.* Reprinted in U.S. Congress, House. Committee on Foreign Affairs, *Human Rights and U.S. Foreign Policy: Hearings before the Sub-Committee on International Organization of the Committee on Foreign Affairs,* 96th Cong., 1st sess., 1979.

————. *Toward an Integrated Human Rights Policy.* New York, 1979.

————. *Ethnic Conflict and Violence in Sri Lanka,* by Virginia A. Leary. Geneva: International Commission of Jurists, 1981.

————. *Ethnic Violence in Sri Lanka, 1981–1983,* Submission to the Sub-Commission on Prevention of Discrimination and Protection of Minorities, Aug. 1983.

International League for Human Rights and the Federation Internationale des Droits de l'Homme. *Strategies for Strengthening the Implementation of Human Rights: The Role of the National and International NGO's.* New York: International League for Human Rights, 1979.

Jolliffe, Jill. *East Timor: Nationalism and Colonialism.* St. Lucia, Queensland: University of Queensland Press, 1978.

Kaelas, Aleksander. *Human Rights and Genocide in the Baltic States.* Stockholm: Estonian Information Centre, 1950.

Katz, Fred E. "Implementation of the Holocaust: The Behavior of Nazi Officials." *Comparative Studies in Society and History,* 24 (July 1982), 510–529.

Kazemzadeh, Firuz. "The Terror Facing the Bahá'ís." *New York Review of Books*, 13 May 1982, pp. 43–44.

Kennedy, Edward M., and Mark O. Hatfield. *Freeze! How You Can Help Prevent Nuclear War*. New York: Bantam Books, 1982.

Khan, Prince Sadruddin Aga. *Study on Human Rights and Massive Exoduses*. United Nations, E/CN.4/1503, dated 31 Dec. 1981.

Kiernan, Ben. "Pol Pot and the Kampuchean Communist Movement." In Kiernan and Boua, *Peasants and Politics in Kampuchea, 1942–1981*, 1982, pp. 227–317.

Kiernan, Ben, and Chanthou Boua, eds. *Peasants and Politics in Kampuchea, 1942–1981*. London: Zed Press, 1982.

Koestler, Arthur. *Janus: A Summing Up*. London: Hutchinson, 1978.

Komarow, Gary. "Individual Responsibility under International Law: The Nuremberg Principles in Domestic Legal Systems." *International and Comparative Law Quarterly*, 29 (Jan. 1980), 21–37.

Kramer, David, and David Weissbrodt. "The 1980 U.N. Commission on Human Rights and the Disappeared." *Human Rights Quarterly*, 3 (Feb. 1981), 18–33.

Krawchenko, Bohdan. "The Great Famine of 1932–33 in the Soviet Ukraine." *One World* (Calgary), 20 (Spring 1982), 17–23.

Kruger, Hans Christian. "The European Commission of Human Rights." *Human Rights Law Journal*, 1, nos. 1–4 (1980), 66–87.

Kuper, Leo. *Race, Class and Power*. London: Duckworth, 1974.

———. *The Pity of It All*. London: Duckworth, 1977.

———. *South Africa: Human Rights and Genocide*. Hans Wolff Memorial Lecture, African Studies Program. Bloomington: Indiana University, 1981.

———. *Genocide: Its Political Use in the Twentieth Century*. London: Penguin Books, 1981; New Haven: Yale University Press, 1982.

———. *International Action against Genocide*. London: Minority Rights Group, 1982.

Kuper, Leo, and M. G. Smith, eds. *Pluralism in Africa*. Berkeley and Los Angeles: University of California Press, 1969.

Kutner, Luis. "World Habeas Corpus: Ombudsman for Mankind." *University of Miami Law Review*, 24 (Winter 1970), 352–387.

———. "A World Genocide Tribunal: Rampart against Future Genocide: Proposal for Planetary Preventive Measures Supplementing a Genocide Early Warning System." Paper presented to the International Conference on the Holocaust and Genocide, Tel Aviv, June 1982.

Kyemba, Henry. *State of Blood*. Preface by Godfrey Lule. London: Transworld Publishers, 1977.

Lane, Eric. "Mass Killing by Governments: Lawful in the World Legal Order?" *New York University International Law and Politics*, 12 (Fall 1979), 239–280.

Lang, David Marshall, and Christopher Walker. *The Armenians*. London: Minority Rights Group, 1981.

Laqueur, Walter. *The Terrible Secret*. London: Weidenfeld & Nicolson, 1980.

Laqueur, Walter, and Barry Rubin. *The Human Rights Reader*. Philadelphia: Temple University Press, 1979.

Leary, Virginia A. *Ethnic Conflict and Violence in Sri Lanka*. Geneva: International Commission of Jurists, 1981.

Lemarchand, René. *Rwanda and Burundi*. New York: Praeger, 1970.

Lemarchand, René, and David Martin. *Selective Genocide in Burundi*. London: Minority Rights Group, 1974.

Lemkin, Raphael. *Axis Rule in Occupied Europe*. Washington: Carnegie Endowment for World Peace, 1944.

Lepsius, Johannes. *Le rapport secret du Johannes Lepsius . . . sur les massacres d'Arménie*. Paris: Payot, 1918.

Levak, Albert E. "Provincial Conflict and Nation-Building in Pakistan." In Bell and Freeman, *Ethnicity and Nation-Building*, 1974, pp. 203–222.

————. "Discrimination in Pakistan: National, Provincial, Tribal." In Foundation for the Study of Plural Societies, *Case Studies on Human Rights and Fundamental Freedoms*, vol. 1, 1975, pp. 281–308.

Lewis, Bernard. "The Anti-Zionist Resolution." *Foreign Affairs*, 55 (Jan. 1977), 54–64.

Lewis, Norman. "The Camp at Cecilio Baez." In Arens, *Genocide in Paraguay*, 1976, pp. 58–68.

Leys, Simon. *Chinese Shadows*. London: Penguin, 1978.

Lifton, Robert Jay, and Richard Falk: *Indefensible Weapons: The Political and Psychological Case Against Nuclearism*. New York: Basic Books, 1982.

Lijphart, Arend. *Democracy in Plural Societies*. New Haven: Yale University Press, 1977.

Lillich, Richard B., ed. *Humanitarian Intervention and the United Nations*. Charlottesville: University Press of Virginia, 1973.

————. *U.S. Ratification of the Human Rights Treaties: With or Without Reservations?* Charlottesville: University Press of Virginia, 1981.

Liskofsky, Sidney. "Coping with the 'Question of the Violation of Human Rights and Fundamental Freedoms.'" *Revue des droits de l'homme*, 5 (1975), 883–914.

Loftus, John. *The Belarus Secret*. New York: Alfred A. Knopf, 1982.

Lorenz, Konrad. "On Killing Members of One's Own Species." *Bulletin of the Atomic Scientists*, Oct. 1970, pp. 3–5, 51–56.

————. *On Aggression*. New York: Harcourt, Brace and World, 1977.

Luard, Evan, ed. *The International Protection of Human Rights*. London: Thames & Hudson, 1967.

MacBride, Sean. "Conference of European Jurists on the Individual and the State." *International Lawyer* 3 (1969), 603–615.

McCarthy, Thomas E. "The International Protection of Human Rights: Ritual and Reality." *International and Comparative Law Quarterly*, 25 (1976), 261–291.

MacDonald, R. St. J. "A United Nations High Commissioner for Human Rights: The Decline and Fall of an Initiative." *Canadian Yearbook of International Law*, 10 (1972), 40–64.

McDougal, Myers S., Harold Laswell, and Lung-chu Chen. *The Basic Policies of an International Law of Human Dignity*. New Haven: Yale University Press, 1980.

McNamara, Robert S. *One Hundred Countries, Two Billion People: The Dimensions of Development*. London: Pall Mall Press, 1973.

Manvell, Roger, and Heinrich Fraenkel. *Incomparable Crime: Mass Extermination in the 20th Century; The Legacy of Guilt*. London: Heinemann, 1967.

Martin, David. *General Amin*. London: Faber, 1974.

Mascarenhas, Anthony. *The Rape of Bangladesh*. Delhi: Vikas Publications, 1971.

M'Baye, K. "Les réalites du monde noir et les droits de l'homme." *Human Rights Journal*, 2 (1969), 382–394.

Medvedev, Roy, and Zhores Medvedev. "The USSR and the Arms Race." In New Left Review, ed., *Exterminism and Cold War*, 1982, pp. 153–173.

Melson, Robert. "A Theoretical Inquiry into the Armenian Masacres of 1894–1896." *Comparative Studies in Society and History*, 24 (July 1982), 481–509.

————. "A Theoretical Inquiry into the Armenian Genocide of 1915." To be published.

Menaul, Stewart. "Survival in Nuclear War." *Contemporary Review*, 239, 1387 (Aug. 1981), 66–70.

Minority Rights Group. *What Future for the Amerindians of South America?* by Hugh O'Shaughnessy and Stephen Corry. London: Minority Rights Group, 1977.

————. *Constitutional Law and Minorities*, by Claire Palley. London: Minority Rights Group, 1978.

————. *The International Protection of Minorities*, by James Fawcett. London: Minority Rights Group, 1979.

————. *The Armenians*, by David Marshall Lang and Christopher Walker. London: Minority Rights Group, 1981.

————. *The Tibetans*, by Chris Mullin. London: Minority Rights Group, 1981.

————. *West Iran, East Timor and Indonesia*, by Keith Suter. London: Minority Rights Group, 1981.

Mojekwu, Christopher C. "The African Perspective." In Alexander and Friedlander, *Self-Determination*, 1980, pp. 221–239.

Moore, John Norton, ed. *Law and Civil War in the Modern World*. Baltimore: Johns Hopkins Press, 1974.

Morgenthau, Henry. *Ambassador Morgenthau's Story*. New York: Doubleday, 1918.

Morris-Jones, W. H. "Pakistan Post-Mortem and the Roots of Bangladesh." *Political Quarterly*, 43 (Apr. 1972), 187–200.

Moynihan, Daniel P. "The Politics of Human Rights." *Commentary*, 63 (Apr. 1977).

Mullin, Chris. *The Tibetans*. London: Minority Rights Group, 1981.

Murphy, John F. "Self-Determination: United States Perspectives." In Alexander and Friedlander, *Self-Determination*, 1980, pp. 43–61.

Nafziger, E. W., and W. L. Richter. "Biafra and Bangladesh: The Political Economy of Secessionist Conflict." *Journal of Peace Research*, 13, no. 2 (1976), 91–109.

Nairn, Allan. "Choices in Guatemala." *New York Times*, 4 Apr. 1983.

Nanda, Ved. P. "A Critique of the United Nations Inaction in the Bangladesh Crisis." *Denver Law Journal*, 49, no. 1 (1972), 53–67.

————. "Self-Determination in International Law." *American Journal of International Law*, 66 (Apr. 1972), 321–336.

————. "Self-Determination Outside the Colonial Context: The Birth of Bangladesh in Retrospect." In Alexander and Friedlander, *Self-Determination*, 1980, pp. 193–220.

Nanda, Ved. P., James R. Scarritt, and George W. Shepherd. *Global Human Rights: Public Policies, Comparative Measures, and NGO Strategies*. Boulder, Colo.: Westview Press, 1981.

Nash, Henry. "The Bureaucratization of Genocide." In Thompson and Smith, *Protest and Survive*, 1981, pp. 149–160.

Navarro, Vicente. "Genocide in El Salvador." *Monthly Review*, 32 (Apr. 1981), 1–16.

Nayar, M. G. Kaladharan. "Self-Determination beyond the Colonial Context: Biafra in Retrospect." *Texas International Law School*, 10 (Spring 1975), 321–345.

Nelson, Jack L., and Vera M. Green, eds. *International Human Rights: Contemporary Issues*. Stanfordville, N.Y.: Human Rights Publishing Group, 1980.

New Left Review, eds. *Exterminism and Cold War*. London: Verso, 1982.

Nixon, Charles R. "Self-Determination: The Nigeria/Biafra Case." *World Politics*, 24 (July 1972), 473–497.

Nordlinger, Eric A. *Conflict Regulation in Divided Societies*. Occasional Papers in International Affairs 29. Cambridge, Mass.: Center for International Affairs, Harvard University, 1972.

———. "Military Governments in Communally Divided Societies: Their Impact upon National Integration." In Foundation for the Study of Plural Societies, eds., *Case Studies on Human Rights and Fundamental Freedoms*, vol. 3, 1975, pp. 535–564.

Nossiter, Bernard D. "East Timor Case at U.N.: "Depressing." *New York Times*, 9 Feb. 1983.

O'Ballance, Edgar. *The Secret War in the Sudan, 1955–1972*. Hamden, Conn.: Archon Books, 1977.

O'Brien, Conor Cruise. *The United Nations: Sacred Drama*. New York: Simon & Schuster, 1968.

Oestreicher, Paul. "The Humanity Test." *Guardian*, 18 Aug. 1979, p. 9.

Organization of American States. Inter-American Commission on Human Rights. *Report on the Situation of Human Rights in the Republic of Guatemala. Report on the Situation of Human Rights in the Republic of Bolivia*. Washington, D.C.: General Secretariat, Organization of American States, 1981.

O'Shaughnessy, Hugh, and Stephen Corry. *What Future for the Amerindians of South America?* London: Minority Rights Group, 1977.

Owen, David. *Human Rights*. London: Jonathan Cape, 1978.

Owen, J. E. "East Pakistan, 1947–1971." *Contemporary Review*, 221 (July 1972), 23–28.

Palley, Claire. *Constitutional Law and Minorities*. London: Minority Rights Group, 1978.

Palmier, Leslie. *Communism in Indonesia: Power Pursued in Vain*. New York: Doubleday, 1973.

Panter-Brick, S. K. "The Right to Self-Determination: Its Application to Nigeria." *International Affairs*, 44 (Apr. 1968), 254–266.

Paust, Jordan J., and Albert P. Blaustein. "War Crimes Jurisdiction and Due Process: The Bangladesh Experience." *Vanderbilt Journal of Transnational Law*, 11 (Winter 1978), 1–38.

Payne, Robert. *Massacre*. New York: Macmillan, 1973.

Pétéri, Zoltan. "Citizens' Rights and the Natural Law Theory." In Halász, *Socialist Concept of Human Rights*, 1966, pp. 83–119.

Ponchaud, François. *Cambodia Year Zero*. Harmondsworth: Penguin, 1978.

Porter, Jack Nusan, ed. *Genocide and Human Rights: A Global Anthology*. Washington, D.C.: University Press of America, 1982.

Przetacznik, Franciszek. "L'attitude des états socialistes a l'égard de la protection internationale des droits de l'homme." *Revue des droits l'homme*, 7 (1974), 175–206.

Rajan, M. S., and T. Israel. "The United Nations and the Conflict in Vietnam." In Falk, *The International Law of Civil War*, 1971, pp. 114–143.

Ramcharan, Bertrand G. "Implementation of the International Covenant on Economic, Cultural and Social Rights." *Netherlands International Law Review*, 23 (1976), 151–161.

———. "A Critique of the Third World Response to Violations of Human Rights." In Cassese, *U.N. Law/Fundamental Rights*, 1979, pp. 249–258.

———. "The United Nations Response to Urgent Situations of Human Rights." Paper delivered to a Quaker conference in New York, 1981.

———. "The Good Offices of the United Nations Secretary-General in the Field of Human Rights." *American Journal of International Law*, 76 (Jan. 1982), 130–141.

———. *Humanitarian Good Offices in International Law*. The Hague: Martinus Nijhoff, 1983.

Ramcharan, Bertrand G., ed. *Human Rights: Thirty Years after the Universal Declaration*. The Hague: Martinus Nijhoff, 1979.

Reisman, W. Michael, and Burns H. Weston, eds. *Toward World Order and Human Dignity*. New York: Free Press, 1976.

Robertson, A. H. *Human Rights in the World*. Manchester: Manchester University Press, 1972.

———. *Human Rights in Europe*. Manchester: Manchester University Press, 1977.

Robinson, N. *The Genocide Convention*. New York: Institute of Jewish Affairs, 1960.

Rodley, Nigel. "On the Necessity of United States Ratification of the International Human Rights Conventions." In Lillich, *U.S. Ratification of the Human Rights Treaties*, 1981, pp. 3–19.

Ronen, Dov. *The Quest for Self-Determination*. New Haven: Yale University Press, 1979.

Rothschild, Emma. "The Delusions of Deterrence." *New York Review of Books* (14 Apr. 1983), pp. 40–50.

Rousset, Pierre. "Cambodia: Background to Revolution." *Journal of Contemporary Asia*, 7, no. 4 (1977), 513–528.

Rubin, Barry M., and Elizabeth P. Spiro, eds. *Human Rights and U.S. Foreign Policy*. Boulder, Colo.: Westview Press, 1979.

Russell Tribunal. Second International Tribunal. *Found Guilty: The*

Verdict of the Russell Tribunal Section in Brussels. Spokesman Pamphlet 51. Nottingham: Bertrand Russell Peace Foundation, 1975.

———. Third International Tribunal. *Berufsverbote Condemned.* Nottingham: Bertrand Russell Peace Foundation, 1975.

———. Fourth International Tribunal. *The Rights of the Indians of the Americas.* Amsterdam: Workgroup Indian Project, 1980.

Rutgers Society of International Law. "Vietnam and the Nuremberg Principles: A Colloquy on War Crimes." *Rutgers Camden Law Journal,* 5 (Fall 1973), 1–58.

Sachar, Abram Leon. *A History of the Jews.* New York: Alfred A. Knopf, 1967.

Sartre, Jean-Paul. "On Genocide." *Ramparts* (Feb. 1968), pp. 37–42.

Scheer, Robert. *With Enough Shovels: Reagan, Bush and Nuclear War.* New York: Random House, 1982.

Schell, Jonathan. *The Fate of the Earth.* New York: Alfred A. Knopf, 1982.

Schmidt, Péter. "The Citizens' Freedoms." In Halász, *Socialist Concept of Human Rights,* 1966, pp. 227–265.

Schumacher, Edward. "Argentina Justifies Drive in 70's against Left as Needed and Legal." *New York Times,* 29 Apr. 1983, pp. 1, 6.

Sears, William. *A Cry from the Heart.* Oxford: George Roland, 1982.

Shaw, Stanford J., and Ezel Kural Shaw. *History of the Ottoman Empire and Modern Turkey.* 2 vols. Cambridge: Cambridge University Press, 1976–77.

———. "The Authors Respond." *International Journal of Middle East Studies,* 9 (Aug. 1978), 388–400.

Shawcross, William. "Cambodia: Nightmare Without End." *Far Eastern Economic Review,* 100 (14 Apr. 1978), 32–34.

———. "The Third Indochina War." *New York Review of Books* (6 Apr. 1978), pp. 15–22.

———. *Sideshow.* New York: Simon & Schuster, 1979.

Shestack, Jerome J. "Sisyphus Endures: The International Human Rights NGO." *New York Law School Law Review,* 24 (1978), 89–123.

Shestack, Jerome J., and Roberta Cohen. "International Human Rights: A Role for the United States." *Virginia Journal of International Law,* 14, no. 4 (1974), 637–701.

Shulman, Marshall D. "On Learning to Live with Authoritarian Regimes." *Foreign Affairs,* 55 (Jan. 1975), 327–338.

Smith, Bradley F. *The Road to Nuremberg.* New York: Basic Books, 1980.

Smith, M. G. "Social and Cultural Pluralism." *Annals of the New York Academy of Science*, 83 (1960), 763–785.

———. *The Plural Society in the British West Indies*. Berkeley and Los Angeles: University of California Press, 1965.

———. "Institutional and Political Conditions of Pluralism." In Kuper and Smith, *Pluralism in Africa*, 1969, pp. 27–65.

———. "Pluralism in Precolonial African Societies." In Kuper and Smith, *Pluralism in Africa*, 1969, pp. 91–151.

———. "Some Developments in the Analytical Framework of Pluralism." In Kuper and Smith, *Pluralism in Africa*, 1969, pp. 415–458.

Southeast Asia Chronicle. "East Timor's Diplomatic Struggle." 74 (Aug. 1980), 27–28.

Sohn, Louis B., and Thomas Buergenthal. *International Protection of Human Rights*. New York: Bobbs-Merrill, 1973.

Stone, Julius. "Range of Crimes for a Feasible International Jurisdiction." In Stone and Woetzel, *Toward a Feasible International Criminal Court*, 1970, pp. 315–341.

———. *Conflict through Consensus: United Nations Approaches to Aggression*. Baltimore: Johns Hopkins University Press, 1977.

Stone, Julius, and Robert K. Woetzel, eds. *Toward a Feasible International Criminal Court*. Geneva: World Peace through Law Center, 1970.

Sureda, A. Rigo. *The Evolution of the Right of Self-Determination: A Study of United Nations Practice*. Leiden: A. W. Sijthoff, 1973.

Survival International. *Supplement (Paraguay)*, June 1978.

———. *Review*, Spring 1979 and Autumn/Winter 1980.

Suter, Keith. *West Iran, East Timor and Indonesia*. London: Minority Rights Group, 1979.

Temperley, Howard. *British Anti-Slavery*. London: Longman, 1972.

Thompson, E. P., and Dan Smith, eds. *Protest and Survive*. New York: Monthly Review Press, 1981.

Thornberry, Patrick. "Is There a Phoenix in the Ashes? International Law and Minority Rights." *Texas International Law Journal*, 15 (Summer 1980), 421–458.

Tibetan (Dalai Lama's) Government in Exile. Report of the Second Delegation. "Tibetans in Tibet Today." *Tibet News Review*, 1 (Winter 1980/81).

Tomasson, Richard F., ed., *Studies in Sociology*. Vol. 1. Greenwich, Conn.: J.A.I. Press, 1978.

Torrès, Henry. *Le Procès des Pogromes*. Paris: Editions de France, 1928.

Toynbee, Arnold. *Experiences*. London: Oxford University Press, 1969.

Umozurike, U. O. *Self-Determination in International Law*. Hamden, Conn.: Archon Books, 1972.

UNESCO. *Human Rights, Comments and Interpretation: a Symposium*. London and New York: Allan Wingate, 1949.

Union of Concerned Scientists. *The Arms Control Debate*. Cambridge, Mass., 1983.

United Nations. Proceedings and Resolutions of the Security Council, the General Assembly, the Economic and Social Council, the Commission on Human Rights, and the Sub-Commission on Prevention of Discrimination and Protection of Minorities.

————. *Yearbook*. New York: United Nations, 1946–1979.

————. *Monthly Chronicle*. May 1964–Jan. 1983.

————. *Protection of Minorities*. New York: United Nations, 1967 (Sales No. 67.XIV.3).

————. *Proclamation of Teheran*. International Conference on Human Rights, 13 May 1968.

————. *United Nations Action in the Field of Human Rights*. New York: United Nations, 1980 (Sales No. E.79.XIV.6).

————. Commission on Human Rights. *An Investigation of Charges of Torture and Ill-treatment of Prisoners, Detainees, or Persons in Police Custody in South Africa* by Ad Hoc Working Group of Experts. E/CN.4/950, 27 Oct. 1967.

————. *Apartheid and Genocide*. E/CN.4/984/ Add. 18, 28 Feb. 1969.

————. *Human Rights Communication*, no. 478, 29 Sept. 1969.

————. *Study Concerning the Question of Apartheid from the Point of View of International Penal Law*. E/CN.4/1075, 15 Feb. 1972.

————. *Application of the International Convention on the Suppression and Punishment of the Crime of Apartheid*. E/CN 4/1366, 31 Jan. 1980.

————. *Study of the Human Rights Situation in Equatorial Guinea*, by Professor Fernando Jiménez. E/CN.4/1371, 12 Feb. 1980.

————. *Implementation of the International Convention on the Suppression and Punishment of the Crime of Apartheid*. E/CN.4/ 1426, 19 Jan. 1981.

————. *Study on Ways and Means of Insuring the Implementation of International Instruments such as the International Convention on the Suppression and Punishment of the Crime of Apartheid, Including the Establishment of the International Jurisdiction Envisaged by the Convention*. E/CN.4/1426, 19 Jan. 1981.

————. *Situation of Human Rights in Guatemala*, Note by the secretary-general. E/CN.4/1501, 31 Dec. 1981.

————. *Study on Human Rights and Massive Exoduses*, by Prince Sadruddin Aga Khan. E/CN.4/1503, 31 Dec. 1981.

———. *Study on the Human Rights Situation in Bolivia*, by Special Envoy Héctor Gros Espiell. E/CN.4/1500, 31 Dec. 1981.

———. *Progress Report on Apartheid*, by Ad Hoc Working Group of Experts. E/CN.4/1485, 8 Jan. 1982.

———. *Report of the Working Group on Enforced or Involuntary Disappearances*. E/CN.4/1492, 31 Dec. 1981, and Add. 1, 22 Feb. 1982.

———. *Final Report on the Situation of Human Rights in El Salvador*. Submitted by Special Representative José Antonio Pastor Ridruejo. E/CN.4/1502, 18 Jan. 1982.

———. *Annual Report of the Inter-American Commission on Human Rights, 1980–1981*. E/CN.4/1982/2, 25 Jan. 1982.

———. *Implementation of the International Convention on the Suppression and Punishment of the Crime of Apartheid*. E/CN.4/1507, 29 Feb. 1982.

———. General Assembly. *Alternative Approaches and Ways and Means within the United Nations System for Improving the Effective Enjoyment of Human Rights and Fundamental Freedoms*. Resolution 32/130, 16 Dec. 1977.

———. Statement re East Timor by Noam Chomsky to Fourth Committee of General Assembly. A/C.4/33/7 Add. 3, Nov. 1978.

———. General Assembly. Resolutions on Disarmament. Nos. 36/92–100, Dec. 1981, and 37/70–85 and 37/95–100, Dec. 1982.

———. Human Rights Committee. "Consideration of Iran's Report under Article 40 of the Covenant." *Human Rights Law Journal*, 3, nos. 1–4 (1982), 393–403.

———. Secretary-General. *Secretary-General's Summary of Information Regarding Consideration of the Proposal for a High Commissioner for Human Rights*. E/CN.4/Sub.2/1982/26.

———. Sub-Commission on Prevention of Discrimination and Protection of Minorities. *Study of the Question of the Prevention and Punishment of the Crime of Genocide*. Report by Nicodème Ruhashyankiko. E/CN.4/Sub.2/416, 4 July 1978.

———. *Study of the Rights of Persons Belonging to Ethnic, Religious and Linguistic Minorities*. Report by Francesco Capotorti. E/CN.4/Sub.2/ 384 and Add. 1–7, 20–30 June 1977. (Sales No. E.78. XIV.I). New York: United Nations, 1979.

———. *The Right to Self-Determination: Implementation of United Nations Resolutions*. Study prepared by Héctor Gros Espiell. E/CN.4/Sub.2/405/Rev. 1. New York: United Nations, 1980 (Sales No. E.79.XIV.5).

———. *The Right to Self-Determination: Historical and Current Development on the Basis of United Nations Instruments*. Study prepared by Aureliu Cristescu. E/CN.4/Sub.2/404/Rev. 1. New York: United Nations, 1981 (Sales no. E.80.XIV.3).

——. *Updating of the Report on Slavery Submitted to the Sub-Commission in 1966*, by Benjamin Whitaker, E/CN.4/Sub.2/20 and Add. 1, dated July 1982.

——. *Study of the Problem of Discrimination against Indigenous Peoples*. Report submitted by the Special Rapporteur, Jose R. Martinez Cobo. E/CN.4/Sub.2/476 and Add., E/CN.4/Sub.2/1982/2 and Add., and E.CN.4/Sub.2/1983/21 and Add.

——. *Study of the Implications for Human Rights of Recent Developments Concerning Situations known as States of Siege or Emergency*. Report submitted by Nicole Questiaux. E/CN.4/Sub.2/1982/15.

United States Catholic Bishops. "The Challenge of Peace: God's Promise and Our Response." *Origins*, 13 (19 May 1983), 1–32.

United States Congress. *Report on Human Rights Practices in Countries Receiving U.S. Aid by the Department of State to a Joint Committee of the U.S. Congress on Foreign Relations*, 8 Feb. 1979, p. 317.

——. House. *International Protection of Human Rights*. Staff Report by Susan M. Mowle. Hearings before Sub-Committee on International Organizations and Movements of the House Committee on Foreign Affairs, 93d Cong., 1st sess., 1973, App. 32.

——. *International Protection of Human Rights*. Hearings before Sub-Committee on International Organizations and Movements of the Committee on Foreign Affairs. Washington, D.C.: U.S. Government Printing Office, 1974.

——. "The United Nations Commission on Human Rights: A Review of the 36th Session." Testimony by Michael Posner to the Committee on Foreign Affairs, Sub-Committee on International Organizations, House of Representatives, 23 Apr. 1980.

——. Senate Committee on Foreign Relations, International Convention on the Prevention and Punishment of the Crime of Genocide, Senate Executive Report No. 92–6, 92d Cong., 1st sess. (4 May 1971).

Van Boven, Theo. C. "Some Remarks on Special Problems Relating to Human Rights in Developing Countries." *Human Rights Journal*, 3 (1970), 383–396.

——. "Partners in the Promotion and Protection of Human Rights." *Netherlands International Law Review*, 24 (1977), 55–84. Special issue.

——. "United Nations and Human Rights: A Critical Appraisal." In Cassese, *UN Law/Fundamental Rights*, 1979, pp. 119–135.

————. "United Nations Policies and Strategies: Global Perspectives." In Ramcharan, *Human Rights*, 1979, pp. 83–92.

————. "Protection of Human Life." Address at the Opening Session of the United Nations Commission on Human Rights, 1 Feb. 1982.

————. "Des voiz qu'il faut entendre à l'ONU." Talk given in Geneva, Apr. 1982. (Reception given to van Boven on his retirement).

————. *People Matter*. Amsterdam: Meulenhoff, 1982.

Van Boven, Theo. C., and B. G. Ramcharan. *Implementation of International Standards*. Amnesty International Conference on Extra-Legal Executions, Amsterdam, 30 Apr.–2 May, 1982.

Van den Berghe, Pierre. "Pluralism and the Polity: A Theoretical Exploration." In Kuper and Smith, *Pluralism in Africa*, 1969, pp. 67–81.

Vanderhaar, Gerard A. "Genocidal Mentality: Nuclear Weapons on Civilian Populations." Paper presented at the International Conference on the Holocaust and Genocide, Tel Aviv, 20–24 June 1982.

Van Niekerk, Barend V. D. "The Mirage of Liberty." *Human Rights*, 3 (1973), 283–299.

Waldheim, Kurt. *The Challenge of Peace*. London: Weidenfeld & Nicolson, 1980.

Waldock, Humphrey. "The Effectiveness of the System Set Up by the European Convention on Human Rights." *Human Rights Law Journal*, 1, nos. 1–4 (1980), 1–12.

Weatherbee, Donald E. "The Indonesianization of East Timor." Paper presented at the 20th Annual Meeting of the Southeast Conference Association for Asian Studies, 24 Jan. 1981.

Wechsberg, Joseph, ed. *The Murderers among Us: The Simon Wiesenthal Memoirs*. New York: McGraw-Hill, 1967.

Weinstein, Warren, and Robert Schrire. *Political Conflict and Ethnic Strategies: A Case Study of Burundi*. Syracuse: Syracuse University Press, 1976.

Weisbrodt, David. "The Role of International Nongovernmental Organizations in the Implementation of Human Rights." *Texas International Law Journal*, 12 (Spring/Summer 1977), 293–320.

Wertheim, W. F. "Indonesia before and after the Untung Coup." *Pacific Affairs*, 39 (Spring–Summer 1966), 115–127.

Whitaker, Benjamin. *Updating of the Report on Slavery Submitted to the Sub-Commission in 1966*, E/CN.4/Sub.2/1982/20 and Add. 1, dated July 1982.

Whitaker, Benjamin, ed. *The Fourth World: Victims of Group Oppression*. New York: Schocken, 1973.

Wiesenthal, Simon. *The Murderers among Us: The Simon Wiesenthal Memoirs*, ed. Joseph Wechsberg. New York: McGraw-Hill, 1967.

———. "Why the Search for Nazis Must Go On." *Jewish Digest*, 23 (Sept. 1977), 83–88.

Wirsing, Robert, ed. *Protection of Ethnic Minorities*. New York: Pergamon Press, 1981.

Wiseberg, Laurie, and Harry Scoble. "The Moscow Congress of the International Political Science Association." *A Chronicle of Human Rights in the USSR*, 35 (July–Sept. 1979), 35–47.

———. "Problems of Comparative Research on Human Rights," and "Recent Trends in the Expanding Universe of NGOs Dedicated to the Protection of Human Rights." In Nanda, Scarritt, and Shepherd, *Global Human Rights*, 1981, pp. 147–171, 229–260.

———. "An International Strategy for NGOs Pertaining to Extra-Legal Executions." Paper presented to the Amnesty International Conference on Extra-Legal Executions, Amsterdam, Apr.–May 1982.

Young, Crawford. *The Politics of Cultural Pluralism*. Madison: University of Wisconsin Press, 1976.

Index

Aborigines Protection Society, 110
Aché Indians: genocide against in Paraguay, 12, 151, 161
Acholi: genocide against in Uganda, 132, 139
Afghanistan, 214–15
African Charter on Human and Peoples' Rights, 105
Agency for International Development and the World Bank, 198
Aggression: U.N. definition of, 6, 91
Algeria, 82, 155, 156
Allende Gossens, Salvador, 141
American Association for the International Commission of Jurists, 39
American Convention on Human Rights, 5, 99
American Declaration of the Rights and Duties of Man, 5
Amin, Idi, 103, 127, 139, 140, 162, 185; massacres under, 132, 133
Amnesty International, 16, 34, 141, 188, 220; and Cambodia, 135; and Indonesia, 130; role of in early warning system, 224; and Uganda, 133, 140
Angola, 114, 115, 118
Anti-Slavery Conventions, 113–14, 115, 116; obstacles to implementation, 111–12, 113, 119–21, 122–23
Anti-Slavery Society for the Protection of Human Rights, 110, 118, 119, 123, 124
Apartheid, 93, 95, 113, 170; anti-apartheid movements, 227; and genocide, 176–77; U.N. committees con-

cerned with, 175–76, 177–78; world concern with, 175–76. *See also* Slavery; South Africa
Arendt, Hannah, 102*n*
Argentina, 103, 141–42, 194; disappearances in, 144–45
Arlen, Michael J., 149
Armenians: Judgment of the Permanent Peoples' Tribunal on the Genocide of the Armenians, 247–53; Turkish genocide against, 148–49, 189, 192–93
Arrest, arbitrary, 42
Assam, 45
Assassination, 16, 156, 219
Atlantic Charter of August *1941*, 33
Australia, 27, 90, 167, 191, 194
Autonomy. *See* Self-determination of all peoples
Awad, Mohamed, 109, 113
Awami League, 47, 50
Axis Rule in Occupied Europe (Lemkin), 9

Bahá'ís of Iran, 152–53, 170; Bahá'í International Community, 163–64; current urgency of, 222, 223; U.N. protective response to, 163–64
Ball, Desmond, 230–31
Baluchistan, 45, 46
"Banality of evil," 235–36
Bandung Conference, 134
Bangladesh, 17, 20, 76, 78; atrocities in, 47, 48, 50; background for secession, 44–47; issues and conclusions, 71, 83–85; Security Council resolution regard-